THE EUROPEAN SOCIAL QUESTION

Building Progressive Alternatives

Series Editors: David Coates†, Ben Rosamond and Matthew Watson

Bringing together economists, political economists and other social scientists, this series offers pathways to a coherent, credible and progressive economic growth strategy that, when accompanied by an associated set of wider public policies, can inspire and underpin the revival of a successful centre-left politics in advanced capitalist societies.

Published

Corbynism in Perspective: The Labour Party under Jeremy Corbyn
Edited by Andrew S. Roe-Crines

The European Social Question
Amandine Crespy

Flawed Capitalism: The Anglo-American Condition and its Resolution
David Coates

The Political Economy of Industrial Strategy in the UK:
From Productivity Problems to Development Dilemmas
Edited by Craig Berry, Julie Froud and Tom Barker

Race and the Undeserving Poor: From Abolition to Brexit
Robbie Shilliam

Reflections on the Future of the Left
Edited by David Coates

THE EUROPEAN SOCIAL QUESTION

Tackling Key Controversies

AMANDINE CRESPY

agenda
publishing

First published in 2022 by Agenda Publishing

Agenda Publishing Limited
The Core
Bath Lane
Newcastle Helix
Newcastle upon Tyne
NE4 5TF
www.agendapub.com

ISBN 978-1-78821-357-8 (hardcover)
ISBN 978-1-78821-358-5 (paperback)

British Library Cataloguing-in-Publication Data
A catalogue record for this book is available from the British Library

Typeset by Newgen Publishing UK
Printed and bound in the UK by TJ Books

CONTENTS

ACKNOWLEDGEMENTS

This book is in many ways the product of ten years spent researching political contention surrounding socio-economic issues in the European Union (EU). Over the past few years, I have benefited from the support and intellectual input from various institutions, research groups and individual colleagues, whom I would very much like to thank here.

The Université libre de Bruxelles (ULB), especially the Centre d'études de la vie politique (Cevipol) and the Institut d'Etudes Européennes, have provided over the years a very stimulating atmosphere in which to research, teach, work and live. Collaborative research – for instance in the framework of the H2020 project ENLIGHTEN (2014–17) involving Laszlo Andor (Corvinus/ULB), Cornel Ban (CBS), Ramona Coman (ULB), Len Seabrooke (CBS), Vivien Schmidt (BU/ULB) and many others – has fed my thoughts over the transformation of EU socio-economic governance and the acute social issues in the aftermath of the 2008–10 crisis. Vivien Schmidt's work has inspired me for a long time to reflect on what is occurring at the intersection of changing capitalism, democracy and European integration. The Jean Monnet module on solidarity coordinated at ULB by Ramona Coman and Anne Weyembergh (2016–19) provided further opportunities for interdisciplinary exchanges on social issues in Europe.

I am also very thankful to the successive generations of students in the module "The Internal Market and Social Europe" (POLI O416) at ULB. The course has provided both the motivation and the backbone for this book. Through their questions and presentations the students have helped me to conceive of analytical tools in an attempt to bring controversy and nuance, politics and policy together.

The initial work on this book started back in 2018 thanks to a visiting fellowship at the Institute for Social Science Research at the Universiteit van Amsterdam. I would like to thank warmly Jonathan Zeitlin for inviting me and for his advice and challenging input. The work accomplished for the book was supported by funding (research credit) from the Fonds National de la Recherche Scientifique (FNRS).

ACKNOWLEDGEMENTS

In various ways, I have benefited tremendously from discussions with a number of colleagues who have either provided feedback on some aspects of the book or with whom I have had a continuous intellectual dialogue over "Social Europe" more broadly, including Lorenza Antonucci, Paul Copeland, Francesco Corti, François Denuit, Maurizio Ferrera, Janine Goetschy, Caroline de la Porte, Philippe Pochet, David Rinaldi and Bart Vanhercke, among others.

I am deeply indebted to Katya Long, as well as Francisco De Araujo Vasquez and Bastian Kenn for their hard work on translating, proofreading and copy-editing parts of the manuscript. Their help has been invaluable and has contributed to make the book what it is. It has been a real pleasure to work with Agenda Publishing and I am grateful for the team's professionalism, efficiency, helpful advice, kindness and patience throughout.

This book is dedicated to my partner Yves Coudron and our daughter Nina. Nina came into this world and grew up as my work on the book unfolded; this period has therefore been a very rich one, filled with two parallel adventures. We live very happily in this strange and great place called Brussels, in a country that has been at the heart of the social struggles surrounding the unification of Europe. In many ways, Brussels as a city epitomizes the European social question. High unemployment and poverty, inequality reinforced by spatial segregation, societal fragmentation and political polarization coexist with a great deal of indifference vis-à-vis the EU, so close and so far at the same time. But Brussels is also a place of solidarity, exhibiting cultural and economic dynamism, multilingualism, social experimentation and tolerance. It is certainly a place to understand that those calling for a return to twentieth-century-style welfare states supporting homogeneous societies are selling a dangerous delusion. Instead, we need to invent new forms of solidarity and find out what social justice means in twenty-first-century Europe and under the global existential threat of climate change.

ABBREVIATIONS AND ACRONYMS

CAP	Common Agricultural Policy
CEEP	European Centre of Employers and Enterprises Providing Public Services
CJEU	Court of Justice of the European Union
DG	Directorate General (of the European Commission)
ECB	European Central Bank
ECFIN	Directorate General for Economic and Financial Affairs
ECOFIN	Council for Economic and Financial Affairs
ECSC	European Coal and Steel Community
EEC	European Economic Community
EES	European Employment Strategy
EESC	European Economic and Social Committee
EMA	European Medicine Agency
EMCO	Employment Committee of the Council of the European Union
EMPL	Directorate General for Employment, Social Affairs and Inclusion
EMU	Economic and Monetary Union
ENVI	Committee on the Environment, Public Health and Food Safety
EP	European Parliament
EPP	European People's Party
EPSCO	Employment, Social Policy, Health and Consumer Affairs Council
EPSR	European Pillar of Social Rights
EPSU	European Public Services Union
ESF	European Social Fund
ETUC	European Trade Union Confederation
EU	European Union
GDP	gross domestic product
GROW	Directorate General for Internal Market, Industry, Entrepreneurship and SMEs
ILO	International Labour Organization
IMF	International Monetary Fund

MEP	Member of the European Parliament
MoU	memorandum of understanding
NGO	non-governmental organization
OECD	Organization for Economic Cooperation and Development
OMC	open method of coordination
SANCO	Directorate General for Health and Food Safety
SGEI	services of general economic interest
SGI	services of general interest
SPC	Social Policy Committee of the Council of the European Union
TEC	Treaty Establishing the European Community
TEU	Treaty on the European Union
TFEU	Treaty on the Functioning of the European Union
UNICE	Union of Industrial and Employers' Confederations of Europe
WHO	World Health Organization

"If poverty could be eliminated with good intentions, the EU would have long eradicated it."

– Olivier De Schutter, UN special rapporteur on extreme
poverty and human rights, January 2021

INTRODUCTION: "SOCIAL EUROPE" – IRRELEVANT, CATCHING UP OR DANGEROUS?

The European social question arises from a shared diagnosis among most scholars and (arguably) political and social actors that there is something wrong with the social dimension of European integration. In other words, the European Union (EU) exhibits a social deficit in the sense that its law and policies, the action of its institutions and its politics fall short in addressing the pressing social issues faced by individual citizens and national societies. Although Europe remains one of the most developed and wealthiest regions in the world, and the birthplace of institutionalized welfare states, one in five people – over 92.4 million or 21.1 per cent of the population – are still at risk of poverty in the 27 member states of the EU. And inequality levels have remained virtually static since the 2008 crisis. A total of 19.4 million children – representing 23.1 per cent of the population – are at risk of poverty across the EU, an exceedingly high number for developed country standards (De Schutter 2021).

Against this background, this book addresses the following overarching question: does the EU serve to enhance social cohesion at the scale of the continent?[1] Any attempt to answer this question almost inevitably begs for a second, related interrogation about whether addressing the social question *should be* the role of the EU. In order to guarantee a satisfactory level of social cohesion moving forward, should the competences of the EU in the field be enhanced or,

---

1. Defining the contours of the EU's role in the social realm is not an easy task. Scholars will often distinguish between social policy (i.e. EU instruments relating to welfare states as such), employment policy and solidarity among member states (cohesion policy). Taking a broad view of the European social question, this book is grounded in the premise that all these dimensions are relevant in the controversies at stake. The book will therefore refer to "social policy" understood broadly as the general action of the EU to address social issues in their multiple dimensions. As far as the objective of said action is concerned, it will refer to "social cohesion" as an endeavour to reduce social inequality both within and across EU member countries. As far as specific policy fields are concerned, health policy is included but education and culture are not. Finally, the social question will be considered to be strongly embedded in broader economic structures and policies. The various conceptual approaches to the European social question are presented in Chapter 1.

on the contrary, curtailed? To be clear, the European social question is therefore not about whether European societies are suffering from serious social issues (the assumption being that they do), but whether the EU does, can or should do something about it. Surely social cohesion has been at the heart of the very project of regional integration ever since its origins after the Second World War. In fact, claims of a need for a stronger "Social Europe" have been a key component serving to legitimize the unification of the continent. Economic integration, and the intertwined European social policy, have been presented by European elites as a strategy to guarantee ever-higher levels of welfare for all Europeans. Therefore, " 'Social Europe' is an analytical category, an ideological construct, as well as a controversy" (Seeliger & Kiess 2019: 5).

Contentious debates around the European social question have intensified with the turn of the twenty-first century, which has seen the unprecedented territorial enlargement, making the EU more heterogeneous than ever, concomitant with a historic deepening of its policies and institutions, as the effects of the monetary union were coming of age. The internal contradictions dividing Europeans were exacerbated under the influence of external events and self-inflicted problems, precipitating the EU in an era of crises. The weak legitimacy of the EU polity, the financial and debt crisis from 2008–10, the unmanaged intensification of migrants' inflows from 2015 onwards, the exit of the UK from the EU, and the Covid-19 pandemic all have their roots in the European social question. And, in turn, these developments also had a major (mainly negative) impact on social cohesion across the EU. The way the EU has responded to these challenges has further fed into debates of both scholars and political actors on what exactly is wrong about the EU social dimension and how it can be fixed. The purpose of this book is to examine a range of key controversies surrounding the European social question and the assessment of "Social Europe". To give account of the fault lines underpinning these controversies, this introduction will present three main assessments provided by distinct scholarly debates, namely that EU social policy is (a) irrelevant or too weak, (b) slowly catching up and (c) dangerous for welfare states and social cohesion. This reflects the fact that any knowledge about the European social question is inevitably intertwined with explicit or implied normative considerations, which is what European social policy *should* be.

A first group[2] of scholars tends to describe the social policy of the EU as irrelevant, meaning that it is too weak to help European states tackle problems

---

2. The "groups" described in this introduction refer in no way to coherent schools of thought and the scholars included in them may have never worked together. As research findings are always more complex than such categories, scholars will find themselves simultaneously in several groups, which can overlap in several respects. Thus these "groups" or "schools" are only used here with the heuristic aim of shedding light on key lines of interpretation within scholarship, in the hope of remaining faithful to the work cited.

of social cohesion. Descriptions of European social governance inevitably point out that the EU has come nowhere near a European welfare state. Not only is the redistributive dimension trumped and restricted to the EU's structural and investment funds (cohesion policy), but even its regulatory instruments are often weak and only apply in a narrow range of policy issues: essentially free movement, health and safety at work and anti-discrimination. Thus, social cohesion and welfare are still governed primarily at the national level, and no deterministic logic of globalization or Europeanization has forced European welfare states to converge (Kleinman 2002). The EU could therefore be described, at worst, as an "empty shell" (Falkner 2000). Despite – or perhaps because – they operated a pro-European Economic Community (EEC)/EU social-liberal conversion, social democratic parties in Europe failed at building a supranational social market economy when they were in power (Delwit 1995; Vesan *et al.* 2021), mainly because they never shared a "substantive social democratic agenda" (Bailey 2005). The inability of the social democrats in the face of the 2008–10 euro crisis to stop a major degrading of welfare institutions was a blatant illustration of this state of affairs (Bailey *et al.* 2017).

A variation of this argument stresses the idea that EU social policy is fundamentally different from national social policy in its nature and function. It was never conceived as to effectively counterbalance market-making through market-correcting. From the outset in the Treaty of Rome, it was rather an "add-on" (Copeland & Daly 2015; Daly 2017) to economic policy, supposed to allow and ease labour mobility within the single market. Legal scholars have argued that the EU's social objectives had been "displaced" from the realm of social policy to that of economic and fiscal policy, from the legislative to judicial terrain and from the realm of hard law to the realm of soft law (Dawson 2018; Garben 2018). This converges with the idea that Social Europe had been to a large extent left to the judges and the markets (Leibfried 2005). Looking at seven decades of European integration, it clearly shows that social policy has remained a "secondary" policy area (Copeland 2020). Thus, for many scholars, it is fair to say that "Social Europe", understood as a supranational social market economy, including its redistributive and corporatist components, "is dead" (Crespy & Menz 2015b; Ewing 2015). Looking to the past, historians have argued that hoping for a more social Europe has been like "waiting for Godot" (Ramírez Pérez 2020). Looking at the present and to the future, it may also present a "dead end", especially after the euro crisis that has accelerated a "downward spiral" (Lechevallier & Wielgohs 2015).

Shifting the focus from the European to the national level, an important strand of the literature has shown that the effects of EU social policy depend primarily on domestic actors (Graziano *et al.* 2011; Jacquot 2013; Palier 2000). Whether EU social policy translates – if at all – into progressive or regressive reforms of national welfare states depends on the strategic "usages" from national actors seeking to use European cognitive, financial or discursive resources to pursue and legitimize their own agenda (Jacquot & Woll 2004, 2010). This has been especially true in an era that has seen the rise of the open method of coordination (OMC) relying on soft law (Heidenreich & Zeitlin 2009; Zeitlin & Pochet 2005), which opens the door to integrating the EU with the national politics of welfare state reforms (Graziano 2007) and comparing the differentiated impact of Europe on, for instance, the southern and eastern peripheries (Guillen & Palier 2004).

Putting into perspective the irrelevance or weakness, a second group of scholars tends to show how social policy at the EU level is catching up. Studying the developments in the field, they show how EU competences develop incrementally as the interdependency between economies and societies increases. Thus, market-correcting instruments are adopted in a second step of policy-making to match new stages of economic integration. To a certain extent, this echoes the neo-functionalist idea that a spillover from economic (and monetary) integration to social integration exists. This ebb and flow of social policy is particularly visible in the early twenty-first century. The EU experienced a pro-market offensive led by the Court of Justice of the European Union (CJEU) in particular and the European Commission under the leadership of Jose Manuel Barroso (Crespy & Menz 2015a). In this period, liberalization and economic liberties predominantly shaped the European agenda. Legislative initiatives to bring social regulation forward were scant and, when submitted, were impeded by major political disagreements and/or ended in a political deadlock (Graziano & Hartlapp 2019). The era was clearly more favourable to harmless voluntary coordination. When the 2008 financial crisis erupted and turned into a crisis of sovereign debt in Europe, the EU initially promoted an "austeritarian" response that met little resistance (Hyman 2015). Since 2014, however, the EU institutions have taken a clear pro-investment turn, implying a heightened awareness of pressing social matters. Many analyses have shown how the European Semester, the main governance framework for coordinating social and economic policy in the EU, has undergone a process of socialization (Verdun & Zeitlin 2017; Zeitlin & Vanhercke 2014). After their initial marginalization, social policy actors within the European Commission, the Council of the European Union (also known as "the Council") and civil society have fought their way back into economic governance and successfully obtained the inclusion of new benchmarks, instruments and an overall heightened visibility of social issues on the EU's agenda. Since 2014, the European Commission – under the chairmanship of Jean-Claude Juncker (2014–19), followed by Ursula von der Leyen (2019–24) – has clearly shown a renewed entrepreneurship for driving social policy forward (Vesan *et al.* 2021).

The described process of catching up has been mostly depicted as a slow one, shaped by constraints stemming from institutional settings and past decisions, on the one hand, and by the contingency of political actors' mobilization, on the other. From a historical institutionalist perspective, Pierson (1996) famously argued that European social policy was path dependent, meaning that it was building up over time because of the unintended consequences of past decisions. In his seminal article, he referred to the inclusion of Article 119A in the Treaty of Rome requiring "equal pay" between men and women. His account (and that of many others) stresses the importance of political struggles in particular. Only a vivid feminist movement and prominent individual entrepreneurs could make Article 119A the cornerstone of what would become an innovative European policy promoting gender equality. At the same time, social policy enjoys only limited room for change as the field is "best characterized by continuity in form of dominance and of economic over social integration, incremental developments and a focus on soft, non-binding instruments" (Hartlapp 2019: 2112). After ten years of "muddling through" in the face of contestation and the rise of populist anti-European movements (Crespy 2020b), the EU social policy agenda exhibits a renewal, perhaps best illustrated by the European Pillar of Social Rights (EPSR) (Vesan *et al.* 2021) (see Box 7.4, p. 156). Thus, a longitudinal perspective, is useful to understand how the political struggles between "economically oriented actors" and "socially oriented actors" (De la Porte & Pochet 2002) shape phases of progressive policy-making with phases of regressive policy-making. This is visible when considering, for instance, the avatars of social investment in EU policy-making in a historical perspective (De la Porte & Palier forthcoming).

A third group of scholars has analysed the EU's action in the social realm from a very critical angle, implying that European social policy is dangerous for social cohesion. They have done so from various theoretical and disciplinary angles. Anchored in political economy, a "German school"[3] has argued that the EU suffers from an intrinsic pro-market bias built into its institutional and legal architecture. Fritz Scharpf (2010) has famously claimed that the EU *cannot* be a social market economy as market-making through liberalization (negative integration) is bound to prevail over market correction and social regulation (positive integration) in EU politics. According to Scharpf, this is due to the over constitutionalization of the four fundamental freedoms and the prominent institutional position of the European Commission and the CJEU – two competition- and market-oriented actors – coupled with the ever-greater divergence of preferences among the member states trapped into collective action problems in the Council. In the same line of analysis, many others have shown how the CJEU had contributed to debase the national institutions of regulated capitalism, notably by promoting the

---

3. Notably at the Max-Planck Institut für Gesellschaftsforschung established in Cologne.

freedom to provide services over national collective agreements (e.g. Höpner & Schäfer 2010: 401). Having long been sceptical about the capacity of the European social dialogue to spur effective neo-corporatism at the supranational level, owing to the prevalence of business interests at EU level (Streeck 1994), Streeck became one of the harshest critics of the EU, claiming that the history of European social policy was the story of a "progressive regression" (Streeck 2019). Furthermore, the "pessimistic" students of industrial relations have stressed that the structural weakness of trade unions from the former Communist bloc in central and eastern Europe, short of financial and political resources. This has fed into the structural heterogeneity of interests and cultures and has so far prevented the emergence of powerful transnational class mobilization of labour against the offensive of the capital (Seeliger & Kiess 2019).

Applying a different angle, an "English school" of social policy scholars has also emphasized the pro-market bias of EU social policy. This was exemplified through critical accounts of soft coordination, from the OMC to the European Semester (Copeland & Daly 2014; Daly 2006). More broadly, these authors have argued that the more recent developments in EU social policy had only exacerbated the asymmetry between economic and social policy, and questioned the fact that it was ever to be tackled in the face of major "institutional, political and social obstacles" (Bailey 2017; Copeland & Daly 2014; Daly 2006). Analysing the neoliberalization of EU policy-making under its many facets, Whyman *et al.* (2012: 321) conclude that "a Social Europe is an impossible dream".

A similar critique was formulated in the most radical way by the neo-Gramscian scholars of the "Amsterdam school". Following the seminal work of Ryner, Overbeek and Holman (Ryner *et al.* 1998), these authors have analysed how the EU has driven the restructuring of political economies and fed the hegemony of neoliberalism. From a Gramscian perspective, the power of dominant elites is underpinned by the crystallization of a consensus within society on an ideology that fosters their own material interests. This has implied the absorption and neutralization of alternative paradigms such as regulated capitalism and the social market economy (Van Apeldoorn *et al.* 2009). This was notably operated through the collective action of a transnational class of capital holders, including business associations (Van Apeldoorn 2003) – starting with the round table of industrialists, today BusinessEurope – international groups of experts (Horn 2009: 170) and multinational corporations (Horn & Wigger 2016). Focusing less on ideas and more on the material accumulation of capital, neo-Marxist scholars were perhaps the first to pioneer the radical critique of EU integration in the 1980s (Cocks 1980). From this perspective, European social policy is essentially shaped by the transformation of class politics in the long run (Bieler 2005, 2015). Since 1970, the transnationalization of capital accelerated by global financial capitalism allowed economic elites to escape the constraints of national neo-corporatism and labour demands. As a consequence, trade unions have seen their structural political power decline, which was only aggravated by the reforms implemented in response to the 2008–10 euro crisis. So far, the labour movement has proved unable to elaborate strategies of transnational cooperation sufficiently effective to rebalance the power relations between capital and labour (Bieler *et al.* 2015).

In a more eclectic fashion, a "French school" building on history and sociology argues that EU integration is fundamentally a neoliberal project. Promoted vividly by the United States in the aftermath of the Second World War, European unification took an early path to liberalization with the four freedoms enshrined in the Treaty of Rome. Since economic liberalism constitutes the DNA of the EU, as for instance Denord and Schwartz (2009) contend, a "Social Europe" never existed and will never exist. Rather than thwarting market integration, European social policy has only empowered it, serving to legitimize a strategy that relies primarily on financial liberalization (Salais 2013). Far from being the patron of Social Europe's golden age, Jacques Delors thus needs to be reassessed as a figure of the French "second left", namely a group of social liberal technocrats who have shaped financial globalization (Abdelal 2006).[4] In the same vein, the European Trade Union Confederation (ETUC) should be seen as a technocratic structure converted to neoliberalism and detrimental to the way in which industrial relations have traditionally served to regulate class conflict (Gobin 1997: 293; Dufresne & Gobin 2016).[5] Finally, because social policy can only be legitimized by culture, communities and language, it can only be rooted in nation states and local communities, while concepts of social policy can never be translated at EU level (Barbier 2015).

Finally, the "neo-Rokkanian" Italian school looks at the European social question from a socio-historical angle – inspired by the work of Stein Rokkan – on state formation in Europe, cleavages and mass politics (Flora 1999). According to this perspective, EU integration is conceived as the sixth phase of Europe's political structuring, albeit a disruptive one. Ever since the sixteenth century, successive stages of state building, capitalist development, nation formation, democratization and welfare state institutionalization have all implied the consolidation of overlapping territorial, political and social boundaries at the national scale. Within those boundaries, political institutions and solidarity mechanisms have served to mediate conflicts and channel voice (Bartolini 2005). In contrast, EU integration has implied the opening of national boundaries, creating "a tension

---

4. Rawi Abdelal is an American scholar at the Harvard Business School. His research deals with global finance and he has a special expertise on France and the post-Soviet world.
5. Corinne Gobin and Anne Dufresne are specialists of socio-economic governance and the EU from Belgium.

between the project of [a] stateless market at the wider European level and the nationally bounded cultural, redistributive and political capacities" (Bartolini 2005: 375). In other words, the EU has a de-structuring effect on national states and societies because it undermines both state capacity (at the macro level) and political participation (at the micro level). In turn, the re-establishment of politico-administrative and social boundaries at the European level (i.e. the formation of a new "centre" in Brussels) is bound to trigger resistance from peripheral territories and social groups. In this vein, EU integration has implied the opening of "welfare boundaries" threatening the nation-based social systems of redistribution and rights, which are the foundations of social citizenship (Ferrera 2003). The weakness of "Social Europe" epitomizes this unbalanced process of restructuring, which both undermines the EU's capacity to tackle social problems and further fuels the legitimacy crisis (Ferrera 2005). This results in the rise of Euroscepticism, welfare chauvinism within societies and the exacerbation of the centre–periphery cleavage among European states.

Thus, if most scholars probably agree that something is wrong with the role of the EU in social policy, they have presented different arguments as to what exactly this is and why, through a variety of disciplinary and theoretical lenses. These controversies become even more acute when one asks how these problems should be fixed going forward. Is it possible to close the gap between expectations for a more efficient and just European social policy, on the one hand, and actual EU policy-making, on the other? Is Social Europe "an impossible dream" (Whyman *et al.* 2012)?

In an endeavour to present the main lines of the debate in a simple and analytical way (at the risk of oversimplification), three stances will be distinguished here: a *minimal Social Europe* advocated by the "defenders of nation states", the *further build-up of EU social policy* proposed by the "European advisors", and a *major overhaul* of European social policy called for by "Keynesians" and "Habermasians".

Arguing that "Social Europe is a myth" (Höpner 2018), the political economists of the "German school" presented earlier have been the most vocal defenders of nation states as they call for better protection of national social systems against the "destructive dynamics of liberalization", deploring "the fact that a more social EU sometimes needs 'more Europe' but sometimes also needs 'protection against too much Europe' [which] remains a taboo among social democrats and trade unionists even today" (Höpner 2018: n.p.). A key argument has focused on how the Economic and Monetary Union (EMU) has forced contrasted national growth models and social systems to converge; to only see the consequences when the euro crisis required competitive adjustment in the periphery at the expense of internal devaluation driving wages and social standards, thus engineering a social disaster. Scharpf (2016) therefore called to break the EMU into two different currency areas, leaving room for a more flexible mechanism of monetary adjustment. In a confrontational piece criticizing the views of Habermas and the German political establishment alike, Streeck (2014: 213) claimed that:

> the European currency union is not "Europe"; it is a multilateral agreement about a common currency and its administration. Insofar as it does "unify" Europe, it does so by depriving participating states of the possibility of pursuing their own monetary policy fitted to their specific needs.

From a legal perspective, Joerges put forward a critical analysis of the role of the CJEU in the socio-economic realm (Joerges & Rödl 2009) in 2000, to then regard the euro crisis as a perversion of EU law by emergency politics. In other words, legal institutions and professionals had widely served to legitimize discretionary decisions, thus leading to "de-legalization", "de-socialization" and "disenfranchisement" of the EU (Everson & Joerges 2012; see also Joerges 2017). Unfreezing the EU constitutional framework to allow possible conflicts with legitimate national law (e.g. labour law) is accordingly presented as a solution to address the EU's drift towards "executive managerialism". A larger group of scholars further considered the euro crisis as marking "the end of the Eurocrat's dream" of an "ever closer union" (Chalmers *et al.* 2016). In Polanyian terms, many held the view that a countermovement from society to protect itself from the offensive of markets was to be equated with an effective curtailing of the EU's power to intrude into the national realm of socio-economic arrangements. Along this line of reasoning, Crum (2015) defended a vision of European social policy that can be seen as minimal, in the sense that it would essentially *not* overly intrude into national social systems. More specifically, he suggested that the EU has three duties: (a) to guarantee equal access to the economic opportunities arising from integration, (b) to support national social institutions as they aim to fulfil European values and (c) to preserve one's autonomy to decide on social policy arrangements.

Adopting a different stance in this debate, a number of social policy specialists have suggested ways to tackle the weaknesses of European social policy through a further build-up of the EU's capacity. These scholars have often acted as *advisers* of the EU institutions or think tanks close to policy-making circles. Beyond the variety of policy proposals, there is arguably a shared vision relying on moderate reforms that can be undertaken in the current constitutional framework of the EU, and that avoid opening the political Pandora's box of treaty reform. Departing from a call for a federal leap, Ferrera and Vandenbroucke (among others) have promoted a European social union best conceived as a "holding environment" for national welfare states (Ferrera 2018; Vandenbroucke *et al.*

2016). A main point of departure is the idea that the European level is the right scale of governance for protecting welfare states from the retrenchment trends implied by global economic competition. The purpose of the European Social Union is to allow the coexistence of diverse social systems while tackling the risks of detrimental competition because of free movement and ensuring their resilience during crises. This goes hand in hand with the consolidation of social rights in a common space of European citizenship. This vision accommodates two long-standing proposals, namely the adoption at EU level of social investment as a unifying paradigm driving the reforms of welfare states (Hemerijck 2016; Vandenbroucke *et al.* 2011), on the one hand, and the set-up of a European unemployment insurance scheme for stabilizing economies in the face of recession (Andor *et al.* 2014), on the other. More recent debates have spurred critical analyses of socio-economic coordination through the European Semester and suggested how to make it more conducive of social cohesion, for instance by focusing more on progressive taxation (Antonucci & Corti 2020) or by creating a social imbalance procedure mirroring the economic imbalance procedure (Corti *et al.* 2019). Moreover, the potential of the EPSR to catalyse the EU's renewed social policy agenda has also been widely discussed (Cantillon 2019; De la Porte 2019b). Drawing on the lessons from the regressive moment triggered by the euro crisis, but also from Brexit and the ongoing legitimacy crisis of the European project, the social union envisaged should build on a "neighbourhood community" anchored in pragmatic fraternity, reciprocity and the benevolent ethic of responsibility towards the weaker (Ferrera 2017).

Sceptical of small steps for reforming Social Europe at the margins, many voices have called for a major overhaul of EU social policy and its institutions. A widely shared claim among authors with Keynesian views is to shift away from the triangle of fiscal discipline, competitiveness and activation to a return to demand-side policy and the de-commodification of workers and public services (Copeland 2020). Achieving this at European scale implies a fight against two "natural enemies", namely neoliberalism and nationalism (Crouch 2020: 2). However, this does not mean a return to the national Keynesian welfare state of the twentieth century. Rather, there is a need for creative and future-oriented policy solutions; for instance a turn to a new socio-ecological paradigm that can "redefine prosperity without growth" (Pochet 2019: 324) or to address the structural transformations of work driven by technological and societal change (Crouch 2020: 36–41). This group of authors has particularly stressed the need to think of European social policy together with the democratization of the EU. For example, in order to better connect national politics and socio-economic governance, an interdisciplinary group of French scholars has put forward a "Treaty on the Democratization of the Economic and Social Government of the European Union" called "T-Dem" (Hennette *et al.* 2017, 2019). A major proposal in the T-Dem is the creation of an assembly of the euro area composed of members of national parliaments and the European Parliament (EP) entitled to wide decision-making powers in the socio-economic realm. Others have also called into question the independence of the European Central Bank (ECB) to extend its mandate to deal better with redistributive issues and thus really "serve the people" (Dietsch *et al.* 2018). A main claim is the need to make EU institutions more responsive to national politics (including social movements, for instance), when contestation about liberalization and the marketization of welfare arises (Crespy 2012, 2016).

A major overhaul is also advocated by those envisaging the future of the EU from a Habermasian perspective. Ever since his reflections on "the post-national constellation" (Habermas 1998), Habermas has undeniably been the most prominent advocate of the federalization of the EU as the only way to make the EU fully democratic. In his view, socio-economic policy-making and democratic decision-making must fully overlap and be underpinned by shared norms enshrined in a common constitution. In the aftermath of the euro crisis, he criticized what he calls "post-democratic executive federalism", that is inter-governmental decision-making taking place away from citizens' eyes (Habermas 2013a: 12). In the name of interpersonal social justice Europe-wide, the idea of a European basic income, called "Euro-Dividend", has been put forward by Van Parijs and Vanderborght (2017) (see also Denuit 2020). According to its proponents, such an instrument is functionally justified by ties of interdependence and could both support national welfare states and make manifest the elusive European social citizenship.[6] Although an admittedly weak form of intervention, the idea of a guarantee to tackle child poverty and inequality at a young age has, in the meantime, made its way on to the EU's political agenda.[7] Calls to strengthen the EU's redistributive capacity are based on the idea that there is no theoretical ground for restricting distributive justice to – ethnically defined – national communities instead of broader social cooperation and solidarity among distinct *demoi*, as is already the case in multinational states (Rawls & Van Parijs 2003).

After a decade of harsh critiques and widespread despair as to the capacity of the EU in fostering social cohesion, the Covid-19 pandemic has seemingly heralded a new era. The sheer scale of the ongoing recession has led European

---

6. In 2020, a European Citizen Initiative for demanding the establishment of a European basic income was launched.

7. On 24 March 2021, the European Commission made a proposal for a Council Recommendation Establishing a European Child Guarantee (COM 2021: 137). While non-legally binding, the recommendation would see member states commit to guarantee access for all children to essential services (education, including early childhood education and care, healthcare, nutrition and housing, culture and leisure activities).

leaders to adopt a recovery plan that almost doubles the European budget for 2021–27 and relies on an unprecedented creation of common European debt. While there is a lot to say about the new additions to the EU's toolbox, it has also been a reminder that nothing is ever definitively "locked in", as contingent events reconfigure political struggles. At the same time, the last Social Summit held in Porto in May 2021 showed that political conflict lines were enduring as a number of member states have clearly expressed their reluctance vis-à-vis a significant increase in the EU's role in social policy. Thus far, the legitimacy of the EU's action in this area remains fragile and contested. The following chapters in this book will shed light on the more specific controversies underpinning the grand debates of the European social question. The purpose is to provide the relevant historical background, analytical tools and empirical insights enabling the readers to hopefully forge their own views about whether or not the EU can be more conducive to social cohesion.

1

WHAT IS THE EUROPEAN SOCIAL QUESTION?

The European social question concerns both the past and the future of the EU. Compared to other countries in the Organization for Economic Cooperation and Development (OECD), European citizens enjoy the highest level of social protection in the world. Yet, over the past three decades, social cohesion in Europe has been tremendously challenged by economic, technological and demographic change. All European countries are experiencing the degradation of the welfare state (albeit at different paces), the persistence of old and new forms of poverty and the rise of social inequality. The re-commodification of social rights has affected all advanced capitalist economies in the wake of financial capitalism. Against this background, how should we assess the role of the EU and what does it suggest going forward? Has the EU enhanced or, on the contrary, undermined social cohesion? Should its competences in this realm be strengthened or curtailed?

"Solidarity", "equality between men and women" and "full employment and social progress" feature as main principles in the Treaty on the European Union (TEU). Incrementally, the European Community – later the EU – has created new transnational rights for mobile workers and citizens, and it now has a considerable body of regulation based on the principle of non-discrimination. At the same time, the coming of age of a social union in its own right has remained elusive, and the promise of upward convergence was not kept. As the latest financial crisis has shown, what we have been witnessing is a widening of the gap between the continent's wealthy core and its peripheries. The humanitarian crisis provoked by the austerity pushed by the Troika in Greece (see Chapter 3) will remain a dark episode in Europe's history. With the outbreak of Covid-19 in January 2020, Europeans have had to face new challenges. The circulation of the virus led to the suspension of some fundamental liberties granted by the EU, such as the freedom of movement across countries. Although governments and the EU alike have rediscovered the importance of robust healthcare and educations systems – among other collective goods and welfare services – they have had to learn to act jointly vis-à-vis international pharmaceutical corporations to ensure the vaccination of the European population. Last but not least, a historic recession is in the process of unfolding, as most European economies have been put on hold for over a year at the time of writing.

This chapter will lay the groundwork for addressing the European social question and the controversies surrounding it. After presenting the key concepts relating to EU social policy, it will provide a brief overview of the explanations advanced in the literature to explain the weakness of EU social policy-making. The final section looks at the various normative perspectives on the European social question. Ultimately, whether or not the EU should be held accountable for ensuring social justice also depends on what (if anything) binds Europeans together.

Grasping the social question from different conceptual angles

A range of concepts are relevant to the European social question. They differ from each other in that they examine the question from different angles: at the micro/individual, meso/institutional level or macro/polity level. This introductory chapter cannot do justice to the long intellectual history of such concepts. Our purpose is rather to provide some conceptual milestones and to explain how they can be understood in the context of the debates over EU social policy.

Inequality, justice and solidarity

Evidence for the persistence of social inequality in Europe is often the starting point for raising the European social question. A vast body of research in economics and sociology has documented the fact that, since the 1980s, the social gap between the rich and the poor has increased within all advanced capitalist economies (i.e. OECD countries). This is mainly due to the engrained dynamics of financial capitalism that led to the concentration of capital and wealth at the very top of the social ladder. While inequality is mostly conceived of in terms of income inequality, other factors such as disposable income before and after taxation, property wealth and access to public services (such as education and healthcare) should be considered to draw a more faithful picture of social inequalities. In Europe, "the Gini coefficient[1] increased on average from 0.28

---

1. Put forward by the Italian economist and statistician Corrado Gini, the Gini coefficient measures the dispersion of income (or wealth) across social groups as a ratio. It is usually expressed as a value between 0 and 1 where 0 means absolute equality and 1 absolute inequality (or the concentration of wealth in the hands of one person).

in the 1980s to 0.30 in 2014" (OECD 2017: 8), indicating an increase in social polarization across the board with the 10 per cent richest people in Europe earning 9.5 times more than the poorest 10 per cent.[2] Of paramount importance for grasping the European social question is the analytical distinction between (vertical) inequality within European societies, on the one hand, and (horizontal) inequality between or across European societies, on the other (on the latter, see the section on "cohesion and convergence" later in this chapter). When combining vertical and horizontal forms of inequality, it is possible to distinguish three broad social classes across the continent (Hugrée *et al.* 2020): the working class (43 per cent of the European active population), threatened by global financial capitalism and unemployment; the privileged class (19 per cent of the European active population), a relatively homogeneous group of very mobile individuals with high cultural capital; and the intermediate class (38 per cent of the European active population), a mixed group with different orientations. While the majority of the working class is to be found in the south and east of Europe as well as in rural areas, the intermediate and privileged class is more present in the north-west of the continent and is mainly urban.

Tackling social inequality is fundamental to attaining social justice, which is a normative goal whose meaning remains disputed. Notwithstanding, John Rawls's theory of justice has been key to shaping the contemporary conception of social justice in Europe. Reduced to its most basic expression, it relies on fairness and reciprocity in sharing the duties and benefits of social cooperation (Rawls 1971). Whatever that may imply for the EU – this being controversial – it is important for the EU's legitimacy that a majority of Europeans believe that the EU is working to reinforce rather than undermine justice among Europeans.

The struggle against inequality and attempts at social justice at the European level need to be rooted in a sense of solidarity among Europeans. Solidarity is a fundamentally ethical concept that goes beyond moral duty or legal obligation. Relying on a sense of fraternity, solidarity does not exist in natural (i.e. ethnic) communities, but in political – or artificial – communities cemented by trust in predictable reciprocity (Habermas 2013b). For all that, solidarity should not be conflated with altruism, but is rather in tune with the fulfilment of one's long-term self-interest (Habermas 2013b). Whereas solidarity is mentioned multiple times in the EU treaties, it is unclear to what extent it has actually materialized

---

2. "The Nordic countries are among the most equal European countries, but Central Eastern European countries (Slovenia, the Czech and Slovak Republics) also have lower levels of income inequality [see Figure 2.1]. Western European countries, such as France, Germany and the Netherlands, are close to the European average, while the level of income inequality is above average in all southern European countries. The highest levels of income inequality in Europe are reached in the UK and the Baltic States. Inequality in Europe is generally lower than in many non-European countries, in particular the United States and Israel" (OECD 2017: 7).

into the kind of social relations that bind Europeans today. The normative, legal and institutional underpinnings of European solidarity are at the heart of today's controversies surrounding European integration (Coman *et al.* 2019).

Social rights and social citizenship

The EU (previously the EEC) has consistently asserted the ambition of protecting and enhancing individual social rights, albeit in a limited and sometimes ambiguous fashion. In this perspective, a non-binding Community Charter of the Fundamental Social Rights of Workers was adopted in 1989 to address trade unions' demands in terms of working conditions and access to employment. In 2000, a European Convention proclaimed a European Charter of Fundamental Rights, a sort of Magna Carta or Bill of Rights of the EU, which incorporates social rights into a wider body of personal, civil, political and social rights and affirms their indivisibility. In doing so, it deepened the existing social rights (e.g. work–life balance or equality between men and women), on the one hand, and created new ones (e.g. the integration of people with disabilities, or the ban on child labour), on the other (Jacquot 2014: 204).

However, the jurisprudence of the CJEU based on the interpretation of the charter reveals that the court has implicitly established a hierarchy between rights whereby social rights belong mostly to the category of fundamental *principles* rather than genuine rights. This means that they are only invoked if they have already been established in European or national legal provisions (Kenner 2003).

Fundamentally, the notion of social citizenship remains attached to membership in the national community. At the European level, citizenship manifests itself as a market-based citizenship granting rights to individuals as economic agents (workers) as necessary for the development of the single market. Thus, the thin, or even invisible, social dimension of European citizenship has time and again been underlined in contrast with the thick notion of national social citizenship embedded in welfare states (Strath & Magnusson 2004). More specifically, however, European social citizenship can be considered as "nested" in the complex functioning of a multi-level, multi-tiered federal polity (Faist 2001).

EU social rights thus mostly materialize as European citizens are granted access to social rights and protection when they live in a place that is not their country of nationality. The 2004 so-called citizenship directive[3] extended access to the social protection enjoyed by workers to economic inactive categories of

---

3. Directive 2004/38/EC of 29 April 2004 on the right of citizens of the EU and their family members to move and reside freely within the territory of the member states.

people (e.g. retirees or students). Yet, national governments remain powerful gatekeepers who, under the pressure of vivid popular fear of alleged "welfare tourism", have imposed increasing restrictions to access for migrant EU citizens. This trend has been backed by the CJEU. All in all, the openness of national welfare states has remained limited and a pattern of stratification has emerged among EU citizens depending on their individual status, resources and country of origin (Bruzelius & Seeleib-Kaiser 2019).

Welfare states and the European social model

Welfare states find their origins in nineteenth-century Europe (and notably Germany under the chancellorship of Otto von Bismarck) where social protection for the poor and workers started to develop. The welfare state can be defined as the institutionalized form of solidarity within a society based on regulations and the redistribution of resources through a common budget. From a political point of view, the size and shape of the welfare state is the result of confrontations and compromises between various social groups and territories within a state. The emergence of social protection has played a key role in the legitimation of modern states, both before and after the Second World War.

In his seminal book *The Three Worlds of Welfare Capitalism*, the Danish sociologist Gosta Esping-Andersen (1990) distinguishes three models of welfare states in Europe, namely the liberal model, the conservative model and the social democratic model; a typology that was later enriched with a southern or Mediterranean model (Ferrera 1996) and an eastern post-communist model (Kuitto 2016) (see further discussion in Chapter 2). More recently, research has shown that welfare states have been incrementally reshaped by neoliberal retrenchment or social investment while conserving their historically entrenched features (Palier 2010). This book focuses on policy-making at the EU level rather than on the comparative analysis of welfare state reform in Europe. However, the effects of EU policies can only be understood in terms of their differentiated impact across countries as they are "filtered" by historically and culturally rooted national welfare states.

Given the diversity of national welfare states, scholars have contested the very existence of a European social model and the challenges it has faced since the 1990s (Careja *et al.* 2020; Ebbinghaus 1999). The phrase, attributed to Jacques Delors, who was president of the European Commission from 1985 to 1954, has a political connotation meaning that, beyond their specificities, national social models are united by a high level of social protection and an ambition to strive towards social progress rooted in the history of Europe. Although the notion of a European social model has no legal or institutional existence, it is reflected in the values proclaimed in Article 3.3 of the Treaty on the Functioning of the

European Union (TFEU).[4] Since the dawn of the twenty-first century, some scholars and politicians – notably Mario Draghi when he headed the ECB in 2012 (*Wall Street Journal* 2012)– have claimed that the European social model had been extinguished by economic downturns or that it had proved regressive in its actual content (Barbier 2015).

EU socio-economic governance and Social Europe

The socio-economic governance of the EU is at the core of the controversies tackled here. Rather than a homogeneous policy area, social policy at the EU level consists of a complex patchwork of procedures and instruments. It is key to note that, on the basis of EU treaty provisions, the EU has limited competences in social policy as the bulk of competences and financial resources remains with national states.

From a legal point of view, the nature of the EU's social policy competences – mainly laid down in Title X of the TFEU – are twofold. According to Article 153, the EU has a *shared competence* in a number of areas, in which it is entitled to adopt binding legislation via its ordinary legislative procedure. In other areas, it only has a *supporting competence*, meaning that it can only help coordinate the actions of national governments through non-binding recommendations.

Thus, EU social policy consists of a set of public policies in diverse areas, including workers' mobility within the single market, labour law, employment policy, anti-discrimination (including gender equality), the fight against poverty and social exclusion, public health and social protection (including pensions and healthcare). Across these fields, the EU can use a range of instruments rooted in different modes of governance, namely regulation, the social dialogue, redistribution through funds and soft coordination. Furthermore, the EU's socio-economic governance can only be understood in relation to the broader economic framework in which it is nested, namely the single market and the EMU.

"Social Europe", an expression often used to refer to EU-level socio-economic governance, carries an additional political connotation. Deployed as a motto

---

4. "The Union shall establish an internal market. It shall work for the sustainable development of Europe based on balanced economic growth and price stability, a highly competitive social market economy, aiming at full employment and social progress, and a high level of protection and improvement of the quality of the environment. It shall promote scientific and technological advance. It shall combat social exclusion and discrimination, and shall promote social justice and protection, equality between women and men, solidarity between generations and protection of the rights of the child. It shall promote economic, social and territorial cohesion, and solidarity among member states. It shall respect its rich cultural and linguistic diversity, and shall ensure that Europe's cultural heritage is safeguarded and enhanced."

by left-wing political and social actors since the early days of EU integration, Social Europe means that the EU fosters (or ought to foster) progressive social policy-making for enhancing the protection of workers and the vulnerable. As presented in the introduction to this book, various scholars have argued that the pursuit of Social Europe has proved elusive, the most critical arguing that it will never exist, and that the EU has, on the contrary, contributed to the debasing of national social policy and welfare states. Social Europe is there therefore a controversy itself.

In a nutshell, the EU should not be seen as a supranational welfare state. EU social policy exhibits a strong inclination towards regulation with a weak redistributive dimension because of the small size of the EU's budget. While some political actors had hoped that the EU would turn into a fully fledged welfare state over time, they have been sorely disappointed. Current debates focus on how the EU can become a "social union" that would be a "holding environment" for national welfare states (Vandenbroucke *et al.* 2016).

Cohesion and convergence

Mentioned in Article 3 of the TEU, the promotion of "economic, social and territorial cohesion" is an old theme dating back to the early days of the EEC. At the time, cohesion was essentially conceived as the need to foster the economic catch-up of less industrialized territories (especially in Italy, and later in the rest of southern Europe) and it has underpinned the EU's cohesion policy based on the distribution of funds to economically underperforming regions. Historically, an implicit understanding among European decision-makers has prevailed, whereby the EU should promote the integration of markets as convergence towards higher living standards across countries results automatically from economic growth. At the same time, however, Articles 174 and 175 of the TFEU authorize the EU to adopt legislation to foster the "strengthening of its economic, social and territorial cohesion". In the 1990s and 2000s, it was also believed that monetary integration through the creation of the euro would accelerate the convergence Europeans were hoping for. The issue of cohesion and convergence became increasingly acute after the 2004 eastern enlargement.

Although some socio-economic catch-up has taken place – Ireland being a success story in this regard – the 2008 financial crisis revealed that socio-economic structures across the continent had remained profoundly different. The ensuing recession even exacerbated the gap between a wealthy northern and continental core and struggling peripheries in the south, east and the Baltic region (Makszin *et al.* 2020). In addition, the rise of competitive financial capitalism globally brought about an increase in social inequalities across the board.

More recently, the need to foster convergence has crystallized into the idea of "upward convergence", that is the need to improve social welfare both within and between European societies. Insofar as this was the ambition for the founding fathers of the EEC, the capacity of the EU to foster upward convergence across the continent should be the yardstick to assess social policy at the EU level. In this regard, today's state of affairs is disappointing. Looking to the future, it is also concerning that the EU seems dramatically ill-equipped to deal with the challenges facing societies and states in an era of digitalization, eroding social rights and ecological debate.

Explanations for the EU's social deficit

Institutional factors: a fundamental asymmetry between economic and social integration

By combining political economy – and more specifically international trade theory – and rational-choice institutionalism, Fritz Scharpf (1999) has argued that the EU exhibits a structural imbalance between negative and positive integration. Negative integration is geared towards market building and expansion and relies essentially on liberalization and deregulation. It has underpinned the building of a common market through the four freedoms and the suppression of national customs, tariffs and regulations to stimulate cross-border trade in Europe. In contrast, positive integration consists of creating new rules, instruments and resources at the EU level to regulate markets (or correct market failure), govern and redistribute. Negative integration is rooted in rules that have been given constitutional value in the treaties, namely the four freedoms and competition law. The European Commission and the CJEU have strategically used their strong prerogatives in these two areas to enhance market expansion and, at the same time, their own position in the EU institutional system. On the other hand, it has been increasingly difficult for member states with contrasted preferences to agree on market correction and social policy. This is all the more problematic given that a qualified majority (or unanimity) must be reached for the Council to take a decision. This constellation, according to Scharpf (2010), makes it impossible for the EU to become a "social market economy" at the supranational level.

From a historical-institutionalist perspective, it is possible to argue that this fundamental asymmetry is path dependent (Pierson 1996). This means that it reproduces itself over time, as actors tend to find themselves locked into certain configurations as a result of decisions made in the past. For example, when the socio-economic governance framework was overhauled in the aftermath of the financial crisis in 2011, the new framework (the European Semester) reproduced this imbalance between market-making and fiscal discipline, on the one hand, and social policy objectives, on the other (Copeland & Daly 2015). Similarly, lawyers find a continuous asymmetry in the EU's constitutional framework whereby "EU member states are asked to be competitive and lean, but they are pardoned for not being social enough" (De Schutter 2021: n.p.). Examining the EPSR– one of the major policy instruments adopted over the past few years in the realm of social policy – from a legal perspective, it appears that "the Pillar is not capable of addressing the fundamental constitutional asymmetry that underlies European integration's 'social problem'" (Garben 2018: 212) and that it was rather "continuing the displacement of the (national and European) legislator in the internal market and economic governance" (Garben 2018: 210).

Ideational factors: the neoliberal turn and the death of Social Europe

Another line of explanation stresses that institutional constraints do not have mechanistic effects as a lot depends on whether and how agents lead political struggles to defend their ideas (Crespy 2016). An important body of research at the crossroads between international political economy and constructivism shows how the EU has embraced and catalysed the global turn to financial capitalism (McNamara 1998, 2006). Since the 1990s, national leaders have used a discourse stressing the "economic imperative" stemming from globalization as well as EU integration to justify often unpopular socio-economic reforms (Hay & Rosamond 2002). Thus, competitiveness has become omnipresent in the discourses of European leaders and greatly contributes to actors' perceptions of their own economic interests (Rosamond 2002).

When the crisis hit in 2008, the main response was to maintain the supremacy of economic orthodoxy through fiscal discipline and the cutting of public spending, which – more often than not – resulted in the debasing of public services and welfare states. In the end, the answers to the latest crisis of capitalism have been grounded in formulas that have deep roots in the history of economic thought (Blyth 2013). In a poststructuralist perspective inspired by the writings of Claude Lefort or Chantal Mouffe, the invocation that "there is no alternative" served to move the symbolic boundaries of politics by pushing socio-economic issues out of the realm of legitimate political debates in the name of competitiveness and European commitments (Borriello 2017).

Critical historians have gone so far as to argue that economic liberalism – together with the influence of the United States – has constituted the ideological DNA of regional integration since the 1950s and that calling for the advent of a "Social Europe" was fundamentally misconceived (Denord & Schwartz 2009). I have argued elsewhere that "Social Europe" – understood as the development of a fully fledged supranational welfare state inspired by social democratic and corporatist models – was dead (Menz 2015), leaving the lines of a new progressive horizon particularly blurred.

Political factors: joint-decision trap and sovereignty

Eventually, institutional, ideational, material and social factors translate into a complex constellation with many political obstacles to the advancement of social cohesion at a European scale. First, owing to the range of diverse preferences from the member states, the Council is often the victim of the "joint-decision trap" (Scharpf 1988); that is, an impossibility to decide collectively on measures for more market-correcting positive integration. This has certainly been accentuated by the 2004–07 eastern enlargement, which has seen 12 new member states with significantly lower levels of economic development and social protection joining the EU. As a consequence, questions surrounding the mobility of "cheaper" workers, the existence of fair competition in the EU or social dumping through labour mobility of firm relocation has come to the fore and created an east/west cleavage in the EU.

Second, the legitimacy of the EU to act in the realm of social policy has always been fragile owing to the "largely nationally focused *demoi* of each of the EU's member states, and the degree to which member states jealously guard attempts to erode their national sovereignty" (Bailey 2017: 110). The reluctance to equip the EU with new competences or resources in the realm of social policy has become even more salient in contemporary political debates, bringing about conflicts between various conceptions of sovereignty (Brack *et al.* 2019). On the one hand, northern countries with robust welfare states (especially Denmark and Sweden and increasingly the Netherlands and Austria) have sought to curtail the EU's capacity to intervene in order to protect their social model and limit the possible expenses involved with more social solidarity. On the other hand, a range of member states have been consistently averse to EU action in this realm (especially the UK and most member states from central and eastern Europe). In addition, for some citizens in southern countries, the EU's action in social policy has taken the form of brutal retrenchment as imposed by memorandums of understanding (MoUs) and the Troika in the 2010s.

Material and social factors: the hegemony of economic actors

For neo-Marxists and neo-Gramscians, the battles of ideas over Social Europe are fundamentally underpinned by asymmetric social relations that reflect the functioning of financial capitalism. As early as the 1980s, Peter Cocks and Stuart Holland claimed that European integration was intrinsically a project aimed at expanding capital beyond national borders (Bache *et al.* 2011: 69). Thus, theories such as neo-functionalism or federalism did nothing but conceal the fact that the project was above all in line with the interests of capital-owning elites. EU integration has accompanied a great change in class relations over the long term, which has seen the decline of the labour movement and the domination of transnational finance over the economy (Bieler *et al.* 2015). Against this background, the EU has contributed to the consolidation of neoliberal hegemony by fostering the restructuring of national political economies (Holman *et al.* 2004); it has also absorbed, and thereby rendered ineffective, alternative paradigms such as social market economy or regulated capitalism (Van Apeldoorn *et al.* 2009). This trend is reflected in the political influence of a transnational class of capital owners and multinational corporations well organized at the EU level in BusinessEurope (formerly the European round table of industrialists (Horn & Wigger 2016).

Applying the theory forged by Karl Polanyi in 1944 to today, it appears capitalist forces have been able to use regional integration to accelerate the economy's "disembedding" from society. Some scholars have argued that the EU has also provided tools allowing a "countermovement" of social forces to avoid the coming of age of a "market society" (Caporaso & Tarrow 2009). Yet, a greater range of studies stress that these have proved insufficient to counter the triumph of the neoliberal logic of accumulation over workers' claims or the protection of the environment (Bieler *et al.* 2015; Höpner & Schäfer 2010; Savevska 2014).

Reflecting on the normative roots of the European social question

From the perspective of political or social theory, the European social question is concerned with the fair distribution of the burdens and benefits associated with the functioning of the economy and the production of collective goods (safety, well-being, a healthy environment, etc.). The purpose is to define, theoretically, what standards apply to the EU (i.e. what expectations can be formulated towards the EU considering the nature of the social relations stemming from economic and political integration). In other words, the demands for justice towards the EU depend on the extent to which Europeans form a society. Beyond their differences, authors often share the critical view that the EU, as it is today, does not contribute satisfactorily to the promotion of social justice.

The internationalist or intergovernmentalist perspective

From a Rawlsian outlook, the fundamental legitimate unit relevant for social justice is the people, understood as a national society. Social policy is thus rooted in the historical, cultural and social links that provide the moral foundation for solidarity between individuals:

> The social welfare state and democracy primarily – but also the corporatist system of comprehensive and "far-sighted" interest mediation – can be realized only "within borders"; that is, within a mode of socialization limited to the nation-state, whose protagonists recognize each other as worthy of trust and solidarity.   (Offe 2000: 24–5).

However, some consider that not all member states enjoy the benefits of European integration in equal measure (such as access to the single market), in particular because of the variety of social economic systems and their unequal ability to adapt to economic and fiscal competition (Sangiovanni 2013). Furthermore, the EU's most integrated economic policies, such as the four freedoms, competition policy or the EMU, disrupt national arrangements. In some respects, the EU seems to fail to ensure a regime of cooperation, in particular by preserving the integrity of representative democracy at the national level (Bellamy 2013) and avoiding the domination of certain states (e.g. the creditors within the EMU) over others (the debtors) and turning the EU into a regime of domination and asymmetrical sovereignty (Fabbrini 2016).

Hence, there are two different positions for how to counteract these tendencies that undermine social justice in the EU. The first considers that the negative effects of interdependency must be *compensated* through new mechanisms of solidarity (Sangiovanni 2013; Vandenbroucke 2017). The other focuses rather on *limiting* interdependency through institutional reforms, for example de-constitutionalizing the economic rules linked to the single market or broadening the possibilities of opt-outs (Scharpf 2015) to guarantee people's democratic and socio-economic autonomy.

The transnationalist or federalist perspective

Contrary to intergovernmentalists, transnationalists consider that Europeans form a political community in which they may have demands for social justice. The principle of social justice must thus be fulfilled and institutionalized between individuals, irrespective of their country of nationality. This stems from a historical sociology perspective according to which peoples (*demoi*) do not exist naturally and have never entirely pre-existed political and institutional structures but have been, on the contrary, most often shaped and cemented by the latter. Yet, the EU, in its evolution, and even more so since the reforms that followed the crisis of 2008–10, not only does not organize solidarity among Europeans, but also exacerbates social inequalities between and within European societies.

Jürgen Habermas has argued that the emancipating potential for social justice and democracy can only be realized through a qualitative change from an international community to a cosmopolitan community based on the principle of human rights (including social rights) (Habermas 2013a). In the name of interpersonal social justice between Europeans, Philip van Parijs and Yannick Vanderborght (Van Parijs & Vanderborght 2017) promote the implementation of a European basic income that they call Euro-Dividend (i.e. a universal unconditional allowance for all Europeans). Made legitimate by the economic and social interdependence that already exists between Europeans, this type of tool would support national welfare states while also giving body to a European social citizenship that would in turn strengthen the legitimacy of the European *polity*.

Pluralist perspectives

Pluralist approaches have attempted to find a third way between inter-governmentalism and federalism. The debacle of the constitutional experiment,[5] which started with the Convention on the Future of Europe in 2000, and the displays of increasing popular hostility towards the EU have brought to light the resilience of national identities. Over the past 15 years, a group of authors has developed a theory of European *demoi*cracy, according to which the lack of a unified European *demos* does not damn the EU, nor does it exonerate it from demands for democracy and social justice (Cheneval & Nicolaïdis 2017; Cheneval & Schimmelfennig 2013). Rather, multiple *demoi* govern together within a community of peoples, at once a union of citizens and a union of states. This means that the EU must organize the mutual opening of peoples and the management of externalities and interdependencies that come with it, while also preserving the sovereignty and integrity of national communities. Kalypso Nicolaïdis (2007, 2013) suggests that, beyond the principle of non-domination, European *demoi*cracy should be based on mutual transnational recognition.

---

5. The European Convention on the Future of Europe proposed a "Constitution for Europe" later amended and endorsed by the European Council under the label "European Constitutional Treaty" in 2004. Alongside the rationalization of the EU institutions and competences, the treaty was to accentuate and assert the constitutional features of the EU legal and political order. Submitted to citizen's approval in ratification referenda in a number of member states, the treaty was rejected by a majority of voters in France and the Netherlands in May and June 2005. These negative referenda have epitomized popular resentment towards the federalization of the EU in two founding member states.

In a broad sense, mutual recognition may be understood as the far-reaching respect for the diversity of identities, political traditions, social contracts and memorial histories of our European neighbours. It is, however, often difficult to understand how *demoi*cracy can take shape within institutional mechanisms, particularly in matters of social policy.

From a legal theory perspective, the production of collective goods through the EU serves to address demands of social justice and cohesion at three intertwined levels: within states (national solidarity), between states (the distribution of costs and benefits of EU integration) and among individuals (transnational solidarity bonds in a unified European socio-economic space). Some scholars have argued that, in order to diffuse conflicts, demands for justice in one realm may be limited in order to avoid adverse effects in another. For example, it may be legitimate – and in tune with *demoi*cracy – for states to delay or restrict access to welfare benefits for non-national EU citizens in the name of national solidarity or solidarity among states (Bellamy & Lacey 2017; Sangiovanni 2013). Thus, the legal system of the EU, as echoed in the case law of the CJEU, has created a system of transnational social justice through non-discrimination and the granting of individual socio-economic rights allowing people to move freely within the EU. However, transnational justice may be limited to preserve the diversity of national conceptions of justice (De Witte 2012, 2015). The existence of sufficient – economic, political, social – bonds between individuals and the national state or society in which they have migrated to is considered a key element for grounding demands of social rights.

Conclusion

In a nutshell, today the EU is facing an acute social question in the sense that its action in the realm of social policy is widely considered as unsatisfactory given the challenges at stake. In the literature, this social deficit of the EU is conceptualized from many different angles. The EU is not very effective at tackling the rise of social inequality both within European societies (vertical inequality) and between European societies (horizontal inequality). Thus, the EU is not meeting its ambitions to reach a high level of social cohesion across EU countries. While the bulk of social policy instruments and resources remain at the national level, EU socio-economic governance faces difficulties in creating a supporting environment to steer progressive reform of national welfare states and has even sometimes driven regressive reforms. Furthermore, the social dimen-sion of EU citizenship remains embryonic with only a very limited set of social rights granted at the EU level. As a consequence, the existence of a European social model, or the progressive nature of its content, is being challenged.

Scholars have emphasized different explanatory factors for the weakness of EU social policy, ranging from the fundamental institutional bias of the EU architecture to the ideational, material and social factors that strengthen market actors. As presented in the introduction to this volume, scholarly assessments have opposed those who consider "Social Europe" as mainly irrelevant, those who see it as a succession of rebalancing acts for catching up with market-making and those who see it as a dangerous project for national societies. In any event, the action of the EU in the social realm is bound to develop over time insofar as it is linked to the logic of market expansion (Daly 2017: 101).

Ultimately, assessments depend on how one normatively apprehends the very nature of the EU and its social underpinnings. Those who see national states and societies as the unsurpassable, most legitimate form of organization tend to argue that the role of the EU in the realm of social policy should be limited, or better delineated. This also implies protecting national societies' political autonomy vis-à-vis negative externalities or political domination stemming from their European neighbours. In contrast, it is possible that the ever-deeper interdependence between European societies requires the EU to effectively address demands for justice between individuals and across national boundaries. How this will be done remains to be seen.

Can this only be done by enhancing the federal features of the EU with significantly more resources and stringent procedures to materialize solidarity? Creating a social union that safeguards the social foundations of national social policy and complements it with transnational and international forms seems the best way to go forward today. Yet, its operationalization in practice remains contentious and elusive.

Further reading

- David Bailey, "Obstacles to 'Social Europe'". In Patricia Kennett and Noemi Lendvai-Bainton (eds), *Handbook of European Social Policy* (Cheltenham: Edward Elgar, 2017), 108–25.
- Wolfgang Streeck, "Progressive regression: metamorphoses of European social policy". *New Left Review* 118 (Jul./Aug. 2019), 117–39.
- Franck Vandenbroucke, "The idea of a European Social Union: a normative introduction". In Frank Vandenbroucke, Catherine Barnard and Geert De Baere (eds), *A European Social Union after the Crisis* (Cambridge: Cambridge University Press, 2017), 3–46.

Questions to debate

- Does a European social model exist?
- Why does the EU exhibit a social deficit?

2

IS THE EU A KEY PLAYER IN ADDRESSING SOCIAL ISSUES?

Only very few citizens are aware that the EU plays a role in social policy. This is because of the multi-level and piecemeal nature of European social policy-making. From a legal perspective, the EU can only act in a limited number of areas as specified in the TFEU. The literature offers contrasted accounts of how relevant the EU's role is. The EU intervenes in a range of policy areas, but through differentiated procedures and modes of governance implying various degrees of constraint for member states. The roots of European social policy lie in provisions facilitating the free movement of workers and, later, of citizens at large (e.g. the coordination of social security). Labour law and non-discrimination (including equality between men and women) have progressively also become important areas for European law-making. The EU has promoted territorial and social cohesion through cohesion policy. Dedicated structural funds ensure a redistribution from wealthy to poorer regions through the EU budget. Since the 2000s, welfare state reforms (labour markets, education, pensions) and policies related to poverty and social inclusion are coordinated through soft mechanisms relying on benchmarking and the diffusion of best practices. Every sequence in the history of EU integration has driven new normative views, discourses, policies and institutional developments in social policy.

Yet, European social policy is in no way developing into a European welfare state. The bulk of social policy remains the prerogative of national states and the various types of welfare states (whether continental, Scandinavian, liberal or southern) have proved very resilient. The resources available from the EU budget are in no way comparable to national ones. Most importantly perhaps, social policy at the EU level cannot be considered as an autonomous policy area isolated from economic policy. From the outset, it has been subjected to the imperatives of economic integration, free movement and monetary integration in particular. Thus, it is of paramount importance to consider the interaction between EU economic and social policy. As the introduction to this book sets out, experts on social policy in the EU disagree on the effectiveness (whether it is irrelevant or catching up) and the nature (progressive or dangerous) of the EU's social action. They also disagree about what the EU should do in the future to best address the social question: should it offer minimal support to the autonomous functioning of national welfare states or further build up the EU's capacities to address externalities and interdependencies stemming from regional integration, or is a major overhaul required, taking the EU in a Keynesian and/or Habermasian direction?

To enlighten the reader on the realities underpinning these controversies, this chapter aims to give an overview of what the EU does (and does not do) in the realm of social policy. To this end, it defines EU social policy-making through four constitutive components: (a) the policy areas in which the EU intervenes, (b) the modes of governance used, (c) the normative contours of the underlying political project and (d) the models of national welfare states that form the infrastructure of EU social policy-making.

Piecemeal prerogatives across policy areas

A first peculiarity of the EU is that, unlike national states, it cannot act in every area of social policy. Although this presents a substantial limitation, it is also the result of competence distribution across levels of governance, as is the case in other federal systems. As far as social policy is concerned, the EU treaties fundamentally distinguish between shared and supporting competences (see Table 2.1). In this regard, it is striking that the EU's competences are strongest when related to the single market. This corroborates the thesis that EU social policy action has been essentially an "add-on" to or even "dependent on" economic integration (Copeland & Daly 2015). Thus, the continuous extension of the EU's competence in the social domain has been shaped by a path dependency in which social policy objectives have never constituted a strong, autonomous agenda as such.

The rules relating to *free movement* are the historical nucleus of a Social Europe and have accompanied the evolutions of the single market. At first, freedom of movement was centred on workers. When it was extended to people in general, there was a need to establish rules for the coordination of social security and pension systems. This would ensure the portability of rights during mobility and guarantee the access of non-nationals to social benefits in the country in which they work or simply reside. The EU has also gradually established *minimum labour law standards* pertaining to working conditions, health and safety, working time, parental leave, the right to information and consultation of workers in large groups and the creation of European work councils.

Anti-discrimination is an essential part of EU social policy. The quest for gender equality gave rise to a series of pioneering policies, not only through a large body of legislation but also through specific programmes to support women. The EU has also adopted a legislative arsenal to combat discrimination on the grounds of race and ethnic origin or employment discrimination because of religion, age, disability or sexual orientation. Yet, its implementation remains tentative.

The EU's social objectives are generally pursued within the framework of a *cohesion policy*, which occurs through the distribution of so-called structural and investment funds to support regions or groups of vulnerable people. Today, the programmes financed by the European Social Fund (ESF) mainly focus on combatting unemployment and enhancing human capital. Practically, this means that the funds are granted to organizations offering continuing education or helping social inclusion and access to employment.

Public health is a hybrid area in which the EU has both shared and supporting competences. It is not generally considered to be a strong competence of the EU, which should mainly "encourage cooperation between the member states" (Article 168 TFEU). Yet, the Maastricht Treaty conferred a regulatory competence in essentially three fields: (a) the quality of veterinary and phytosanitary products, blood and human organs and the rules on the quality and marketing of medication; (b) prevention in the fight against addictions; (c) monitoring,

Table 2.1 Competences of the EU in the field of social policy

Shared competences: the EU supports and complements the action of member states (it may enact legislation)	Improving the work environment (protecting the health and safety of workers)
	Working conditions
	Social security and workers' benefits
	Protection of workers in case of termination of the work contract
	Information and consultation of workers
	Representation and collective protection of workers' and employers' interests
	Rules for the employment of nationals of third countries
	Integration of persons excluded from the labour market
	Gender equality at work
	Territorial, social and economic cohesion
	European social dialogue
	Public health
Supporting competences: the EU assists member states in coordinating their policies (it may not enact legislation)	Employment policy
	Fight against social exclusion
	Social security (including pensions, healthcare, long-term care)
	Public health

evaluation and warning systems of contagious diseases and epidemics. The differentiated competences have crucial implications in terms of the significance of the EU's action vis-à-vis national policy-making. For instance, while the European Medicine Agency (EMA) established in 1995 is responsible for the centralized procedure for the marketing authorization of medicines; in contrast, the European Centre for Disease Prevention and Control created in 2005 acts merely as a hub for information and networking in relation with risks associated with infectious diseases. During the Covid-19 pandemic, it has offered guidance and recommendations to national authorities but has not had the power to impose constraining decisions or to strictly coordinate the EU member states' efforts to tackle the pandemic.

In its four other fields of action, the EU only has supporting competences and limits itself to encouraging the coordination of member states' policies. In matters of *employment*, the Treaty of Amsterdam (1997) set up the European Employment Strategy (EES). The aim has been to monitor the evolution of national labour markets and to draft opinions and recommendations that help national governments achieve European objectives in combatting unemployment. Since 2000, the EU has also attempted to coordinate *social security reforms*, including pensions, healthcare and long-term care. Finally, the fight against poverty is the last important area in which the EU endeavours to promote common objectives. Since 2011, the coordination of employment and social policies happens within the framework of the European Semester, a process that has strongly emphasized the deregulation of labour markets in response to the recession and the lack of competitiveness of certain European economies. The main leitmotivs at the EU level have been flexicurity, social investment and social inclusion. Outcomes remain underwhelming, as illustrated by the so-called poverty target that only helped 3.1 million people out of poverty in 2017 with an objective of 20 million set for 2020.

Differentiated modes of policy-making and governance

Beyond policy areas, it is also possible to distinguish between various modes of policy-making and governance implying different procedures and instruments through which the EU is acting in the social realm. EU social policy is mainly based on regulation (i.e. the promulgation of rules to control economic and social activities), as opposed to (re)distributive policies relying on collective fiscal resources (i.e. the budget) to tackle social inequality by redistributing large amounts of resources through social benefits and public services.

From the Treaty of Rome (1957) and the beginning of European integration, European institutions have been using *regulation* to allow the mobility of workers within the EEC. In addition to legislation, the EU body of social law also includes the broader provisions in European treaties, as well as the jurisprudence of the CJEU. The CJEU has often been called on to rule on the rights of individuals in cases of transnational mobility, thus creating new European rights for workers, persons with disabilities or granting access to social benefits or healthcare in a European country other than one's own. However, the defence of individual rights (free movement of persons) or economic rights (free movement of services) enshrined in the European treaties sometimes conflict with, and may weaken, national rules at the collective level (trade union rights) or the institutional level (states).

European regulation in social matters should be considered as the counterpoint to the *deregulation* that goes with EU liberalization policies. In other words, the opening of borders with the single market, and the free movement of persons and services, leads to the abolition of national rules, which are, to a certain extent, replaced by common rules at the European level. Liberalization nevertheless often comes with minimal regulation, thus giving full rein to the market. Most public services, for example, have been recast as services of general economic interest (SGEI) in EU law. The recognition of their economic nature means that they are most often subject to the rules of European competition law (i.e. they operate in competitive markets where public funding [state aid] must be limited and justified by obligations of public service). From the late 1980s, the sectors of telecommunications, transport (air, rail, local), television and radio, energy distribution (gas and electricity) and postal services have undergone a gradual liberalization (i.e. the end of state monopoly and the competition with private or public operators, be they national or foreign). Although this has not been systematic and was always left to the free choice of national governments, liberalization has often led to the (partial or total) privatization of public services. These profound transformations question the ability of states (or of the EU) to regulate markets in ways that guarantee the basic principles of continuity, quality, fairness and geographical accessibility of public services.

Whereas the redistribution of resources through the welfare state is the main mode of national-level public action in the social field, it remains marginal at the EU level with a budget equivalent to about 1 per cent of the European gross domestic product (GDP). The main form of social redistribution in the EU is through the structural and investment funds, in particular from the European Regional Development Fund, which aims to stimulate balanced socio-economic development in the various regions of Europe, and the ESF that supports projects related to employment and investment in human capital. Evaluating the impact of these redistributive instruments remains a challenge. Criticized for their inefficiency, overly managerial aspects or even the risks of local corruption they carry, the European funds are nonetheless the only way to try to help (at the local level) the most disadvantaged territories and social groups and those who are socially excluded and discriminated against in access to employment, particularly young people, job seekers or minority groups.

Although policy instruments implied by regulation and redistribution can be found in national policy-making, European policy-making in the social realm relies on specific modes of governance, namely the community method, the European social dialogue and soft coordination. These different modes of governance tend to emerge and prevail at certain times, thus allowing us to grasp the dynamics within Social Europe over the six decades of European integration. Different modes of policy-making and governance can be intertwined in a single policy area, as illustrated by the complex example of health policy in Table 2.2.

Historically, the *community method* is the mode of governance that gives the EU some aspects of a supranational political system in which the European Commission, a community institution independent from the states, proposes legislation to the Council who adopts it. Since 1992 and the implementation of co-decision by the Maastricht Treaty, the EP is systematically associated to the Council. With the Treaty of Lisbon, this has become the ordinary legislative procedure. Thus, all the social regulations relating to the protection and representation of workers, their rights in cases of mobility within the single market, the regulation of public health and non-discrimination are adopted via the community method as directives and regulations. Directives set out a framework that

Table 2.2 Modes of EU policy-making and governance in the area of health policy

Sub-domain	Type of competence and legal base in TFEU	Modes of policy-making/ governance	Policy	Impact of EU on national policy-making
Health and safety at work	Shared	Regulation (community method)	Safety standards (including protection of pregnant workers)	Medium
Public health	Shared	Regulation (community method)	Prevention and management of cross-border health threats	Medium
	Supporting	Coordination	Safety standards regarding human substances, veterinary and sanitary products	High
Healthcare	Shared	Community method Liberalization, regulation	Cross-border healthcare services	Low, potentially strong if strong increase in cross-border healthcare
	Supporting	Soft coordination	Reform of healthcare systems: (quality versus financial sustainability tension)	Low

is transposed and implemented according to the practical and legal modalities chosen by member states while regulations apply directly within national legal orders. In 2009, the *acquis communautaire* in social matters (i.e. the existing body of EU social law) consisted of approximately 80 legislative texts (Falkner 2010), a number that has increased to around 165 today.[1] Studies have shown a slowdown of the EU's regulatory activity in the social realm (Graziano & Hartlapp 2019; Pochet & Degryse 2017). Since 2000, there have been fewer directives initiating new policies proposed and/or adopted while there has been more focus on revising existing texts, which suggests that social policy has become more contentious as the EU has grown larger in the twenty-first century.

The European regulatory arsenal is supplemented by agreements stemming from the *European social dialogue*. This mode of governance is specific in that it operates a kind of delegation of legislative competence to the social partners. Negotiations between social partners (employers and trade unions) on working conditions, as happens in the case of corporatism and national industrial relations, can lead to so-called statutory agreements. The Council can adopt these as such and transform them into binding legislation in the form of a regulation. The European social dialogue also creates so-called autonomous agreements, which are implemented according to modalities defined by actors or authorities at the national and local levels. Established by the Maastricht Treaty (1992), the European social dialogue exists at both the interprofessional and sectoral level, wielding 13 statutory agreements and 9 autonomous agreements (see Table 2.2). There is a wide consensus among scholars that the European social dialogue was only effective during a relatively short period of time in the 1990s and early 2000s when employers saw social regulation as a necessary corollary for fostering the development of the single market and when negotiations mostly occurred under the auspices of a proactive European Commission. Since then, the multiple calls for a "new start" of the European social dialogue have not brought about any tangible outcomes (Degryse 2017).

As indicated earlier in this chapter, the making of social policy at the EU level relies to a large extent on the *soft coordination* of national policies. Soft coordination is also often referred to as the open method of coordination (OMC). Foreshadowed by the EES at the end of the 1990s, it was then formalized when the Lisbon Strategy for Growth and Competitiveness was launched in 2000. In the areas where it only has a supporting competence and therefore may not adopt legislation, the EU seeks to coordinate the policies and reforms carried out by national governments with new instruments such as the exchange of best practices, the use of indicators (benchmarking) and peer review among national experts sent by national administrations. These new modes of governance

---

1. According to the criteria used by the data base from the European Trade Union Institute.

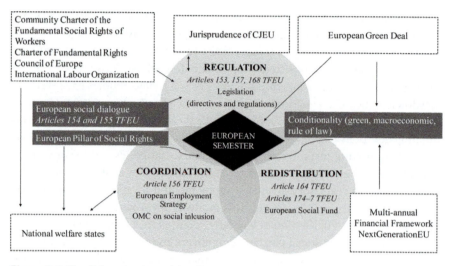

Figure 2.1 The EU's action in social policy

expanded rapidly in the early 2000s to cover social protection and inclusion, pension reform, healthcare and research. Rather than using binding regulation, the OMC aims at generating and diffusing consensual views about common problems and policy solutions to those problems. Scholars tend to disagree on the impact of soft coordination on national policy-making. Some scholars point to the weakness of implementation mechanisms and the inability to bring about effective policy change at the domestic level (Daly 2006; Radaelli & Borras 2010). In contrast, other scholars emphasize the cognitive effects of the OMC among domestic actors and institutional effects implying better territorial coordination and more openness to civil society actors in the making of social policy (Barcevicius *et al.* 2014a).

The reshaping of socio-economic governance after the financial crisis and the debt crisis of 2008–10 has led to hybridized modes of governance (Coman 2017). From 2011, the coordination of fiscal, macroeconomic and social policies has been synchronized in a single annual cycle called the European Semester (see Figure 2.1). This means that the European Semester organizes the procedure by which the conformity of domestic budgets – eventually approved by national parliaments – is checked by the European Commission and the Council. In parallel, the Commission monitors any potentially concerning trends in every country's macroeconomic development. Finally, the OMC on social inclusion and the social objectives set out in the Europe 2020 strategy are also incorporated under the umbrella of the Semester. The European Semester has led to the blurring of boundaries between various modes of policy-making and governance. It combines elements of supranationalism from the community method – the Commission has received, for instance, increased supervisory powers – and elements of intergovernmentalism whereby the Council plays a key role regarding multilateral surveillance. In the same vein, the Semester associates hard law in the fiscal realm with coordination relying on soft law in the social realm.

A failed political project

The complexity and diversity of European governance on social matters must not hide the fundamentally political, or even ideological, dimension of the project of a Social Europe and its evolutions. Since the origins of Europe's unification after the Second World War, the strengthening of the EU's competences in the social realm has been primarily supported by social-democratic actors, including workers' unions, left-wing political parties, and socially minded civil servants and technocrats. "Social Europe" has been a recurrent motto in the European manifestos of left-wing parties and unions for decades. Improving the living conditions of European citizens and promoting social progress have been proclaimed objectives of the EU. From a historical perspective, however, one must acknowledge that the promise of a genuine supranational *social* market economy ensuring social cohesion throughout the continent has been largely disappointed (Ramírez Pérez 2020). Today, there is a dearth of political mobilization as even actors from the social democratic movement show reservations vis-à-vis the strengthening of the EU's role in social policy. There are therefore grounds to claim that, in many respects, the political project dubbed "Social Europe" is dead (Crespy & Menz 2015b).

Broadly, there are three key moments in the history of European social policy.[2] The beginnings and the long period of initial growth of European integration, from the 1950s to the end of the 1980s, are dominated by an economic imperative. The social measures contained in the 1957 Treaty of Rome are essentially intended to accompany the construction of a single market through the liberalization of trade within the EEC. Political elites have great confidence in postwar reconstruction and, in their eyes, the increase in the production of wealth and goods should necessarily lead to an improvement in living and social standards. Furthermore, national leaders at the time believe in a healthy division of labour. The EEC's role was essentially to stimulate economic cooperation, while the conduct of social policy occurred through the then blossoming national welfare states. High wages would be maintained in a context of competition between member states, and compensation and support measures for

---

2. For a social history of European integration, see Leboutte (2008). For a chronological account of European social policy until 2000, see Geyer (2000).

workers affected by the restructuring of certain economic sectors would be provided, for instance by the ESF. Although widely invested in the European project in its early days, trade unions (Social Democrats as well as Christian Democrats) became critical of the liberal turn of the Rome Treaty as early as the 1950s. While the European Coal and Steel Community (ECSC) seemed to promote corporatist governance and a federalist project based on political and social integration, the Treaty of Rome focused on market-making through liberalization and free trade. Trade unions feared this would lead to competition between workers (social dumping) (Verschueren 2013: 51–65). When the construction of the single market is revived at the end of the 1980s the same logic prevailed. After three decades of limited progress in matters of economic and social integration, European politics was dominated by the radical economic liberalism of Margaret Thatcher (the UK joined the EEC in 1973) and in France François Mitterrand's abandoning of Keynesian policy. Nevertheless, the Single European Act of 1986 introduced a crucial institutional change: unanimity as a decision-making rule in the Council was replaced by a qualified majority, which removed the possibility for a single member of the community to block decision-making through a veto.

The decade between the end of the 1980s to the end of the 1990s is often considered the golden age of Social Europe and sometimes dubbed the "Delors moment". Under the impetus of Jacques Delors – a French politician from the liberal wing of the French Socialist Party, who served as president of the European Commission from 1985 to 1994 – European governance in social matters experienced a relative boom. Delors spread awareness about the fact that intensifying market integration must go along with social measures aimed at alleviating the adverse effects of competition in certain territories and social groups. Social Democrats were also aware that the monetary and fiscal constraints[3] induced by the creation of the EMU would have negative social consequences and be unpopular with their electorate (Geyer 2000). During that time, the Commission made strategic use of a qualified majority in order to have the Council approve new regulations for the improvement of health and safety at work. But above all, the Maastricht Treaty paved the way for new possibilities as the Commission obtained the endorsement of a protocol on social policy that had to be appended to the treaty (rather than included in it) as a result of the UK's rejection of new common rules in that area. The protocol espouses the Community Charter of the Fundamental Social Rights of Workers that had been adopted in 1989 and

---

3. On the one hand, that national governments can no longer use monetary devaluation to stimulate the economy in times of crisis and loss of competitiveness. On the other hand, they need to comply with fiscal discipline and thus limit deficit by reducing public spending (and/or increase taxes).

that proclaimed several fundamental social rights in the EEC.[4] More importantly, the protocol gave the European social dialogue institutional recognition by making it possible to transform agreements negotiated by the social partners at the EU level into binding legislation adopted by the Council.

Although it does not transfer any significant social competences to the EU, the Treaty of Amsterdam of 1997 confirmed that the political climate of the 1990s was favourable to the advancement of European social policy as three prosperous member states with a particularly strong social democratic welfare state (i.e. Austria, Finland and Sweden) were joining the EU. At the same time, the British Labour Party came to power with Tony Blair, who agreed to put an end to the British opt-out from the Social protocol, which could therefore become a proper chapter for the Treaty Establishing the European Community (TEC). The EU's role in combatting discrimination was reinforced and a new chapter on employment was also included. Soft coordination was inaugurated with the EES in a context in which most European countries faced mass unemployment. This is also when many non-governmental organizations (NGOs) and associations active in the social field turned to Brussels, notably through the creation, in 1995, of the European social platform, which represents around 40 national organizations.

Although this period is probably the most dynamic in matters of social policy in Europe, the widespread idea of a social "golden age" should be put into perspective. In the late 1990s, 10 of the 15 EU member states were led by Social Democrats. Yet this political domination did not result in a significant leap in the rules, competences or financial resources available to EU social policy. In fact, the leaders in power at the time largely embraced the neoliberal reforms of the welfare state domestically. The programmatic renewal of social democracy towards a resolutely liberal and centrist "Third Way"[5] was proclaimed by Tony Blair and Gerhardt Schröder in their 1999 joint statement.

Against this background, the 2000s marked a neoliberal turning point. A third phase opened with the decline of the social democratic political project of a Social Europe. Soft coordination was presented as an institutional innovation, but its role was above all to overcome the lack of consensus on new transfers of social policy competences to the EU. Social democratic parties have been experiencing a long electoral decline while conservative, Eurosceptic and far-right parties have consistently gained ground in elections and within the EU

---

4. Free movement of workers, fair remuneration, improved living and working conditions, right to social protection, freedom of association and of collective bargaining, right to vocational training, gender equality, information, consultation and participation of workers, health protection and safety in the workplace, protection of children and adolescents, pension rights for the elderly and the social and professional integration of people with disabilities.

5. *Third Way* in the UK and *Neue Mitte* in Germany.

institutions. The financial crisis of 2008 and the debt crisis of 2010 reinforced the subordination of social policies to the economic imperatives of budgetary discipline and competitiveness. The implementation of drastic austerity plans in countries receiving loans from European and international institutions to bail out their debt had dramatic effects, which were combined with the explosion of unemployment, especially among young people. Aware of the profound crisis of legitimacy and the devastating political effects caused by the continuing rise in social inequality, some European leaders have sought to put social issues on the agenda. Yet, this has yielded limited results for various reasons, including the continuing emphasis on fiscal discipline, the lack of fiscal resources at the national level and salient mistrust vis-à-vis the EU among certain parties and parts of the European publics. In that context, Ursula von der Leyen, who has chaired the European Commission since 2019, has reframed the EU agenda around the Green Deal and the issues related to a socially fair transition to a more ecologically minded economy.

Meanwhile, the European response to the Covid-19 pandemic and its socio-economic consequences has arguably led to a reconfiguration, where fiscal discipline has been – at least – temporarily suspended and new resources have been generated to help member states fight against the new ongoing recession. One open question is to what extent access to these resources will be conditional upon compliance with a European agenda and whether such an agenda would be consistent with tackling social inequality and fostering social cohesion.

The EU and national welfare states

To the extent that the EU's social competences and resources are very limited, it is necessarily dependent on the preservation of the traditionally strong welfare states and the strengthening of those who developed later and are less robust for both economic and political reasons.

The evolutions of the social dimension of Europe cannot be grasped without a good understanding of the national social models and their evolution since the mid-twentieth century. In his book *The Three Worlds of Welfare Capitalism* (Esping-Andersen 1990), the Danish sociologist Gosta Esping-Andersen laid the groundwork for a sociological approach to the welfare states in Europe, a framework that has been continuously developed since then.[6] Esping-Andersen outlines three models: liberal, corporatist and social democrat.

In the liberal model, often also called Anglo-Saxon, the state's main role is to encourage the smooth functioning of the market. Individuals are considered

---

6. For a contextualization of the different welfare state models in the EU, see Kleinman (2002).

to be responsible for the satisfaction of their needs, which is why the idea of social assistance is often viewed negatively. This model favours the flexibility of the labour market, which leads to higher employment levels (less unemployment), while a larger number of individuals have low incomes (large low-wage sector). The level of social protection is rather low, residual in nature and trade unions are relatively weak. Countries that have adopted the liberal model, such as the United States, Australia, the UK and Ireland, suffer from higher levels of social inequality.

In the corporatist, or conservative model, the state's mission is to remedy market failures to ensure a reasonable level of well-being for the population. The nature of social rights is associated with one's class and status in the employment market. Historically, this model is strongly influenced by traditional values, excluding women from work for example. In the corporatist model, the labour market is relatively rigid because workers' rights are defended by trade unions that actively participate in socio-economic decision-making. The welfare state is financed by an insurance system (called the "Bismarckian" system) into which employers and workers pay important contributions. In the countries of continental Europe (Germany, Austria, Belgium, France) with a corporatist model, social inequalities are average.

In the social democratic or Nordic model, the welfare state actively promotes social equality and universal rights. A high level of social protection is financed by the heavy tax-based contribution of all citizens to the state finances. The state strongly regulates the labour market and conducts active education and training policies. Trade unions are central to socio-economic governance and enjoy high levels of membership. In the European countries with this model (Denmark, Finland, Sweden and, to some extent, the Netherlands), the level of social inequality is among the lowest in the world.

Other researchers have completed the initial typology of Esping-Andersen to acknowledge the diversity of welfare states in the EU. One can indeed distinguish a Mediterranean, or "southern" model (Ferrera 1996), a witness to a later development of the welfare state where the family was long regarded as the main social institution. Thus, public intervention as well as the level of social assistance is limited and focused on pensions. As in the corporatist model, the labour market is traditionally rigid, and the role of trade unions is important, particularly regarding wage negotiations. In the Mediterranean countries (Spain, Greece, Italy, Portugal), social inequalities were contained for a long time.

Finally, there are debates about the existence of a *post-communist model* in central and eastern Europe, where capitalism was only introduced after the fall of the USSR and the dismantling of its sphere of influence. Here, the picture seems mixed because these countries most often combine pre-communist elements of the corporatist model (such as a Bismarckian insurance system), communist components (universalism and egalitarianism) and post-communist aspects (introduction of market mechanisms in the functioning of the welfare state). Thus, the countries of the former Eastern bloc show some similarities. They all have, for example, a universalist healthcare system as well as a similar pension system set up with the help of the World Bank. Above all, their socio-economic model has often been referred to as "dependent capitalism" (Nolke & Vliegenhart 2009) because of the investments from stronger economies, particularly those from western Europe. On the other hand, they are very heterogeneous in other aspects, such as employment and family policy. Apart from a few exceptions, the average level of protection in central and eastern Europe and the Baltic states is much lower than in the rest of Europe.

Despite their diversity, the different European social models face the same challenges brought on by technological change and globalization: deindustrialization, competition from cheaper workforces in other parts of the world, digitalization and robotization, fiscal competition between states to attract capital and investment. By decreasing the employment rate, increasing the precariousness of certain groups and reducing available public resources, all these developments generate considerable pressure on the sustainability of welfare states as well as on the preservation of a distinctively protective European social model.

Scholars studying the Europeanization of social policy, that is the impact of EU social policy on national policies, have shown how national welfare states act as a filter that generates a differentiated reception of EU social policy and various degrees of change. In their comparative study, Guillen and Palier (2004) explain that southern welfare states, which had developed a Bismarckian model prior to their accession to the EEC, only had to pursue adaptation to EU norms; in contrast, the Bismarckian welfare state in central and central and eastern European states had been profoundly altered by decades of communism. Their accession to EU membership has therefore implied a more radical transformation from building an entirely new system, followed by a sequence of privatization of the social system, ending with attempts to rebalance the functioning of the welfare state (Guillen & Palier 2004). Furthermore, domestic institutions and politics determine which "usage" national actors will make of EU rules, resources and recommendations (Jacquot & Woll 2010). The Europeanization of social policy should be conceived both as a bottom-up process as well as in terms of top-down effects. National decision-makers prove instrumental in using the EU to advance their own agenda. In Italy, for example, reformist politicians have typically invoked the constraints coming from the EU (e.g. the Maastricht criteria or the pressure exerted from the EU institutions) to enforce unpopular pension reforms (Natali 2004).

Conclusion

As the centre of gravity still lies at the national (and regional) level, social policy cannot be considered as an area where the action of the EU is preponderant. But this does not make the EU's role irrelevant. The difficulty in addressing this question is that analytical arguments – what does the EU do? – are almost inevitably intertwined with normative arguments – does it do it well? Should it do more or less? The phrase "European social model" encapsulates this pervasive ambiguity: is there such a thing as a European model empirically? Is it a progressive or regressive model from the point of view of Europe-wide social justice and cohesion? When trying to understand the EU's role in social policy, one should not wonder whether the glass is half full of half empty. By explaining what the EU does and does not do, this chapter has brought forth three types of arguments.

First, empirically, EU social policy has primarily existed in response to a functional need. The competences of the EU and the – regulatory as well as financial – resources available to tackle social issues Europe-wide have only increased as the expanding and deepening of the single market has raised a series of social issues relating to the free circulation of people and services in particular, as well as stemming from fiscal and monetary integration. It is therefore hardly possible to identify an autonomous EU social policy agenda able to promote social cohesion on the same foot as market-making.

Second, social policy remains strongly rooted in national cultures and political arenas. This explains that the Europeanization of the field has been mainly incremental and piecemeal. As a result, the EU has limited competences across policy areas, relying on relatively weak resources and differentiated modes of governance implying contrasted levels of constraint vis-à-vis national authorities. Therefore, the outcomes of EU social policy depend on how it is received in national arenas, filtered by national institutions and used by national political actors.

Third, from a normative point of view, the EU social policy agenda is bound to reflect the ideational and power struggles shaping domestic and EU politics alike. The prevailing neoliberal approach to welfare state reform since the 1990s, the electoral decline of social democracy and the resurgence of nationalism have all concurred to shape the EU social policy agenda in a way that has undermined its capacity to address social issues. Whether residual or maximalist, this agenda has remained crucial to legitimize the EU as a whole and, in particular, visions for a more politically integrated polity (Pochet 2019).

To sum up, EU social policy shows important limitations owing to the piecemeal nature of its competences across the various subareas of social policy, with a historical dependence on market integration, the complex patchwork of modes of governance used across said policy areas and the "filtering" operated by national social systems. Whether good or bad, the EU's impact in the realm of social policy takes many indirect routes but is far from irrelevant. Going beyond abstract concepts policy and governance, the next chapter looks at those political and social actors who make, contest, resist or filter EU social policy.

Further reading

- Amandine Crespy, "Is the EU doing enough to tackle inequalities?" In Ramona Coman, Amandine Crespy and Vivien A. Schmidt (eds), *Governance and Politics in the Post Crisis European Union* (Cambridge: Cambridge University Press, 2020), 196–216.
- Mary Daly, "The dynamics of European Union social policy". In Patricia Kennet and Noemi Lendvai-Bainton (eds), *Handbook of European Social Policy* (Cheltenham: Edward Elgar, 2017), 93–107.
- Miriam Hartlapp, "European Union social policy". In Sonja Blum, Joanna Kuhlmann and Klaus Schubert (eds), *Routledge Handbook of European Welfare Systems* (Abingdon: Routledge, 2019), 545–59.

Questions to debate

- Why is the EU not regarded as a European welfare state?
- Should the EU regulate minimum wages?

3

ARE SOCIALLY MINDED ACTORS TOO WEAK IN EU POLICY-MAKING?

As in other federal systems such as the United States or Canada, social policy within the EU is not the purview of a specific institution but is shaped in a fragmented way by a multiplicity of actors (Leibfried & Pierson 1995). These sometimes form alliances in public policy networks and communities and depend on each other in the framework of the multi-level governance that characterizes the EU. Yet, beyond legal prerogatives and institutional dynamics, the making of EU social policy is the product of underlying political struggles. As highlighted in the previous chapters, the area of social policy has always been one of symbolic projection for normative debates around social justice and solidarity among European citizens and states. Thus, the pursuit of a (more) "Social Europe" has been historically supported by some actors and resisted by others. And those struggles have been in flux.

In the early days of EU integration in the 1950s and 1960s, entrepreneurs of social policy at the EU level actively promoted the emergence of a distinct body of EU social law (Fertikh 2016). Although representatives of trade unions were relatively marginalized in the new architecture of the EEC (compared to that of the ECSC), lawyers, experts and officials within the Directorate General (DG) of the European Commission for Employment, Social Affairs and Inclusion (EMPL) have drawn on specialized knowledge to build a transnational policy field, which was nevertheless perceived as relatively weak compared with other areas such as competition policy, finance or trade. These actors engaged in interpretation struggles over the Treaty of Rome, intrinsically rooted in economic liberalism with the assertion of the four freedoms, and progressively succeeded in asserting a space for embryonic European public policy in the social realm (Fertikh 2017). Some 60 years on, what does it look like?

Today's literature is populated with contrasting assessments of the EU institutions and their role vis-à-vis social policy. The EU Commission has been depicted as a social policy entrepreneur (Pierson 1996; Wendon 1998) or as an agent focused on market-making and liberalization (Crespy & Menz 2015a).

In the context of the euro crisis, at least parts of the Commission (especially in the DG for Economic and Financial Affairs of the European Commission [ECFIN]) were assimilated with the "ayattolahs of austerity" denounced by the Italian prime minister Enrico Letta in 2013 (Schmidt 2020: ch. 7). Similarly, the CJEU has been seen at times as a vector of transnational solidarity (De Witte 2015) and at others as the champion of market freedom over social regulation and workers' rights (Seikel 2015). Even the representatives of workers' unions are seen as builders of transnational labour solidarity (Gajewska 2009) or as Europeanized bureaucrats lacking legitimacy in the eyes of the grassroots (Wagner 2013).

This chapter provides insights into the prerogatives and role of the EU institutions, the member states and civil society organizations in social policy-making. It also shows how their respective roles and views vis-à-vis social policy have changed over time. Looking at power relations and their dynamics, it may be argued that the agency supporting an ambitious social policy agenda exhibits weakness. The entrepreneurship displayed by the two key supranational institutions, namely the European Commission and the CJEU, has proved changeable depending on the broader political and ideological context as well as on the sub-areas of social policy at stake. National governments have proved consistently reluctant to strengthen the action of the EU and have embraced differentiation in the implementation of social policy where possible. Meanwhile, civil society organizations established at the EU level are still struggling for significance and political weight. Workers' unions, in particular, seem especially affected by structural decline combined with a lack of unity Europe-wide.

The institutional triangle

The European Commission

Two DGs within the European Commission have the main responsibility for social policy. The DG EMPL's portfolio covers all aspects relevant to employment (social dialogue, European Semester, employment policies coordination, labour regulations), worker mobility (free movement, coordination of social security schemes within the EU), social affairs (social investment, modernization of social protection systems, fight against exclusion), along with education and training (recognition of qualifications, apprenticeships and further training), as well as investment via the ESF and the European Globalization Adjustment Fund, including the operational management of these funds. For its part, the DG for Health and Food Safety (SANCO) is responsible for policies related to healthcare systems and medications (performance of national systems, cross-border care, prevention, e-health), the management of health crises and food safety (chemicals, plants, veterinary issues).

In matters of social policy, the European Commission has three main missions. First, it proposes legislation and takes the initiative when it comes to the regulatory dimension of social policy. Second, the Commission plays an important role in the coordination of national policies. In the framework of the OMC, and more recently, of the European Semester, the Commission organizes multilateral surveillance and the exchange of good practices between member states by sitting in the committees of the Council (see next section), formulating reform recommendations and producing and diffusing knowledge and data on national policies. Third, as the "guardian of treaties", the Commission oversees the transposition of social regulation into the national legal orders. When it finds, after complaints by citizens or interested parties, that a member state has not transposed European directives or has done so improperly, and if the concerned authorities do not take satisfactory measures, it may initiate an infringement proceeding before the CJEU. Although sanctions are very seldomly levied, this procedure is crucial to guaranteeing the effectiveness of European law – as shown by the 25 infringement proceedings initiated over the two anti-discrimination directives adopted in 2000.

From an internal balance of power perspective, many policies and initiatives lead to power struggles and sectoral conflicts between DGs whose portfolios, institutional interests and political visions differ. In this respect, DGs EMPL and SANCO are less powerful than more established DGs such as ECFIN and the DG for Internal Market, Industry, Entrepreneurship and SMEs (GROW). Differing ideology and sectoral interests tend to overlap. Since 1958, DG EMPL has been under the purview of a social democrat Commissioner two-thirds of the time, whereas GROW or the DG for Competition (COMP) are most often under the administration of a conservative or liberal commissioner (Hartlapp *et al.* 2014: 51). As stressed in the previous chapters, the history of EU integration has entailed the subordination of social policy to economic objectives. This is reflected in the hold "economic" DGs have over "social" DGs within the European Commission, which is also due to the entanglement of their missions. For example, the issue of the financial sustainability of national healthcare systems is mostly the purview of DG ECFIN, which publishes reports and provides recommendations on the necessary reforms to health systems.

That being said, one should not espouse a simplistic view of the complex dynamics of the functioning of the European Commission. Hartlapp *et al.* (2014) studied the power relations and internal coordination within this institution. Their study revealed that the formulation of legislative proposals is based on three distinct but combined logics: a technocratic logic focused on the resolution of problems, a competence-seeking logic aimed at extending or retaining the Commission's prerogatives and a policy-seeking logic grounded in the pursuit of normative and ideological goals. The prevalence of one or the other of these depends on the specific context of each dossier. The technocratic logic dominates the initial positioning of each DG, but normative or opportunistic logics appear when conflicts in competence or ideological disagreements emerge between DGs. This is particularly true when, as is often the case in social matters, the issues at hand are salient to the public debate and can even become the subject of intense politicization (Hartlapp *et al.* 2014: 293).

In the late 1980s and 1990s, the Commission asserted itself as an entrepreneur of social policies by very opportunistically using the legal basis of the EEC treaty to introduce social regulations within the internal market (Cram 1993; Wendon 1998). However, it became increasingly difficult for the Commission to initiate social policy regulation for political and institutional reasons (divisions within a larger council, the decline of social democracy, the rise of sovereignty concerns, etc.). Over the past 15 years, initiatives entailing constraining provisions for more social regulation have proved contentious[1] and sometimes ended in deadlock[2] because of a lack of majority backing in the Council and the EP. Despite unfavourable internal power dynamics, commissioners for employment and social affairs most often seek to maintain the social activism of the Commission. For example, in the Barroso II Commission (2009–14), Lazlo Andor introduced the package on social investment (see Box 8.1, p. 169), proposed the Youth Guarantee scheme (see Box 8.2, p. 171) and attempted to start a debate on a potential European fund to fight unemployment. Claiming to pursue a "social triple A" for the EU, the Commission under Jean-Claude Juncker (2014–18) promoted a more vivid social policy agenda, albeit with mitigated success. The proclamation of the EPSR, including both legislative initiatives and soft coordination, was presented as a major political milestone for reviving the social policy agenda. Yet, with the exception of two directives passed in 2019, it remains unclear whether and how the 20 principles proclaimed in the EPSR will lead to tangible policy initiatives. Often faced with a lack of political will among the governments of the member states in the Council, the ability of the Commission to steer the social policy agenda has proved to be limited over the past 15 years.

---

1. One can think of the revision of the directive on the posting of workers of 2016 or the directive on work–life balance for parents and carers of 2019.
2. Here, the directive on gender balance in boards of stock exchange companies proposed in 2012 or the revision of the regulation for the coordination of social security put forward in 2016 (still pending at the time of writing) are good examples.

The Council

The Council's sectoral configuration in matters of social policy is the Employment, Social Policy, Health and Consumer Affairs Council (EPSCO). It brings together the national ministers with the relevant purviews approximately four times a year in Brussels. Prior to the ministerial meetings, the Committee of Permanent Representatives (Coreper I) prepares the discussions at the level of the national ambassadors to the EU. But it is mainly at the lower level, that of the committees, that the technical work of amending legislative texts and of the multilateral surveillance of national policies is carried out. The existence of two committees is provided for by the treaties: the Employment Committee (Van Schaik *et al.* 2020) (Article 150 TFEU) and the Committee on Social Protection (SPC) (Article 160 TFEU). They are composed of two representatives per member state (officials of the relevant ministries) and two members of the European Commission. Although formally Council bodies, the committees operate independently with a two-year presidency, a bureau and a secretariat. The Employment Committee of the Council of the European Union (EMCO) conducts analysis and technical observation work, mostly based on EU-level social policy indicators. It directs the employment guidelines and prepares the joint employment report (as part of the EES), prepares the Council conclusions and the country-specific recommendations for the European Semester, as well as monitoring the implementation of the Youth Guarantee. For its part, the Social Policy Committee of the Council of the European Union (SPC) deals with the evolution of social protection systems in member states within the framework of the social OMC and monitors the implementation of the objectives of the Europe 2020 strategy. In the same way, it prepares the Council conclusions and country-specific recommendations for the European Semester. Committees are therefore the real backbone of EU social policy-making and work closely with the social partners (employers and trade unions).

Although the committees can make use of the formal procedures of the Council (including voting) when specific decisions are on the agenda, many researchers have emphasized the informal nature of the discussions and interactions that have taken place within some of the committees. This is because the OMC is essentially grounded in the pooling of expertise based on common indicators and the sharing of best practices, thereby creating a learning process that is more a new form of "experimental governance" (Sabel & Zeitlin 2008) than classical intergovernmentalism, which is often understood as the confrontation of solidified national interests. Members of the committees thus form genuine epistemic communities, that is networks of professionals with recognized expertise and competence in a particular field as well as the authority to wield the necessary knowledge for decision-making on public policies related to this area

(Haas 1992: 3). According to Uwe Puetter (2014: 180–8), the cohesion of EPSCO (socialization between ministers, their interest in Council meetings, deliberative practices, etc.) is much weaker than that of the Council for Economic and Financial Affairs (ECOFIN) or the External Affairs Council. Puetter (2014) suggests that this is due to several factors, including:

- the multiplicity of policies included in the portfolio and involving different ministries (employment, social affairs, health) and the internal competition that sometimes occurs between different ministries within member states;
- the duality of decision-making methods between the community method for the adoption of legislation and deliberation in areas of national policy coordination;
- the bureaucratic burden of the work of the preparatory bodies (the committees); and
- competition with the powerful ECOFIN.

According to Puetter (2014), this explains the difficulties faced by EPSCO in taking a leadership role in the European-level coordination of social policy. This was particularly evident during the crisis management sequence of 2009–10, during which EPSCO failed to prioritize social issues on the agenda of the European Council. Meanwhile, some catching up occurred when the EPSCO council (EMCO and SPC) asserted their role alongside that of ECOFIN in the routine functioning of the European Semester (Zeitlin & Vanhercke 2017). This does not, however, change the fact that it is primarily actors from the ECOFIN "sector" that steer the European Semester, which also affects social policy alongside fiscal and macroeconomic policy.

The European Parliament

Since its accession to the status of co-legislator with the Maastricht Treaty, the EP in particular has attempted to profile itself as the only legitimate representative of European citizens. Supporting the advancement of social regulation has been part of this institutional strategy. In the EP, it is mainly EMPL that decides on social policy issues, while the Committee on the Environment, Public Health and Food Safety (ENVI) deals with health policy debates. Because of the sectoral interests of Members of the EP (MEPs), the EMPL committee is most often chaired by those belonging to political groups from the left and centre left. Starting from the discussions on the Working Time Directive in 1993, the EP voted in favour of regulation in accordance to the law of the host country (often more generous) and not of the country of origin of the workers (Martinsen 2015: 191–2). In the resounding conflict over the Services Directive (also known as the "Bolkestein Directive") between 2004 and 2006, the EP opposed the radical understanding of the liberalization of services advocated by the Commission and, for the first time in the EU's history, largely redrafted the Commission's proposal.

The political role of the EP in social matters is largely linked to its relations with organized civil society, be it trade unions or NGOs active on social issues. The EP has often made itself the echo chamber for grievances born in the street through important citizen mobilizations. Furthermore, intergroups allow for the relatively informal gathering of members of all political groups on issues of a social nature. Between 1999 and 2009, intergroups on social rights and human rights represented one-quarter of all intergroups on average, and the Trade Union Intergroup is one of the oldest in the assembly.

However, the propensity of the EP to support social claims in the past decade must be relativized. In the context of the Great Recession that started with the financial crisis of 2008, the EP has not acted as the spokesperson of the citizens and organizations critical of the austerity policies implemented throughout Europe as a response to the crisis. While many citizens and unions mobilized against the hardship entailed by cuts in wages and public services, the EP was not vocal in criticizing the actions of the Troika (see Box 3.1). In fact, it found itself marginalized in the recast of socio-economic governance in the aftermath of the

---

BOX 3.1 THE TROIKA

Originally referring to a political regime dominated by three powerful individuals (triumvirate) in the Soviet Union or Russia, the term "Troika" has served to refer to the association of the European Commission, the ECB and the IMF during the euro crisis (2010–15).

The three institutions provided assistance to overindebted Greece in 2010 and later to Ireland, Portugal, Cyprus and Spain. Conditions for receiving loans from the Troika were set in MoUs containing detailed prescriptions and conditions for structural reforms implying large-scale privatization of public assets, freezing of wages, cuts in the public sector and infrastructure, labour market deregulation, etc.

The actions of the Troika have been criticized mainly on three points. First, the measures advocated in MoUs were rooted in misconceived neoliberal dogmas and proved counterproductive with regard to the recovery of these countries. Second, the nature of the Troika was legally dubious and its presence in guiding national administrations to reform amounted to violations of sovereignty. Third, its demands were deleterious to a number of fundamental social rights enshrined in EU and international law. Alongside trade unions, both the Council of Europe and the International Labour Organization (ILO) deplored the actions of the Troika.

2008–10 euro crisis. However, in an area where its powers have been increased, namely the approval of free trade agreements, the EP did not support the Europe-wide movements of 2016–17 protesting against the Comprehensive Economic and Trade Agreement between Canada and the EU and the Transatlantic Trade and Investment Partnership with the United States.

This less prominent role of the EP in social matters is mainly explained by the political make-up of the assembly. Looking at the results of European elections since 1999, there has been a clear shift to the right, with social democracy losing a lot of ground and the exponential growth of nationalist forces. Unlike their predecessors from the pro-European Christian democracy, significant sections within the Conservatives of the European People's Party (EPP) have been hostile to an agenda seeking to deepen social policy integration at the EU level and are less prone to compromise.

All in all, the formation of majorities within the EP is determined ad hoc by the multiple political divisions within it. While the traditional divide between political groups from the left and the right is naturally salient on social issues, votes also often oppose the pro-integration political groups of the centre (Conservatives, Social Democrats and Liberals) to the more peripheral left- and right-wing groups often hostile to an increase in Europe's social portfolio (especially on the right). MEPs are also divided along national lines depending on which welfare model they promote (whether neoliberal or more regulated). For example, members of the British Labour Party or the Social Democrats of the Baltic countries are often less favourable to social regulation than some French or German Liberals or Conservatives. Finally, the voting patterns on the EP resolution on the EPSR in January 2017 shows divisions between MEPs from the creditor countries at the heart of Europe (Germany, Austria, Scandinavia), opposed to a socially ambitious version of the EPSR, and MEPs from debtor countries (especially from southern Europe), more broadly in favour of setting up new European social policy instruments (Vesan & Corti 2017).

The independent institutions

The Court of Justice of the European Union

The Court of Justice of the European Union (CJEU) is undeniably a key player in social policy. Through its jurisprudence on social matters, it has heavily shaped the contours of European citizenship. Socio-historical research on judges and lawyers in the EU by Vauchez (2012) has shown how the CJEU has relied on national and transnational powerful professional networks to legitimize its integrationist jurisprudence. Indeed, the construction of EU law was always "embedded in a complex legal and political struggle over the nature and future of Europe" (Cohen & Vauchez 2011: n.p.; see also Vauchez 2010). The CJEU's jurisprudence has enriched and sometimes even preceded the social regulation of the single market, largely based on freedom of movement and establishment as well as the equal treatment of all citizens.

The influence of the CJEU in social matters revolves mainly around three issues: (a) the reciprocal influence between judges and legislators, (b) the distribution of competences between the EU and the member states and (c) the equilibrium between the market and social rights.

The phrase "integration through law" encapsulates the powerful dynamic of political change brought about by the CJEU's jurisprudence. After a phase of trial and error during which the judges struggled to define their role in the young EEC, the activism of the CJEU became particularly marked in the initial phase of building the single market between the Treaty of Rome in 1957 and the Maastricht Treaty in 1992 (Saurugger & Terpan 2017: ch. 2). Fundamental rights and social regulation in the framework of the single market were areas of strong activism from the 1970s. Rather than being based on the unilateral action of the CJEU alone, the dynamic of social integration through law is based on a mechanism called codification, through which European legislators (the Council and EP) incorporate elements developed by jurisprudence into the legislation *ex post*. One can observe a dynamic of codification in the areas of coordination of social security regimes for migrant workers, equal treatment or patient mobility (Saurugger & Terpan 2017: 189–95). This may reflect a "judicialization of politics" in the sense that the jurisprudence acts as a strong constraint on European and national legislators by limiting the available public policy options. Recent research shows that, because of the over-constitutionalization of EU law, it is very difficult for the latter to contest, override or disregard the CJEU's jurisprudence. In matters relating to free movement and the welfare state, national administrations and courts have to adjust their rules and practices to comply with EU law and they often face political dilemmas (Blauberger & Schmidt 2017). Despite the constitutional status and equal treatment, the EU remains an "unequal union" owing to gaps in EU law as well as differentiated and limited compliance within the member states (Schmidt *et al.* 2018).

Furthermore, the CJEU and its decisions are in no way immune from politics, nor do they shape political decisions in a systematic fashion. To start with, a significant proportion (currently more than one-third) of judges and advocates-general appointed by national governments have held functions in political institutions or the senior public service (Saurugger & Terpan 2017: 55–8). This does not mean that the Luxembourg judges are controlled by their governments, but rather that they are not in any way isolated from the evolution of social preferences or the politicization of certain issues in the public debate. Thus, in most cases, the decisions of the CJEU do not differ fundamentally from member states' preferences. Prior to decisions, they produce written comments on the cases submitted to the CJEU and, according to several researchers, threats of legislative reprisals or non-compliance with European law deter the Luxembourg judges from opposing member states head-on (Carruba & Gabel 2014). The decisions of the CJEU regarding the access of non-nationals to social benefits in Germany and the UK between 2013 and 2016 are a case in point. In a climate in which public opinion was agitated by possible "benefits' tourism" because of freedom of residence within the EU, the CJEU clearly halted the extension of individual rights by giving states the opportunity to limit the access of the jobless to unemployment benefit or family allowance. Rendered a week before the referendum on Brexit, the CJEU's decision in the *Commission v United Kingdom* case is textbook in this respect. In that regard, the judges in Luxembourg have proved sensitive to today's political climate within society and the political class in many European countries (Blauberger *et al.* 2018).

Furthermore, political responses to CJEU rulings can be diverse. In her study of 22 legislative texts adopted between 1988 and 2012, Martinsen (2015) found that only 13 have led to the codification of the jurisprudence into legislation. In five of the cases, legislators amended the provisions of the rulings; in three cases, the Council and the EP could not agree on how to respond to case law, which led to the non-adoption of legislation and legal uncertainty; and one case ended with a reversal of the jurisprudence. Thus, if the influence of the CJEU is evident in half the cases, legislators (governments and MEPs) can also use various means to alter, circumvent or ignore it.

Regarding the legal and institutional equilibrium underpinning EU social policy, one should distinguish the influence of case law on two continuums, namely an EU integration versus national autonomy axis, on the one hand, and a social rights versus economic freedom axis, on the other. Regarding the former, the CJEU shows, unsurprisingly, mostly a pro-integration bias. As far as the latter is concerned, the jurisprudence oscillates between different considerations and diverse socio-economic models. In the years 2007–09, the CJEU created a considerable commotion with decisions (famously known as the *Viking, Laval, Rüffert*, and *Luxembourg* cases), which gave prominence to the freedom to provide cross-border services over national labour laws, especially the prerogatives of trade unions in collective bargaining and industrial action. Furthermore, while the EU Charter of Fundamental Rights had some potential for the expansion of transnational social rights, both the drafters of the charter and the CJEU acted to contain this possibility, so as to not create obligations on states with regard to social rights and policies (see Chapter 4). Therefore, the EU Charter of Fundamental Rights has not altered the disequilibrium that underpins the European legal structure. This balance stems from the fact that economic rights within the single market were enshrined in the treaties as early as 1957 and are the norm, whereas the protection of social rights is defined primarily at the national level and mainly falls under a regime of exception (De Schutter 2006: 150). Although some progress has been made on the topic of discrimination, for example, the CJEU has sought to maintain the balance between the views of conservatives and progressives who had reached a compromise on the charter (Bailleux 2014: 289). In recent years, the CJEU has arguably sought to avoid excessive activism.

The European Central Bank

Endowed with political independence and the exclusive power to conduct the common monetary policy of the euro area, the European Central Bank (ECB) is *a priori* scarcely involved in social policy. However, the financial crisis of 2008, which evolved into a sovereign debt crisis that destabilized the eurozone, has considerably strengthened the ECB's weight in European governance and revealed how it indirectly influences social policy choices. Through its capacity for action and its expertise in monetary and financial matters, the ECB strengthened its moral authority in the face of member states' governments (Fontan 2014). Even though anti-austerity protests were limited in scope, the ECB itself has been targeted several times as a symbol of austerity and of the power of finance by demonstrations and protests in Frankfurt in 2010, 2012 and 2015.

On the one hand, the ECB impacts social stratification through its monetary policy choices. From a Keynesian perspective, the monetary policy pursued by the ECB, based on maintaining interest rates at historically low levels and then on increasing monetary liquidity, may be considered to have maintained easy access to credit for businesses and households. However, ECB officials, as well as their American and British counterparts, have acknowledged that repurchasing large-scale assets contributes to deepening social inequalities as it increases the assets detained by capital holders. They have nevertheless consistently argued that such anti-redistributive effects were unintended and collateral, temporary and exceptional, and that the fight against social inequalities is not the job of central bankers but of legislators and politicians (Dietsch *et al.* 2018). Furthermore, the ECB has promoted "solutions" to the crisis, which have strengthened the centrality of major banks in the functioning of the economy. Through complex mechanisms of intervention in the financial markets, the intertwining of the public authority embodied by the ECB and the private actors operating in those markets has been increased. This has given the financial sector an "infrastructural" power that guarantees the preservation of its interests by the ECB (Braun 2018).

On the other hand, the ECB has been especially influential indirectly through the promotion of "structural reforms". Mindful of the limits of monetary policy, the ECB has been a proactive advocate for the ordoliberal doctrine that fiscal discipline (i.e. the strict limitation of deficit and debt) guarantees the stability of the single currency. The ECB's fiscal doctrine comes with a focus on "structural reforms" (i.e. organizational rather than ad hoc reforms) that would limit public spending and make European economies more competitive. Inherited from the neoliberal agenda promoted by the International Monetary Fund (IMF) or the World Bank in the 1980s and 1990s in developing countries, structural reforms have become central to the EU's economic governance where they take the form of a pervasive and ambiguous catchword. Although they crystallize around three main types of restructuring – the liberalization of markets for goods and services, the flexibilization and deregulation of labour markets and the rationalization of public administrations – this agenda has also absorbed more progressive elements such as social investment and social inclusion (Crespy & Vanheuverzwijn 2017).

The harshest form of pressure was exerted on states that receive financial support from the EU through bailouts. The most salient aspect of the ECB's political role has therefore been its participation in the Troika – along with the European Commission and the IMF – which attached conditionality to financial help. Indeed, the MoU signed between the Troika and the governments of the affected countries stated that financial assistance was conditional on the implementation of a macroeconomic adjustment programme, namely the adoption of drastic savings to reduce the level of debt. With a strong economic recession leading to an increase in mass unemployment, this conditionality mechanism caused entire sections of the welfare state to be dismantled. There were cuts to the number of civil servants in national education and health services, pension reforms, limits on healthcare coverage, cuts in social benefits, a dismemberment of the industrial relations system between employers and employees, the privatization of infrastructure and public services and more. Therefore, they imply a major intrusion into the socio-economic policy-making of EU countries.

Furthermore, the ECB has increased its political hold by using unofficial conditionality on the Spanish and Italian governments in connection with its securities buyback operations in 2011. The letter sent by the then ECB president Jean-Claude Trichet to Silvio Berlusconi, for example, states that:

> The full liberalization of local public services and of professional services is needed. This should apply particularly to the provision of local services through large-scale privatizations. (b) There is also a need to further reform the collective wage bargaining system allowing firm-level agreements to tailor wages and working conditions to firms' specific needs and increasing their relevance with respect to other layers of negotiations. (c) A thorough review of the rules regulating the hiring

and dismissal of employees should be adopted in conjunction with the establishment of an unemployment insurance system and a set of active labour market policies capable of easing the reallocation of resources towards the more competitive firms and sectors [...] we regard as crucial that all actions listed in section 1 and 2 above be taken as soon as possible with decree-laws, followed by Parliamentary ratification by end September 2011. A constitutional reform tightening fiscal rules would also be appropriate.   (Trichet quoted in Fontan 2013: 32–4)

The way in which such political pressure was exerted created a stir in public opinion and triggered an investigation by the European Ombudsman (in the case of Spain).

Thus, in the aftermath of the 2008 financial crisis, the ECB has opportunistically increased its prerogatives both in the monetary and macroeconomic fields. Although its missions do not directly concern social policy, it is up to the other institutions to uphold and develop the "social dimension" of the EMU. This debate, although revived in 2013 under the leadership of the Belgian Herman van Rompuy, then president of the European Council, is now stalled.

The member states

Political coalitions and socio-economic models

As in foreign policy in general, the preferences of European states are relatively stable in matters of European social policy. Therefore, there are recurring dynamics of coalitions between states. Schematically, the central and southern European countries with a culture of regulated capitalism (Mediterranean and corporatist model) have often been opposed to the countries of the north and east who support neoliberal capitalism (Scandinavian, liberal and dependent model). France has often found itself leading a coalition advocating for more social regulations at the European level. Germany often has a pivotal role as a Franco-German alliance is decisive in terms of the qualified majority in the Council owing to the demographic weight of both countries. With its traditional Rhenan neo-corporatist model of regulated capitalism, which has undergone major rounds of neoliberal reforms in the 2000s, Germany is arguably located at the EU's political centre of gravity. Under Angela Merkel's leadership, it has essentially supported the regulation of a pan-European labour market (to facilitate labour mobility while tackling social dumping) but been largely reluctant towards extending the EU's competence in welfare state matters as such. The Scandinavian countries, and increasingly the Netherlands, have proved hostile to

European intervention in social matters. In 2019 and 2020, Danish and Swedish governments and unions alike were vocal against the EU directive on work–life balance,[3] and they have been even more so against the directive proposal on fair minimum wages,[4] which is still under discussion at the time of writing. With robust welfare states, the leaders of these countries fear that European regulations will disrupt and even weaken their social model. Preferences thus play out both on a left–right axis and on an integration–subsidiarity axis. The enlargements of 2004 and 2007 undoubtedly accentuated the "clash of capitalisms" and strengthened the camp of those wishing to curb European social regulation (Copeland 2014). Just a few days before the last Social Summit held in Porto in May 2021, a group of 11 member states issued a political statement claiming that

> targeted EU-level action can complement national action, but … any action on EU level should fully respect the division of competences of the Union, its member states and the social partners. Any EU initiative in these areas should be in line with the principles of subsidiarity and proportionality and needs careful consideration of different national starting points, challenges and institutional setups. Setting EU-level headline targets could help to steer national debates, policies and reforms.[5]

The purpose was clearly to send a political signal and trump the ambitions of the Portuguese presidency to recognize the EU as a key actor for addressing Europe's social problems.

Political events and changes in leadership can decidedly upset the European agenda, especially when the politicization of European issues puts national leaders on the spot. In 2005, for example, the referendum campaign on the ratification of the European Constitutional Treaty in France focused on the Services Directive and the left-wing movements made it the symbol of a neoliberal Europe pitting western and eastern workers against each other. The mobilizations were transnational and affected Germany and Belgium, as well as Sweden, where the problem of social dumping erupted around the *Laval* case (see Box 5.1, p. 97). These events and the headlines they created provoked the reversal of the German, French and Swedish governments who were initially in favour of a further liberalization of services as

---

3. Directive (EU) 2019/1158 of the European Parliament and of the Council on Work–Life Balance for Parents and Carers, 20 June 2019.

4. Proposal for a Directive of the European Parliament and the Council on Adequate Minimum Wages in the European Union, COM(2020)682, 28 October 2020.

5. "Social summit: non-paper by Austria, Bulgaria, Denmark, Estonia, Finland, Ireland, Latvia, Lithuania, Malta, the Netherlands and Sweden", Politico, www.politico.eu/wp-content/uploads/2021/04/22/Non-paper-Social-Summit.pdf (accessed 16 September 2021).

proposed by the Commission (Crespy 2010). More recently, the revision of the directive on the posting of workers was politicized in Emmanuel Macron's campaign for the French presidential election of 2017.

The institutional dynamics within member states also play a key role. It is first of all a matter of territorial and political specificities. In federal states such as Germany and Belgium, regions can be "veto points" (Scharpf 1988), which block the EU decision-making process. For example, the German *Länder* have taken position against the adoption of a European framework directive regulating the quality and accessibility of public services (Crespy 2016: ch. 4). Moreover, the logic of institutional inertia, according to which states are reluctant to change their own regulations or policies to adopt new European standards, pushes governments to often seek to transpose (or upload) their own policy models at the European level. In the debates around the 1994 directive establishing European works councils, for instance, Germany long sought to impose its model of codetermination between workers and employers. In the end, the directive offered three options reflecting the German, the French and Italian, and the Scandinavian model (Bulmer *et al.* 2007: 119). Finally, there are also more diffuse phenomena of policy transfers between European countries. This was the case with the Danish and Dutch models of flexicurity, for example, which acquired the status of a European model and whose aspects were exported, subject to national translations, in Portugal (Caune 2014).

The implementation of social policies

After decisions have been made at the European level within the Council, member states ensure the transposition and implementation of European social regulation. As discussed earlier, the European Commission monitors the respect of European law by the member states. Between 1961 and 2014, the Commission initiated 1,025 infringement proceedings before the CJEU, placing social policy in third place (after agriculture and the free movement of goods) of fields with the most judicial procedures (Martinsen 2015: 11).

Examining the transposition of labour law in particular shows us that violations of European law are linked to political motives of opposition to the European text in only a minority of cases, whereas it is most often explained by a lack of administrative capacity or problems of interpretation. Overall, member states can be classified into three groups (Falkner *et al.* 2007): those who comply with the rules;[6] those where national politics or institutional difficulties impede

---

6. Denmark, Finland and Sweden.

implementation;[7] and those who most often are negligent for political, cultural and administrative reasons.[8] Research focusing on the new member states who joined the EU in 2004 and 2007 shows that, if they are indeed among the least observant states, they do not form a category per se (Leiber 2007). As social policy regulation has become more and more contentious, opt-outs and derogations are sometimes a way to circumvent political deadlocks, as in the case of the Working Time Directive. Increased differentiation in the implementation across member states nevertheless implies important drawbacks in terms of (un)equal social rights granted to people and the instrumental use of (less protective) social policy as a competitive advantage (Martinsen & Wessel 2014).

Beyond the mere transposition of social regulation, the implementation of social policy, in all its dimensions, does contribute to the emergence of a European administrative space. In the framework of soft coordination, the absorption of the social OMC into the European Semester has led to an intensification of relations between national administrations and European institutions with frequent exchanges over the drafting of country reports by the Commission or the adoption by member states of national reform plans. However, ownership of EU objectives and instruments by domestic political and social actors is still very limited, as the European coordination remains an essentially bureaucratic exercise (Vanheuverzwijn & Crespy 2018).

With regard to cohesion policy, ESF funds are distributed to and managed by regional and local authorities. European institutions seek to establish a partnership with subnational authorities, in which the funds serve the major strategic objectives defined at the European level, such as improved access to employment and training (especially for young people), the fight against discrimination and the strengthening of public services. European funds thus help to shape administrative practices at the regional level through mechanisms such as calls for grants and competition between "project leaders", performance measures and evaluation of the use of funds. According to Fanny Sbaraglia (2018), the logic of project management fosters the paradigm of social investment while, at the same time, reconfiguring power relations among levels of governance. While the objectives of cohesion policy are increasingly defined at the EU level, the local authorities bear the heavy bureaucratic management of projects.

In a nutshell, member states leave their imprint on social policy both upstream from the policy process – when they have to agree in the Council – and downstream when they implement social policy on the ground. Whether regulation, the distribution of funds through projects or soft coordination of welfare state reforms are at stake, the implementation of social policy has known significant

---

7. Germany, Austria, Belgium, Spain, the Netherlands and the UK.
8. France, Greece, Luxemburg and Portugal.

impediments linked to diverging preferences on how much social regulation over markets is desirable, and how much EU intervention is desirable.

Organized civil society

The European Economic and Social Committee

The European Economic and Social Committee (EESC) is an institutionalized form of civil society representation. It has 350 members appointed by the member states at the pro rata of their demographic weight. Members are drawn from various sectors but are assembled into three groups within the assembly: the employers' group with representatives from the various sectors of the economy (agriculture, industry, services); the workers' group, made up of representatives of national or sectoral trade unions and confederations; and the "miscellaneous activities" group, which brings together representatives of consumer associations, artisans and small and medium-sized businesses, the social economy and social and environmental NGOs. The EESC is also organized into six thematic sections specializing in public policy areas.[9]

The EESC is an advisory body, which renders between 150 and 200 non-binding opinions every year that are sent to the Commission, the Council, and the EP. These opinions may be required by the EU decision-making process or formulated on the EESC's own initiative. Established by the Treaty of Rome of 1957, the EESC has seen its prerogatives strengthened by successive treaties, even if its opinions remain non-binding. Under the Lisbon Treaty, the EESC's consultation is compulsory within the framework of the ordinary EU legislative procedure in some 30 areas. The EESC defines its missions around three axes: a consultative mission to the EU institutions, a liaison mission between civil society and the European institutions along with a better participation of the former in European political processes, and a strengthening of civil society in third countries and in particular the promotion of the European model of consultation between social partners.[10] The EESC wishes to be a progressive player engaged in the promotion of socio-economic development.

Created at a time when there was little representation of socio-economic and societal interests within European institutions, the EESC's *raison d'être* is now

---

9. Economic and monetary union, economic and social cohesion, key enabling technologies (KET), production and consumption, transport, energy, infrastructure and the information society, external relations, agriculture, rural development and the environment, employment, social affairs and citizenship and the Consultative Commission on Industrial Change.

10. European Economic and Social Committee, "EESC mission statement", www.eesc.europa.eu/en/about (accessed 15 September 2021).

in question. Today, thousands of associations, platforms and interest groups are set up in Brussels and promote the interests of organized civil society towards the European institutions. Starting with the social partners (employers and trade unions), they all have more informal and effective channels to exert their influence on the EU's decision-making process. Other factors weaken the action of the EESC: for example, the fact that its opinions are often rendered after the important compromises have already been reached between the decisive political actors in the Commission, the Council and the EP, or the fact that the members of the EESC only occupy their function part-time (and not full-time), which reduces their capacity for action. This indicates that the EESC is one source of expertise from "the field" among others for EU institutions, rather than a fully fledged political player capable of influencing the decision-making process.

Trade unions

The European Trade Union Confederation (ETUC) is the most visible face of unionism on a European scale. Based in Brussels, it represents 89 national confederations and 10 European sectoral federations (see Box 3.2). Through the slogan of a Social Europe, ETUC aims to defend "quality jobs, workers' rights and a fair society".

It focuses on the EU's areas of action, namely mobility and workers' rights within the single market, European social dialogue, non-discrimination, macroeconomic coordination, the EPSR on social rights that are under negotiation and social issues related to trade policy. ETUC has several institutionalized channels it can use to influence the European decision-making process. Since 2001, it has participated in the Social Summits, which bring together the European Council, the social partners, and the six-month rotating presidency of the EU Council to discuss the broad guidelines of the EU social agenda. At the legislative level, the European Commission is required to consult ETUC on all employment and social policy proposals. ETUC also maintains links with European parliamentarians, notably through the EP Trade Union Intergroup, and coordinates the participation of trade union organizations in the EESC. Additionally, it represents workers within the framework of the European social dialogue at a cross-sectoral level. Finally, it conducts ad hoc campaigns on topical political issues at the European level on subjects such as wages, the fight against tax havens, decent work and the protection of whistle-blowers.

ETUC began playing a significant role in the 1990s when the Maastricht Treaty established the European social dialogue, on the one hand, and defined the criteria for the socio-economic convergence that would lead to the single currency, on the other. As it then engaged in a process of consensual dialogue

BOX 3.2 THE EUROPEAN TRADE UNION CONFEDERATION

The European Trade Union Confederation (ETUC) was created in 1973 as a replacement for union coordination structures at the European level. It consists of 89 national trade union confederations from 39 countries as well as 10 European sectoral federations:

EAEA: European Arts and Entertainment Alliance
EFBWW/FETBB: European Federation of Building and Woodworkers
EFFAT: European Federation of Trade Unions in the Food, Agriculture and Tourism
EFJ/FEJ: European Federation of Journalists
EPSU: European Federation of Public Service Unions
ETF: European Transport Workers' Federation
ETUCE/CSEE: European Trade Union Committee for Education
EUROCOP: European Confederation of Police
IndustriAll: European Federation for Industry and Manufacturing workers
UNI-EUROPA: European Trade Union Federation for Services and Communication.

The ETUC congress takes place every four years. It determines the organization's general policy. It elects the members of the Executive Committee, the president, the general secretary, the two deputy general secretaries and the four confederal secretaries. The Executive Committee is made up of representatives of ETUC's member organizations, proportional to their membership. It meets four times a year and can adopt joint positions and agree on actions in support of its demands. The Executive Committee also has the power to decide on the mandate and composition of the delegations that negotiate with the European employers' organizations.

The Steering Committee decides on measures to implement the policies adopted by the Executive Committee. It meets eight times a year.

---

and participation in European governance, it is often described as a technocratic actor (Erne 2008; Gobin 1997).

In the context of the emergence of the EMU, ETUC participated in the macroeconomic dialogue and accompanied the policy of wage moderation (i.e. wage stagnation). Promoted by the European institutions, this agenda was also pursued by national trade unions, in particular the German ones who adopted a strategy of "competitive corporatism" in the 1990s and 2000s, seeking to increase the competitiveness of German workers in the single market through wage moderation (Erne 2008). In the mid-2000s, ETUC contributed more widely to the Europeanization of the trade union movement by participating in EU-wide protest actions, such as the Euro-demonstrations. The confederation also intensified its relations with civil society organizations often more radical and critical of the EU by participating in European social forums. Autonomously, but within the framework of ETUC, European sectoral federations have played a pioneering role in the Europeanization of trade union actions. One example is the European Transport Federation, which organized multiple protest actions against the effects of rail transport liberalization including two marches in Brussels in 1996 and 1998, a Euro-strike (a strike action taking place in several European countries in order to secure a common outcome) in 1998 and a "train of cooperation and solidarity" in 2001 (Hilal 2007: 64). Additionally, the European federations were the ones who initiated a European coordination in matters of collective bargaining. In the early 1990s, coordinating committees were created under the impetus of the European Metalworkers' Federation (now IndustriALL) with the objective of defining common standards for wages and working conditions and evaluating collective bargaining. However, these efforts produced little effective coordination (Dufresne 2015).

The literature on Euro-unionism has often pointed to the structural obstacles to the emergence of a powerful union movement at the European level. They relate essentially to the ideological context, limited resources and the diversity of national trade union cultures (Kiess & Seeliger 2019; Martin & Ross 1999). National trade union organizations were greatly weakened by the end of Keynesian policies in the 1980s and then the neoliberal turn of the 2000s. The creation of the single currency strengthened the competitiveness paradigm based on wage moderation and the decentralization of negotiations between the social partners, which increasingly happen at the company level where trade unions have less bargaining power. This trend has further accelerated with the reforms for making labour markets more "flexible" in many European countries over the past ten years. Weakly endowed by the contributions of its affiliates, ETUC depends in part on financing from the European institutions, which goes hand in hand with its technocratic profile and its search for legitimacy vis-à-vis these institutions. Sociological research shows that the type of resources required to be involved in the multiple arenas where the European social dialogue takes place tends to create a gap within the movement between an elite, endowed with a distinct type of cognitive and educational capital (notably the ability to speak foreign languages), and the grassroots (Wagner 2013).

But it is mainly the diversity of national trade union cultures that appears to be an obstacle to the unity of the union movement at the European level. In the continental and Scandinavian model countries, trade unions have often sought to preserve their autonomy in national collective bargaining rather than foster pan-European strategies. In the countries of southern Europe and France, or even in Belgium, a more confrontational trade union culture has tried to oppose the deregulation of labour markets head-on but has been unable to stop it. In central and eastern Europe, trade unions are weak in the post-communist context and struggle to formulate a defensive discourse in the face of the neoliberal restructuring promoted by European integration. The emerging picture is a complex one, in which union representatives may find themselves torn between the national construction of interests and European socialization. The conflict that erupted in Waxholm, Sweden in 2006 (see Box 5.1, p. 97) has illustrated how, on the ground, workers' interests seemed to be in contradiction along national lines. On one hand, issues related to workers' mobility (mainly from the "east" to the "west" of the union) have seen unions from central and eastern Europe opposed to stricter regulation to preserve jobs. On the other hand, unions from western unions have instrumentally invoked "Social Europe" as they called for tighter regulation to tackle social dumping through workers' mobility; but they have been vocal against the proposed EU regulation of minimum wages that would mainly benefit eastern workers on the grounds that it would undermine their own autonomy in wage bargaining (Seeliger & Kiess 2019).

However, the transnational mobilization of labour is not completely impossible. Examples such as the mobilization of dockers against the Port Services Directive in 2006, protests against the services directive proposed in 2004 or the simultaneous strike actions against mass redundancies by workers at the production sites of General Motors between 2002 and 2006 in Germany, Belgium, Great Britain, Poland and Sweden show that transnational mobilization can be effective. Two elements seem key to allowing unions to articulate a transnational discourse based on class interests in a cross-border perspective rather than on national strategies. First, the existence of institutional channels of mobilization and influence (such as European works councils) and, second, the existence of spaces of European socialization for trade unionists outside the technocratic circles of Brussels (Gajewska 2008). However, these two channels do not seem to be available in the context of the current recession. In the aftermath of the financial crisis, ETUC coordinated demonstrations against austerity and for employment and solidarity several times a year. Yet, the opposition between northern creditor countries and debtor countries was not conducive to a strong coordination among workers faced with contrasting problems (constrained emigration, social dumping, wage restraint, etc.). Although the Covid-19 pandemic is causing yet another recession, it remains to be seen whether the labour movement will formulate common claims at the EU level in order to avoid a new episode of social regression like the one that followed the 2008 financial crisis.

Non-governmental organizations

Representatives of economic interests and the various professional groups were the first to set up offices in Brussels as early as the 1980s but non-governmental organizations (NGOs) defending public or citizens' interests caught up significantly in the 1990s. NGOs focused on social issues (anti-discrimination, poverty, disability, education, families, children and youth, health, development, etc.) are now an essential part of the so-called organized civil society that is active around the European institutions. The European Social Platform, created in 1995, is the largest forum for the representation of NGOs in the sector, with 47 members acting for some 2,800 national and local organizations. The umbrella organization includes other broad platforms such as Solidar, representing 28 associations active in the field of social services, or the European Anti-Poverty Network that, since 1990, has united national and European organizations fighting poverty.

Alongside representative democracy, the EU recognizes and embodies a model of pluralist democracy based on the activity of many – private as well as public – interest groups trying to influence decision-makers through advocacy or lobbying. Article 11 of the TEU states that "the institutions maintain an open, transparent and regular dialogue with representative associations and civil society". Overall, NGOs perform various functions related to participation, representation and deliberation within the EU (Kohler-Koch 2012). First, NGOs participate in decision-making through online consultation processes or expert groups convened by the European Commission. On more confrontational issues, they can also participate in mobilizations and protest campaigns. In general, NGOs help to strengthen the representation of specific groups of citizens who have a limited capacity for mobilization and representation. They do this particularly through the creation of upward and downward communication channels between citizens and the European institutions. Lastly, NGOs contribute to the political deliberations at the European level and thus to the consolidation of a European public sphere beyond the institutions.

That being said, empirical research on organized civil society in the EU has often critically underlined the limits of its contribution to European democracy (Saurugger 2008). A first limitation stems from the relation of mutual dependency between European institutions and NGOs. Often accused of colluding with powerful corporate actors, the EU institutions have sought to enhance their legitimacy by displaying greater openness towards representatives of citizens' interests. Around the turn of the new century, the European Commission was particularly keen to fight its image as a technocratic body and widely promoted "civil dialogue" in a competition with the EP (Saurugger 2008). On the other hand, the vast majority of NGO platforms at the European level are largely dependent on European funding, since 43 per cent of their budget on average – and often much

Table 3.1 Top ten social NGOs receiving the most EU funding (millions of euros)

NGO	European funds	Total budget
European Youth Forum	2.4 (79 per cent)	3
European Consumer Organization	2.3 (59 per cent)	3.9
AGE Platform Europe	1.3 (85 per cent)	1.5
European Anti-Poverty Network	1.2 (86 per cent)	1.4
European Network Against Racism	1.2 (85 per cent)	1.4
Friends of the Earth Europe	1.2 (42 per cent)	2.8
European Region of the International Lesbian, Gay, Bisexual, Trans and Intersex Association	1 (60 per cent)	1.8
European Federation of National Organizations Working with the Homeless	1 (85 per cent)	1.2
European Disability Forum	0.8 (76 per cent)	1.1
European Women's Lobby	0.8 (84 per cent)	0.9

Source: Sanchez Salgado (2014: 347).

more (see Table 3.1) – comes from European Commission funds (Greenwood & Dreger 2013). The extent to which this constrains them in their ability to criticize the policies initiated by the European institutions remains largely open to consideration. According to Rosa Sanchez Salgado (2014), the European funding system for social NGOs positively corrects the European political system by allowing the representation of excluded groups who have few resources. In this way, the European Commission also promotes operating standards such as the representativeness and autonomy of NGOs, without restricting their freedom of action.

That being said, however, it also feeds into a bureaucratic modus operandi whereby civil society organizations are seen more as a source of expertise for EU officials rather than as a genuine channel for participation or representation. In fact, bureaucrats who work for the umbrella organizations in Brussels are "professionals of Europe" often remote from grassroots concerns and identities. In that sense, the EU may be described as a "stakeholders' democracy" (Aldrin & Hubé 2016).

The question of whether NGOs from the social sector are able to influence European decision-makers remains largely unexplored. They undoubtedly contribute to stimulating the EU's social agenda and, occasionally, to politicizing certain issues. Louisa Parks's work in which she compares several European mobilization campaigns shows that the impact of civil society is more important when it engages in a process of confrontational politicization widely involving national actors, rather than the more technical campaigns confined to the "Brussels bubble" (the political microcosm surrounding the EU institutions), in which NGOs are more likely to serve as purveyors of expertise (Parks 2015).

When the 2009–10 financial crisis hit Europe and was largely framed by decision-makers as a crisis of public debt caused by profligate and uncompetitive southern states, the organized civil society of Brussels had little to offer the largely disenfranchised "99 per cent" who would bear the costs of internal devaluation and fiscal discipline. As underlined by Della Porta (2017: 28), the "democracy of the squares", which ensued in the following years, reflected a deep lack of trust in all established institutions, including political parties, unions and organized civil society. This anti-system movement remained to a large extent local and/or national and no significant Europeanization of mobilization took place. Unlike the global justice movement of the late 1990s and early 2000s, today's movements are geared more towards experimenting with new forms of participatory democracy at the local level, as illustrated by the occupation of squares by the various Occupy groups that flourished in 2011–12, the occupation of the Place de la République in 2016 in Paris in protest about the reform of Labour law by the French government or the occupation of roundabouts by the *gilets jaunes* in 2019–20. Over the past three decades, grievances have consistently concerned the commodification of labour and public services and the rise of inequality. But meanwhile, the entanglement of EU and national decisions and policies have made it virtually impossible for the grassroots to attribute responsibility across levels of governments and articulate specific demands towards decision-makers at the EU level in particular. Therefore, yesterday's claims for a "more social Europe" have turned into mainly indifference or hostility towards the EU. Whether only an exit from the EU (or the eurozone) will pave the way to progressive policy-making has indeed become a bone of contention within the Left across Europe, including in the UK where the advocates of *Lexit* supported the exit from the EU on the grounds that it could serve to enhance social cohesion in the country (see Chapter 9).

Conclusion

In 2000, Stefan Leibfried and Paul Pierson claimed that the EU's social policy had been left to courts and the markets (Leibried & Pierson 2000). With this claim they were pointing out the leading role of the CJEU's jurisprudence, on the one hand, and that of the single market, on the other, in driving the development of EU social policy. This implies the weakness of political actors in the social policy field, in contrast to the national level, where the state, political parties and trade unions are key players in the running of the welfare state. What is the situation today? Undeniably, the CJEU continues to play a fundamental role by ruling over contentious legislation, pursuing member states who do not implement EU law or setting out the legal implications of the Charter of

Fundamental Rights. Furthermore, people's mobility within the single market continues to provide functional incentives for the continuous creation of a body of EU social law. However, two main developments have brought politics back into EU social policy-making. First, as explained in Chapter 2, the toolbox of the EU has expanded far beyond regulation to include soft coordination of welfare state reform against the backdrop of fiscal discipline. Second, the EU's eastern enlargement of 2004–07 has resulted in a much larger set of preferences in the Council among member states with various ideas and interests around social policy. Finally, when the EU's financial and debt crisis hit, a coalition of northern creditor countries pushed for an austeritarian response that has de facto led to dramatic cuts and underinvestment in public services and, in many EU countries, freezing or cuts in wages and social rights.

Against this backdrop, the social policy agenda at the EU level has not been supported by strong agency. The Commission and CJEU have proved versatile, with decisions and initiatives that have at times served to sustain an ambitious protective agenda, but have sometimes also undermined – directly or indirectly – the rules or resources underpinning the social protection of Europeans. By taking on a political role during the eurozone crisis, the ECB has put the emphasis on structural reforms. More often than not, this has led to dramatic cuts in national welfare services and benefits in some countries and in welfare state recalibration motivated by efficiency gains. More progressive reforms have also taken place as a community of academics, experts and policy-makers[11] has conceptualized and promoted an approach through social investment (see Box 8.1, p. 169). However, these networks were not able to garner enough political support to sustain a coherent and salient agenda steered at the European level. While the Council has increasingly become a force of inertia, the EP itself has become increasingly lukewarm over time, as the conservatives, the liberals and the nationalists have gained more ground in the assembly. Finally, trade unions have been struggling with little success to assert the importance of the European social dialogue in the context of a triumphant financial neoliberalism combined with declining and divided national labour movements. The professionalized bureaucrats within the organized civil society contribute to producing knowledge and articulate claims for EU action to foster social cohesion. Yet, they remain disconnected from the grassroots and the social movements that occasionally erupt and voice strong social grievances, like that of the *gilets jaunes* in 2018 in France. Thus, it is fair to conclude that social policy suffers from a lack of dynamic agency that is

---

11. We can mention, for instance, personalities of academia specializing in social policy, experts gathered in the European Social Policy Network sponsored by the European Commission, researchers of the European Social Observatory, EU officials notably at DG EMPL, or various personalities notably within social democracy who have occupied posts in national and EU politics.

able to provide a new impetus for making the issues of social cohesion a priority for the EU. Furthermore, if the area of social policy is arguably bound to remain a field shaped by the confrontation between actors with diverging ideas and interests, it seems to be one of an uneven struggle in today's EU.

Further reading

Andreas Bieler *et al.*, *Labour and Transnational Action in Times of Crisis* (London: Rowman & Littlefield, 2015).

Michael Blauberger *et al.*, "ECJ judges read the morning papers: explaining the turnaround of European citizenship jurisprudence". *Journal of European Public Policy* 25:10 (2018), 1422–41.

Stefan Leibfried, "Social policy: left to the judges and the markets?" In H. Wallace, W. Wallace and M. Pollack (eds), *Policy Making in the European Union* (Oxford: Oxford University Press, 2005), 243–77.

Questions to debate

- Can the European Commission be regarded as an entrepreneur in the field of social policy?
- Do EU member states act as a driver of or a brake on European social policy?

4

IS EUROPEAN SOCIAL REGULATION A THING OF THE PAST?

In neo-functionalist terms, EU social policy appears to be a *spillover* from economic integration. It has expanded as the deepening of the single market through the four freedoms has brought on new regulatory needs at a European scale. Social regulation can be understood as the hard core of the EU's social governance. Its purpose has been to mitigate the negative effects of economic competition and create a level playing field (i.e. avoid the distortion of competition because of contrasted social standards) between European countries with diverse levels and models of social protection. Whereas harmonizing social rules quickly proved to be impossible, European regulation has helped create new transnational social rights. A historical institutionalist approach (Pierson 1996: 188) helps to understand how some unintended consequences of past decisions combined with activism from socially minded actors have fed the continuous growth of social regulation in the EU. Today, the body of EU social law amounts to over 160 legally binding acts.[1]

However, the EU's regulatory activity has slowed down since the mid-2000s, as shown in several studies (Graziano & Hartlapp 2019; Pochet & Degryse 2017). Although the absolute number of social regulations and directives has not declined significantly, recent legislation tends to focus mainly on technical changes or minor revisions. The number of directives adopted and new initiatives to address new problems has fallen significantly since the end of the 1990s. On the other hand, the number of directives proposed but not adopted has also dropped considerably, which seems to indicate that the Commission has been less and less adventurous on the social front, proposing a text only when it is sure it has the backing of a majority in the Council and Parliament. Furthermore, a careful analysis of the nature of the regulation adopted shows that the EU's legislative output has been increasingly geared towards flanking the single market – especially by regulating workers' mobility – rather than towards

---

1. According to the criteria used by the database from the European Trade Union Institute.

social policy objectives per se (Hartlapp 2019). With the inclusion of social issues in the Lisbon Strategy proclaimed in 2000, the lesser dynamism of social regulation has gone hand in hand with the rise of soft coordination through non-binding recommendations, benchmarks and peer review.

At the same time, the European Commission, under Jean-Claude Juncker and Ursula von der Leyen, has given the regulatory agenda a new impetus with legislative proposals on the transparency of working conditions, parental leave, the posting of workers, the creation of a European labour authority and the revised coordination of social security. But these have proved contentious and some of them have been watered down or are still pending at the time of writing. Finally, with the so-called EPSR, the regulatory agenda has been merged with soft law and coordination. Thus, should one consider that regulation is a thing of the past and can no longer drive progressive social integration in the future? To address this question, this chapter traces the development of EU social regulation across the treaties, legislation and case law. It emphasizes the interactions between those three domains in the advancement or hindering of progress on social regulation as well as the underlying political struggles.

The patchy rise of social issues in the EU's primary law

A gradual build up in the treaties

The study of treaty change since the origins of the EEC shows an ascending curve of the regulatory powers conferred to the EU on an increasing number of sub-areas within the social realm, with shifts from unanimity to qualified majority voting. On the other side of the coin, it highlights how piecemeal and limited these prerogatives remain. Above all, they have essentially served to adopt measures that flank the single market. Article 117 of the Treaty of Rome (1957) promised "to promote the improvement of workers' living and working conditions in order to allow for their harmonization in progress" and essentially created two regulatory tools: a system of social security coordination for migrant workers, on the one hand, and the requirement of equal pay for women and men on the other. While the former would enable workers' mobility, the latter would prevent social dumping through the employment of a female labour force; two objectives that were meant to accompany the creation of the customs union and the common market. These two lines of action (i.e. regulating mobility and preventing discrimination) were then strengthened over successive treaty changes (see Table 4.1). The Maastricht Treaty was an important step forward with its protocol on social policy, which allowed the EU to adopt regulatory provisions in a number of areas by qualified majority in the Council and under the newly introduced co-decision procedure with the EP. These provisions had to be included in a separate protocol on social policy appended to the treaty because of the UK's refusal to follow these developments.

The Treaty of Lisbon did not bring about any leap forward in the field of social policy. Besides meagre advances regarding workers' rights and anti-discrimination, the only new power granted to the EU was the ability to legislate in order to guarantee optimal conditions for the provision of services of general interest (SGI) (Article 14 TFEU). At the same time, however, a separate protocol on SGI, adopted at the request of the Netherlands, emphasizes the diversity of public services and the preservation of regional and national competences, which seems to contradict Article 14 and has de facto deterred EU action in this field.

The Lisbon Treaty has strengthened the symbolic recognition of social objectives, through a horizontal social clause in the new Article 9 TFEU, which states that

> in defining and implementing its policies and actions, the Union shall take into account requirements linked to the promotion of a high level of employment, the guarantee of adequate social protection, the fight against social exclusion, and a high level of education, training and protection of human health.

The practical relevance of such a clause is nevertheless difficult to assess. This adds to the horizontal clauses on gender-based discrimination (Article 8) and all forms of discrimination (Article 10). The aim of these horizontal clauses is to encourage mainstreaming of (i.e. consideration of) these social issues in the definition and implementation of all European policies. Although they provide a rhetorical basis for the actors seeking to strengthen EU social policy, whether they produce any tangible effect remains an open question.

The advent of EU-wide fundamental social rights?

The mention of social rights in the declaratory texts accompanying the treaties led to the growing assertion of principles and rights that serve to interpret and shape EU law. Nevertheless, the accession of social rights to the status of fundamental rights happened in a gradual, limited and, in some respects, ambivalent way.

Inspired by the European Social Charter adopted by the Council of Europe in 1961, the EEC, under the stewardship of the Delors Commission, adopted a Community Charter of the Fundamental Social Rights of Workers in 1989. It was signed in Strasbourg by the heads of state and government of the member states.

Table 4.1 Development of social policy provisions in the EU treaties

	Mobility and protection of workers	Combatting discrimination	Public health
Treaty of Rome (1957)	Article 48 TEC: Free movement of workers and non-discrimination on the basis of nationality Article 49 TEC: The Council can adopt measures (unanimity) Article 51 TEC: Coordination of social security systems for migrant workers Article 117 TEC: Acknowledges the need to promote the improvement of living and working conditions for the workforce	Article 119 TEC: Wage equality between male and female workers Article 7 TEC: Non-discrimination on the basis of nationality	
Single European Act (1986)	Article 118A TEC: Regulatory powers (qualified majority) to adopt minimum provisions to promote "improvements, especially in the working environment, as regards the health and safety of workers"		
Treaty of Maastricht (1992)	Social Policy Protocol: Regulatory powers (qualified majority co-decision) to adopt measures To improve the living and working conditions (health and safety), information and consultation of workers, the integration of people locked out of the labour market (UK opt-out) Regulatory powers (unanimity) to adopt measures on social security and the protection of workers, the protection of workers after the end of the labour contract, the representation and collective interests of workers and employers, hiring conditions for third-country nationals (UK opt-out)		Article 129a TEC: Regulatory powers (qualified majority co-decision) to ensure a high level of health protection, of illness, epidemic and addiction prevention, research on their causes and transmission, and contribution to information and education on health matters

Table 4.1 (*Continued*)

	Mobility and protection of workers	*Combatting discrimination*	*Public health*
Treaty of Amsterdam (1997)	Social Policy Protocol integrated in the body of the treaty (end of the UK's opt-out)	Article 2 TEC: Equality between women and men as a principle of the EU Article 13 TEC: Regulatory powers (unanimity) to combat all discrimination based on gender, race or ethnicity, religion or beliefs, disability, age or sexual orientation Article 119: Measures relative to wage equality between women and men and equal treatment in the workplace are decided by qualified majority and co-decision	Article 152 TEC: Horizontal clause for the protection of human health in the definition and implementation of all European policies Extension of scope of EU's action to drugs-related health damage, including information and prevention Regulatory powers (qualified majority co-decision) to (a) fix quality and safety standards for human organs and substances, blood and its derivatives; (b) measures in the veterinary and phytosanitary fields; (c) incentive measures designed to protect and improve human health, excluding any harmonization of the laws and regulations of the member states.
Treaty of Lisbon (2007)	Article 48 TFEU: Measures relative to the social protection of migrant workers may be adopted to the benefit of salaried or non-salaried workers	Article 19 TFEU: Regulatory powers (qualified majority co-decision) to adopt measures to encourage and support anti-discrimination provisions by member states	Article 168 TFEU: Extension of scope of the EU's action to the prevention of physical and mental illness and diseases, as well as to early warning of and combatting serious cross-border threats to health Extension of regulatory powers (ordinary legislative procedure) to prevention, management and monitoring of scourges and cross-border health threats, and to the prevention of tobacco use and abuse of alcohol

In its proposal for a "Social Charter" the European Commission had put forward a broad vision guaranteeing all European citizens – irrespective of whether they are workers or not – a series of social rights, such as access to social protection, the right to a pension, to education, etc. This far-reaching conception of European social citizenship containing the germs of an autonomous European welfare state was defeated by the member states. The charter that was ultimately adopted focuses instead on social rights dealing with working conditions and access to employment, only superficially answering unions' demands (Kenner 2003: 8). The Commission nonetheless was able to use the charter to ground its legislative initiatives in the field of social policy. It was an interpretative aid to the CJEU in cases relating to fundamental rights, and it also inspired the revision of the treaties, in particular the adoption of the social protocol annexed to the Maastricht Treaty (Kenner 2003: 11).

In 2000, a new Charter of Fundamental Rights was proclaimed by the European Convention against the backdrop of the drafting of a European constitution. Today appended to the Treaty of Lisbon, the new charter was meant to be a sort of Magna Carta or Bill of Rights of the EU. The charter incorporates social rights into a wider body of personal, civil, political and social rights and affirms the indivisibility of these different types of rights. By doing so, it deepens the existing social rights, on the one hand, and creates new ones, on the other (see Table 4.2).

Many legal scholars, however, underline the limited scope of declaratory texts and "the reticence of the judges of the Union to ensure the effectiveness of the fundamental social rights" (Benlolo-Carabot 2012: 90). It is striking that the charter itself stipulates that the rights it invokes should be circumscribed within the limits laid down by the treaties (Article 52), therefore preventing the creation of new EU prerogatives. Contrary to civil and political rights, which are mostly consensual in Europe, the protection of social rights often requires a positive intervention in the form of politically motivated public policy. The CJEU was therefore left with the delicate task of defining the degree to which the charter could be invoked to extend or define new rights. It has done so by establishing a hierarchy between fundamental rights – notably the four freedoms, equality between men and women, or non-discrimination on the basis of age – and fundamental principles that can only be invoked if they have already been established in EU or national law (see Table 4.2). Considering the political debates surrounding the charter,

> the distinction between rights and principles is the result of a difficult compromise between those who wished to see social and economic rights figure in the charter and those who feared that their consecration would lead to creating new obligations for States and to increasing the scope of powers of European judges and legislators.
>
> (Bailleux 2014: 290)

Table 4.2 The CJEU's jurisprudence and the recognition of social rights in the Charter of Fundamental Rights

Charter article	Type of recognition	Jurisprudence
Article 21 Equality and non-discrimination	**Right/general principle of EU law**: Can be invoked as such in a dispute between private parties	Judgment of the Court of 19 January 2010, *Kücükdeveci*, C-555/07, EU:C:2010:21; Judgment of the Court of 17 April 2018, *Egenberger*, C-414/16, EU:C:2018:257.
Article 23 Equality between women and men	**Right/general principle of EU law**: Can be invoked as such between private parties because of the general principle of EU law of equality	Judgment of the Court of 25 May 1971, *Gabrielle Defrenne v Belgian State*, 80/70, ECLI:EU:C:1971:55; Judgment of the Court of 8 April 1976, *Defrenne v Sabena*, 43/75, EU:C:1976:56; Judgment of the Court of 15 June 1978, *Defrenne v Sabena*, 149/77, EU:C:1978:130.
Article 27 Workers' right to information and consultation in companies	**Principle**: Cannot be invoked as such between private parties	Judgment of the Court of 15 January 2014, *Association de médiation sociale*, C-176/12, EU:C:2014:2.
Article 28 Right of collective bargaining and action	**Right/general principle of EU law**: Can be invoked as such between private parties	Judgment of the Court of 11 December 2007, *International Transport Workers' Federation v Viking Line*, C-438/05, EU:C:2007:772.
Article 29 Right of access to placement services	Unknown	
Article 30 Protection in the event of unjustified dismissal	Unknown	
Article 31 Fair and just working conditions	**Right**: Can be invoked as such in a dispute between private parties	Judgment of the Court of 6 November 2018, *Max-Planck v Shimizu*, C-684/16, EU:C:2018:874.
Article 33 Family and professional life	Unknown	
Article 34 Social security and social assistance	Both elements of right and principle	Explanations relating to Article 52 of the charter

Source: Adapted from Bribosia *et al.* (2019).

The laborious extension of social regulation through legislation

Based on the competences established in the treaties, it is by legislative means that the EU has established the regulatory framework of the single market regarding social matters. Since Maastricht, the ordinary legislative procedure implies that the European Commission initiates legislation (mostly after consulting social partners) with the Council – deciding mainly by qualified majority voting with some exceptions (see Table 2.1, p. 31) – and the EP amending, adopting or rejecting the proposed acts. In the late 1980s and 1990s, the Commission was able to use opportunistically the established competence on health and safety to initiate social regulation. Its *raison d'être* was essentially to provide a level playing field throughout the single market and prevent any social dumping caused by the fact that workers from some regions enjoy fewer rights and a lower level of protection. This includes coordination in situations of mobility. Non-discrimination on the basis of nationality spilled over into a much wider range of discriminations, with gender equality at the forefront. Binding social regulation at the European level was *always* contentious as any attempt to broaden its boundaries and assert social objectives as such consistently triggered political battles. Successive enlargements – to the north in the 1970s and 1990s, the south in the 1980s, and the east in the 2000s – only made agreement among the legislators more difficult as it was becoming more necessary.

Free movement and labour law

Historically, European regulation in social matters has focused on the world of labour. The first two regulations, dating from 1958 (3/58 and 4/58), were aimed at promoting mobility and regulating the rights of migrant workers throughout the EEC by organizing the coordination of social security systems. To ensure the continuity of rights and avoid social dumping, non-national workers are covered by the social security system of the country in which they work. These regulations were revised in 1971 (1408/71) and then 2004 (883/2004). The rights related to free movement were consolidated in the 1960s and 1970s by a series of regulations that guaranteed mobility and the right to family reunification.[2] These texts are based on four principles: equal treatment between nationals and non-nationals, the aggregation of benefits accrued in different countries, the portability of these rights and the non-overlap of protection regimes and contributions in different member states (Anderson 2015: 91). These rights only concern a small minority of mobile Europeans, but whose numbers grow steadily. Today, approximately 17 million Europeans live or work in another member state than their country of origin, which is twice as much as ten years ago.[3] In the 1990s and 2000s, these provisions were consolidated and extended in two directions: the rights of mobile workers to social benefits increased (early retirement, unemployment,

---

2. Regulation of 16 August 1961, regulation 38/1964, regulation 1612/68, directive 68/360, regulation 1251/70, regulation 1408/71.
3. See European Labour Authority at www.ela.europa.eu/ (accessed 15 September 2021).

etc.), on the one hand, and access to these rights has been extended to other categories of non-nationals (students, unemployed, pensioners), on the other. The so-called citizenship directive of 2004 (2004/38/EC) established the right for non-nationals to access social benefits, but this right was later curtailed by the CJEU in several judgments in the 2010s (see Chapter 5).

Furthermore, the regulation of the posting of workers abroad by companies in the framework of the freedom to provide services has been the subject of political confrontations between all EU institutions since the early 1990s (see Chapter 5). A fragile equilibrium between the freedom to provide services and compliance with national social regulation was established in the revised directive on posted workers in 2018 (18/957/EU). After heated debates over the nature and scope of its competences, a European Labour Authority was created in 2019 to facilitate the application and enforcement of EU law on mobility and social security for all Europeans living or working in another EU country.

The second area of EU regulatory action touches upon labour law, based on the treaty item "health and safety at work", an area where agreement can be reached with a qualified majority in the Council since the 1986 Single European Act. This led to a series of directives on health and safety, which the Commission understood in a broad sense to include regulation of, for instance, the protection of fixed-term or temporary contract workers (91/383/EEC), pregnant workers (92/85/EEC) and young people (94/33/EEC).

Two political and legal "sagas" are highly illustrative of the battles that have taken place in the field of health and safety. Those related to working time, on the one hand, and maternity leave, on the other. The regulation of working time through an EU directive dates back to 1993 and was contested from the outset by the UK government. The UK obtained not only the exemption of many sectors from the directive but also a general opt-out from the key provision, namely the 48-hour working-time weekly limit. The directive was revised in 2000 and 2003[4] to remove most of the sectoral exemptions. However, in the meantime, it was challenged before the CJEU. The issue raised was whether on-call time was to be considered as working time or not. Although the CJEU consistently adopted a maximalist pro-regulation stance – recognizing that on-call time should be included in working time if workers had to be present at their workplace – up to 11 member states asked for opt-outs for some or all sectors. In 2004, the Commission launched an initial attempt to address these discrepancies through legislation. This effort failed in 2009, after five years of contentious negotiations because the EP objected to the continued possibility for governments to opt out.

---

4. It limits the weekly working time to 48 hours on average, imposes a minimum rest period of 11 consecutive hours per 24-hour period, a minimum weekly rest period of 24 hours per seven-day period, a paid annual leave of at least four weeks and extra protection for night work.

As early as 2010, the Commission picked up the issue again and, this time, the social partners agreed to engage in autonomous negotiations before handing the lead over to the Commission (which they had refused to do six years earlier). Yet, BusinessEurope aligned with the prevailing coalition of member states and proved unwilling to compromise on a possible suppression of the opt-out. To this day, the 2003 directive has not been revised. This means that EU legislation on working time has turned into Swiss cheese with the multiplication of opt-outs resulting in differentiated and partial application of EU rules (Martinsen & Wessel 2014).

The maternity leave directive, a key legislative piece in the EU body of social law, finds itself at the intersection of labour law and family policy, an area where the EU has enjoyed weak legitimacy to act and that has long been divisive "along ideological lines both within and between countries" (Hantrais 1995: 79). The maternity leave directive remains in the legislative records of the EU as an instance of intractable conflict between the Council and the EP. In 2008, the European Commission proposed revising the 1992 directive on maternity leave. In tune with the Lisbon Strategy agenda, one main objective was to increase the rate of participation of women in the labour market. This was to be achieved by extending the minimum length of maternity leave from 14 to 18 weeks and through enhanced rights in term of pay rate and employment. However, the rapporteur in the EP, the Portuguese Socialist Edite Estrela, shaped a radically different text. Grounded in a gender-equality perspective, it included a longer duration of maternity leave at full pay and created a novel two-week paternity leave. This version was unacceptable for the Council, a broad coalition of states saw the provisions on extended maternity and paternity leave as being much too costly and, fundamentally, infringing on the principles of subsidiarity and pro-portionality. The text also unleashed cultural resistance regarding the defence of traditional family values. At the same time, some among the progressives were wondering whether a longer maternity leave would actually promote women's rights or rather consolidate the traditional family model. After the Council blocked the text for four years, it was withdrawn by the Commission in 2015.

These two examples show that, after the adoption of initial, embryonic regulations in the 1990s, the modernization of the social *acquis* has proved to be contentious and difficult in recent decades. This is further illustrated by two recent initiatives on the coordination of social security and on minimum wages (still in deliberation at the time of writing).

In 2016, the European Commission submitted a proposal for revising the 2004 regulation.[5] The main novelty in the proposal was a provision to shift the

---

5. Proposal for a Regulation of the European Parliament and the Council Amending Regulation (EC) No. 883/2004 on the Coordination of Social Security Systems and Regulation (EC) No. 987/ 2009 Laying Down the Procedure for Implementing Regulation (EC) no. 883/2004, COM/2016/ 0815, 13 December 2016.

responsibility of paying unemployment benefits from the country of long-term residence or nationality to the country of activity. This particular provision triggered resistance from the German government together with a blocking minority formed by the so-called like-minded states in the Council.[6] The German government proved sensitive to the popular resentment towards alleged massive benefit tourism in the EU and sought to impede the export of social security benefits back to workers' home country. Moreover, together with Austria and Denmark, Germany was pushing for the introduction of an index for linking the level of child benefits to the living standards in the country where the children of migrant workers reside. In the EP, where the conservative EPP found itself divided along national lines, the German rapporteur, Robert Schulze (CDU/CSU) tabled an amendment for introducing the mentioned index when the EP's first reading vote should have taken place, on 19 April 2019, one of the last sessions of the EP's eighth legislature. Because of the high levels of controversy, however, the vote did not take place. As of June 2021 and following the election of a new assembly in 2019, the piece is still pending.

A further controversial legislative initiative has been the Commission's proposal for a directive on adequate minimum wages put forward in October 2020.[7] The motive for the proposal lies in the fact that 22 EU countries currently have a minimum wage that is below 60 per cent of the (gross) median wage, the benchmark recommended by the ILO. In relation to the implementation of the EPSR, Ursula von der Leyen had pledged to take action to tackle poverty, including in-work poverty, when she took office in October 2019. Far from setting the level of minimum wages (let alone a uniform level across the EU), the proposal obliges national governments to "ensure that the setting and updating of statutory minimum wages are guided by criteria set to promote adequacy with the aim to achieve decent working and living conditions, social cohesion and upward convergence" (Article 5). These criteria include "(a) the purchasing power of statutory minimum wages, taking into account the cost of living and the contribution of taxes and social benefits; (b) the general level of gross wages and their distribution; (c) the growth rate of gross wages; (d) labour productivity developments", therefore constituting a relatively constraining framework. Moreover, the proposal does not seek to constrain the six countries[8] where minimum wages are set through collective agreements to introduce a statutory minimum wage through law.

Long before the draft directive was officially proposed, it was contested both by actors hostile to more regulation for higher minimum wages, and by

---

6. Austria, Belgium, the Czech Republic, Denmark, Luxembourg, the Netherlands, Sweden.
7. Proposal for a Directive of the European Parliament and the Council on Adequate Minimum Wages in the European Union, COM(2020)682, 28 October 2020.
8. Austria, Cyprus, Denmark, Finland, Italy and Sweden.

those hostile to greater involvement of the EU in the domain of work and pay. Among the latter, the unions from Denmark and Sweden have been particularly adamant in claiming that the EU has no competence to act in this area.[9] They are contesting the legality of the proposal on the grounds that Article 153.5 TFEU explicitly states that pay is excluded from the area of competence of the EU. From a policy point of view, they have argued that any interference in complex systems of wage setting may be disruptive and damage national systems that are working well. From a political stance, they have argued that there was a major risk that the directive could be used to decrease wages in times of crisis and they have pointed to the socially regressive role of the EU with references to the *Laval*, *Viking*, and *Rüffert* decisions of the CJEU. To conclude, it is interesting to note that, with this proposal on minimum wages, the European Commission is attempting to break a major taboo in social policy-making. In order to overcome major political resistance, it is not seeking to regulate directly what is going on in the member states. Rather, it is using what scholars have called governance through data, rules and numbers (Crespy 2020b; Schmidt 2020; Supiot 2015) in order to promote its own (technocratic) "evidence-based" policy-making culture.

The European history of combatting discrimination initially focused on equality between men and women in the workplace. In 1966, the workers of the national armament's factory in Herstal, near Liège, Belgium, went on strike to demand that the principle of equal pay for men and women enshrined in Article 119 of the Treaty of Rome be implemented. This episode resulted in a wave of feminist mobilization and a series of cases brought before the CJEU in favour of women (see next section). The principles set out by the court were then codified in an important legislative body of 15 directives and regulations adopted between 1975 and 2010 (Jacquot 2015: 208). The first texts focused on equal pay, broadly understood, and access to social security and pension rights. In 1992, Directive 92/85/EEC established a minimum of 14 continuous weeks for maternity leave. The 1976 directive on equality between men and women with regard to access to employment, training, professional promotion and working conditions was revised in 2006 to consider indirect discrimination and sexual harassment (2006/54/EC).

With the new regulatory competence introduced by the Treaty of Amsterdam (Article 13 TEC), the EU's field of action extended beyond gender equality. On the one hand, Directive 2000/78/EC on equal treatment in the field of employment (dubbed "the employment equality directive") covers discrimination based

---

9. See, for example, Therese Svanström, "Why EU minimum wage is actually a bad idea for workers", euobserver, 13 January 2020, https://euobserver.com/opinion/147050 (accessed 15 September 2021).

on religion, disability, age or sexual orientation. On the other hand, Directive 2000/43/EC on equality irrespective of race or ethnic origin (dubbed the "Racial Equality Directive") applies not only to employment and training, but also to access to social protection or to goods and services in general.

Yet, progress soon stalled. In 2008, the European Commission submitted a proposal to extend the fight against discrimination based on religion, disability, age or sexual orientation beyond the field of employment to social protection, education and access to goods and services that are commercially available to the public. Despite a majority of MEPs voting in favour of the text in 2009, the issue has now been blocked in the Council for almost a decade. As in other areas, EU regulation on discrimination has become more divisive over time.

Health

As underscored by Karen Anderson (2015: 173), the provisions on public health introduced by the Treaties of Maastricht (Article 129 TEC) and Amsterdam (Article 152 TEC) are ambiguous. On the one hand, they establish a regulatory competence for the EU, but, on the other hand, they also emphasize the principle of subsidiarity and the idea that EU action must aim essentially at supporting and encouraging coordination among member states. As in other areas, the Commission has made opportunistic use of the legal possibilities offered by the treaties and, in the end, European public health regulations have taken various forms. First, harmonized standards have been introduced for the safety and quality of blood (and its derivatives; 2002/98/EC) and human tissues and cells (2004/23/EC), as well as for phytosanitary products (e.g. pesticides: 2009/120/EC and 2009/1107 abrogating 79/117/EC and 91/414/EEC) and veterinary checks governing the trade in animals (96/90/EC, 96/43/EC, 1760/2000). This salvo of European regulations (sometimes replacing earlier less stringent legislation) was adopted in response to several health crises, in particular the contaminated blood scandal in France in the 1980s – in which hundreds of patients had been transfused with blood contaminated with HIV and hepatitis C – and the "mad cow" (bovine spongiform encephalopathy) crisis, which began in the UK in 1996 and spread to other European countries via beef exports causing more than 200 human deaths. Regulatory measures to coordinate member states' action on cross-border risk management and control such as epidemics were also adopted (1082/2013/EU). However, the current procedures have proved to be rather ineffective in bringing about a coordinated response to the outbreak of Covid-19 in the spring of 2020. This has led the current president of the European Commission to propose strengthening the existing agencies and instruments or even creating new competences that would build a genuine "European Health Union" (see Chapter 9).

Second, the EU has a regulatory arsenal to control the marketing of medical goods. Set up in 1993, the centralized marketing authorization procedure (726/2004) is the culmination of the drug coordination dating back to 1960s. The EMA, set up in London in 1995 (now located in Amsterdam), supervises this procedure and ensures that the quality criteria laid down in Directive 2001/83/EC are met. European regulations also cover the approximation of national rules regarding clinical trials (2001/20/EC), medicines for rare diseases (141/2000), medicines for children (1901/2006) and innovative therapy medicines (2001/83/EC as amended by 2394/2007).

Lastly, the Commission opportunistically used the legal basis for the convergence of legislations in the internal market (Article 114 TFEU) to submit a directive banning tobacco advertising (on the grounds of harmonizing the rules governing trade). Particularly disputed, this directive was submitted in 1989 and adopted only in 1998 and then annulled by the CJEU, which sided with the German government in 2000. A directive banning only the direct (and not the indirect) advertising of tobacco was adopted in 2002 (2003/33/EC). In other areas, however, the EU fails to advance legislation for protecting human health. In 2017, the renewal of the authorization of glyphosate, a powerful and toxic herbicide, proved that both the Commission and the Council were unable to legislate in favour of human health in the face of major industrial interests.

The key role of case law

On many occasions, the cases brought to the CJEU led the court to delineate the boundaries of EU provisions and rights, thus putting in motion powerful political dynamics. This has implied the mobilization of activists or actions by individuals seeking to consolidate and extend transnational rights. Reactions from member state governments seeking to tighten or, on the contrary, loosen social regulation have also tapped into a – sometimes contentious – dialogue between case law and legislation. Long seen as a mainly progressive force driving the extension of social rights for about three decades, the CJEU has come to show a different face, more cautious from a societal point of view and even aggressively pro-market at times. Insofar as the CJEU seems to be mirroring the divided and sometimes regressive European politics, we are reminded that, despite legal rationality, judges can never be fully independent from politics and society. This section will not provide an exhaustive overview of the existing social jurisprudence, but will rather focus on a few important areas and decisions that illustrate the interactions between case law and legislation.

The codification of case law through legislation

The codification of jurisprudence, that is the subsequent incorporation of the principles and arguments articulated in the rulings of the CJEU into legislation, has been a main catalyser of social regulation. Gender equality and patient mobility within the single market are two paradigmatic examples of this.

The 8 April 1976 decision C-43/75, *Defrenne v Sabena*, marks the beginning of the EU's policy on equality between men and women. Eliane Vogel-Polsky, a Belgian law professor, lawyer and feminist activist (see Box 4.1), introduced two cases in the name of Gabrielle Defrenne, an air hostess working for the Belgian public airline Sabena. She argued that, by forcing its female employees to cease their activity

---

BOX 4.1 ELIANE VOGEL-POLSKY

Eliane Vogel-Polsky (1926–2015) embodies the fight for women's emancipation, equality and parity between men and women after the Second World War. In the war's aftermath, she studied law at the Université libre de Bruxelles (ULB) and finished her interdisciplinary curriculum as one of the first alumni of the ULB's Institute for European Studies in 1965.

As the Treaty of Rome had been signed in 1957, paving the way for the single market, her commitment to equal pay between men and women flourished. The treaty included Article 119 stipulating that men and women should be paid equally for the same work. As Eliane Vogel-Polsky was diffusing her knowledge of EU law in trade union meetings, Article 119 triggered a unique social conflict in the history of EU integration. In February 1966, women from the national armament production site in Herstal started a strike to obtain equal pay between male and female workers. This conflict reinforced Eliane Vogel-Polsky's belief that judicial struggles needed to be fought at the European level to obtain the direct application of Article 119.

The story of Gabrielle Defrenne became the symbol of this struggle as the two decisions on the case would remain among the most famous in CJEU case law. On the grounds of Article 119, Vogel-Polsky argued that Defrenne had not been treated equally vis-à-vis male workers by her employer Sabena. A first decision in 1971 was not satisfactory for the Belgian lawyer who continued to work on the case. A second decision in 1976 turned out much more favourable and asserted that equal pay is a touchstone of the European legal order.

Source: Nicolas Verschueren, "Eliane Vogel-Polsky: mère de l'Europe sociale", 8 January 2019, www.iee-ulb.eu/blog (accessed 15 September 2021).

---

when they reached the age of 40 (compared to 55 for men) with pension rights lower than those of their male colleagues, the company was violating the Treaty of Rome. In 1976, the CJEU boldly ruled that Article 119 of the Treaty of Rome on the equal treatment of men and women (Article 157 TFEU) should apply directly in the member states and that pension rights were an integral part of remuneration. In 1984, in its decision on the *Razzouk and Beydoun* case (C-75/82), the court recognized equality between men and women as a fundamental right. Two years later, with the *Bilka* case (C-170/84), judges strengthened the protection of women by holding that

> Article 119 of the treaty is infringed by an undertaking which excludes part-time employees from its occupational pension scheme, where that exclusion affects a far greater number of women than men, unless the undertaking shows that the exclusion is based on objectively justified factors unrelated to any discrimination on grounds of sex.[10]

Although Article 119 TEC narrowly focused on wage dumping, the CJEU used it to lay the groundwork for an ambitious European legislative framework on gender equality (as presented above), with rights extending to transsexuals in 1996.[11]

Similarly, when, in 2008, the Commission proposed the directive on the rights of patients in cross-border healthcare (adopted in 2011), its aim was to adapt the legislation to the progress made by the CJEU's case law. The reimbursement of care received abroad had until then been governed by the regulations on the coordination of social security systems revised in 2004. According to these texts, patients had to ask their national administration for prior authorization in order to be reimbursed, but national authorities had the obligation to grant it (only) if the required treatment could not be provided in the state of origin within a reasonable delay. This principle was, however, widely challenged in a way favourable to patients by the CJEU. In 1998, in two comparable cases involving the reimbursement of medical care received respectively in Belgium and Germany by Luxembourg nationals, *Decker* (C-120/95) and *Kohll* (C-158/96), the court had held that the lack of reimbursement as well as the refusal to grant prior authorization for reimbursement were obstacles to the free movement of persons and the freedom to provide services. In the case of hospital care, the judges ruled, in a series of cases during the 2000s,[12] that social security administrations could maintain the requirement for prior authorization but within strict limitations, thus

---

10. Judgment of the Court of 13 May 1986, *Bilka – Kaufhaus GmbH v Karin Weber von Hartz*, C-170/84, EU:C:1986:204.

11. *P v S and Cornwall County Council* (C-13/94).

12. *Vanbraekel* (C-368/98), *Smits and Peerbooms* (C-157/99), *Müller-Fauré* (C 385/99), *Inizan* (C-56/01).

rendering authorization quasi-automatic. As a result, the directive on patients' rights in cross-border healthcare adopted in 2011 mainly served to enshrine jurisprudence and ensure a clear and coherent legal framework for cross-border care.

Strengthening legislation through case law

Besides codification, jurisprudence has often served to guarantee the effectiveness of EU law by ensuring, for example, that the acts of transposition into national law do not contradict rights set out in EU legislation. This was the case, for instance, in 2001 when the CJEU challenged an article in the British Transposition Act of the EU 1993 Working Time Directive whereby the right to paid leave would only be effective after a period of employment of 13 weeks, thus discriminating against workers in the television and film industry who are often hired under short-term contracts.

In recent years, case law on non-discrimination has been crucial to ensure the effectiveness of the two directives adopted in 2000 (2000/78/EC and 2000/43/EC), the transposition of which in all member states has only recently been completed. With the Mangold decision of 2005 (C-144/04), the CJEU consolidated the principle of non-discrimination based on age by rejecting a German law allowing the conclusion of fixed-term employment contracts once a worker reached the age of 52. In the *Ingeniorforeningen i Danmark* case (C-499/08), the CJEU ruled that it is discriminatory to refuse to pay severance to an employee because he or she can receive a pension. The confirmation of the Mangold jurisprudence has provoked the resistance of the Danish Supreme Court who refused to submit to the CJEU's judgment (Rorive & Bribosia 2017: 206).

In terms of discrimination on the grounds of race or ethnic origin, the CJEU took a decision for the first time in 2015 on discrimination against Roma. In the *Chez* case (C-83/14), the court ruled that the Bulgarian electricity distribution company Chez had to put an end to its discriminatory practices towards the population living in Roma neighbourhoods (Rorive & Bribosia 2015).

In June 2018, the CJEU ruled in a major case relating to discrimination based on sexual orientation (*Adrian Coman*, C-673/16). A Romanian-American male couple had married in Brussels and subsequently wanted to live in Romania. The Romanian authorities refused to grant Adrian Coman's American husband resident status on the grounds that same-sex marriage is not lawful in the country. The EU judges nevertheless decided in favour of the couple, considering that although some member states do not authorize same-sex marriage, they cannot impede the freedom of establishment of EU citizens by not granting residency rights to their partners. This decision means that the CJEU is de facto imposing the recognition of the legal effects of "gay marriage" across the EU. In the realm of non-discrimination, the CJEU is drawing to a large extent from the corpus of international law, in particular the European Convention on Human Rights (and the jurisprudence of the Council of Europe's Court in Strasbourg), as well as on the various charters and conventions of the United Nations. All this shows that, until recently, the CJEU has played a key role in allowing social regulation to effectively come to fruition in terms of guaranteeing social rights and enhancing social cohesion.

From extending to curtailing social rights?

A progressive linear extension of social rights through case law should not, however, be taken for granted. The CJEU has proved sensitive to context by being at times proactive in the deepening of rights and at others more cautious or even going so far as to encourage the curtailing of rights (Martinsen 2015: 39–40; Saurugger & Terpan 2017: 3–5). This has been visible in three fields especially.

The CJEU's jurisprudence on the posting of workers in the 2000s created outrage within the labour movement and the connected legal and intellectual circles. With four decisions – the now famous *Laval*, *Viking*, *Rüffert* and *Luxembourg* – the judges ruled that the freedom to provide services across national borders should not be hindered by the obligation to respect collective agreements and that industrial action to protest the hiring of cheaper foreign workers was not compliant with EU treaties.

Furthermore, from 2013 onwards, there has been a clear shift in the jurisprudence over the rights of non-national EU citizens to access social benefits in the countries in which they reside. After a period in which rights were broadened, in keeping with the 2004 "citizenship directive" (2004/38/EC), the CJEU granted national governments the right to limit access to social benefits especially to non-active persons (students, the unemployed and their children). This jurisprudence relies on the idea that non-nationals should prove sufficient (economic) ties with the host country in which they reside and should not become a (financial) burden to the national community. This strongly calls the idea of unconditional transnational rights into question. In doing so, the judges of Luxembourg have proved sensitive to the politicization of the matter and to public controversy over "welfare tourism" (Blauberger *et al.* 2018). This was particularly blatant in the run-up to the Brexit referendum in 2017.

Finally, the CJEU's use of the Charter of Fundamental Rights since its entry into force may seem disappointing in several respects. Until the 2000s, the CJEU had consistently extended the scope of national social rights as well as created new enforceable rights that individuals can claim on the basis of EU law (Lenaerts & Foubert 2001). Equal treatment between men and women, notably with regard to pay, is a case in point. Against this backdrop, the adoption of the Charter of Fundamental Rights inevitably raised expectations, only to yield disappointing results. The CJEU endorsed the distinction between fundamental rights and fundamental principles, considering that the latter cannot be invoked directly, and can only maintain or consolidate the rights already established in national or EU law (see Table 4.2). Thus, the judges abstained from judicial activism for the creation of new rights. This is, for instance, reflected in two cases from 2012[13] and 2014[14] in which the CJEU refused to acknowledge the right to maternity leave for breastfeeding mothers whose children had been conceived via surrogacy (neither for the mother who had conceived the child nor for the mother for whom the child had been conceived). As far as social rights and the charter are concerned, the judges of Luxembourg now seem very attentive to the principle of subsidiarity and anxious to respect divergent societal and cultural preferences, waiting for (most) national societies and legal orders to first acknowledge new rights before consecrating them in the CJEU's jurisprudence.

Most importantly perhaps, by restrictively interpreting the Charter of Fundamental Rights, the CJEU failed to contain the debasing of social rights during the euro crisis in 2010–15. Conditionality and the type of structural reforms imposed through the MoU signed between the Troika and the indebted countries inevitably led to the weakening of social protection, but in various forms and extents.

Conclusion

This chapter has shown that social regulation results from the continuous – and sometimes contentious – dialogue between the treaties, the legislation and case law. In the second half of the twentieth century, these interactions have led to the slow yet continuous extension of social regulation. Although primarily concerned with flanking measures for enabling free movement in the single market, regulation gradually extended to a broad vision of anti-discrimination – especially gender equality and, arguably, the recognition of same-sex marriage – and to admittedly limited action in the fields of labour law and public health.

However, the developments at stake over the past two decades show that no progressive path dependency of EU social regulation can be taken for granted. The rise of neoliberalism, the decline of the political left in the domestic and European arenas alike, as well as the successive enlargements of the EU have all concurred to make agreement on social regulation increasingly difficult. If the

---

13. *Z/A Government Department and the Board of Management of a Community School* (C-363/12).
14. *C.D./S.*T (C-167/12).

"joint decision trap" described by Scharpf has been reinforced, however, it is not only for institutional and legal reasons as he has frequently argued, but also for political ones. On the one hand, the Commission and the CJEU have led marked pro-market offensives. On the other, national governments have increasingly been populated by liberal, conservative or even far-right parties who have fed a climate of welfare chauvinism (or been responsive to it) and sought to prevent any further involvement of the EU in social matters. Consequently, the regulatory activity of the EU has waned while other modes of governance have been more dynamic, especially soft coordination. This is illustrated by the EPSR, whose implementation relies on both hard and soft law.

That being said, one may argue that social regulation is far from being a thing of the past, mainly for two reasons. First, the regulatory agenda has been, to a certain extent, revived by the Commission after ten years of muddling through a recession with long-lasting social consequences in terms of poverty and inequality. Under Jean-Claude Juncker's presidency, sensitive regulatory issues including parental leave, posted workers, information on working conditions and the coordination of social security have been put on the legislative agenda.

The second reason ensuring regulation is bound to remain a key mode of governance is the need to tackle the challenges the EU will have to face in the years to come. As mentioned earlier, Ursula von der Leyen and the commissioner for jobs and social affairs, Nicolas Schmit, are pursuing the establishment of a European framework for "fair" minimum wages across the EU on the grounds that it is necessary to tackle poverty (not least in-work poverty). This attempt from the Commission to venture into the realm of wages has triggered much resistance from a number of member states and unions who see the proposal as a violation of subsidiarity. Regulation will also be necessary to guarantee, for instance, that workers in a-typical forms of unemployment (short contracts, self-employment, etc.) also enjoy adequate social protection. In the area of public health, the president of the European Commission has suggested, in her 2020 State of the Union Address "discuss(ing) the health competences", that, in the light of the Covid-19 pandemic, the EU should gain more (regulatory) powers to combat cross-border health threats (see Chapter 9).

Further reading

- Karen Anderson, *Social Policy in the European Union* (Basingstoke: Palgrave Macmillan, 2015), chs 2 and 3.
- Paolo Graziano and Miriam Hartlapp, "The end of Social Europe? Understanding EU social policy change". *Journal of European Public Policy* 26:10 (2018), 1484–501.

- Dorte Sindbjerg Martinsen, *An Ever More Powerful Court? The Political Constraints on Legal Integration in the European Union* (Oxford: Oxford University Press, 2015).

Questions to debate

- Do social fundamental rights exist at the European level?
- In which area is EU social regulation most elaborate?

5
DOES LIBERALIZATION UNDERMINE SOCIAL COHESION?

Liberalization is rarely addressed as one of the components of social policy. On the contrary, political discourses about the EU depict liberalization policies as the embodiment of a "neoliberal Europe" incompatible with the project of a "Social Europe". Moreover, previous chapters have stressed how social policy at the European level has developed as an "add-on" (Copeland & Day 2015) aiming to facilitate market creation. Yet, one should go beyond simplistic oppositions to understand the complex effects of liberalization on social cohesion and inequalities. Liberalization can be defined as the broadening of markets. It therefore stimulates cross-border trade by allowing competition between domestic and foreign economic operators. To do so, two types of barriers to cross-border trade must be lifted: tariffs, on the one hand, and on the other hand, national regulations that do not match the standards of foreign operators, therefore preventing them from offering their goods or services in a particular national market. For this reason, liberalization often comes with deregulation, which can, however, be offset by the establishment of new rules at the European level (re-regulation). Liberalization is at the very heart of the European integration process, which is built from its outset on the four freedoms enshrined in the Treaty of Rome. If the free movement of goods and capital only affects social policy to a limited extent, the free movement of persons and services, in contrast, raises a number of issues that are addressed in this chapter.

There are basically two contrasted ways to conceive of liberalization in relation to social cohesion. A central belief driving EU integration is that liberalization creates opportunities that can enhance social cohesion both nationally and cross-nationally. The founding fathers of the EEC believed firmly that the opening of national markets would drive not only growth but also wages and living standards upward, a recurring theme in the 1957 Treaty of Rome. The free circulation of workers, in particular, has been conceived as a source of opportunity for people from economically depressed regions to seek a better life elsewhere in Europe. Liberalization as opportunity remains a main frame of reference used by the EU institutions to legitimize the pursuit of the completion of the single market, especially in the area of services. It is also valued by scholars (e.g. Andor 2020; Crum 2015). Furthermore, liberalization has led to the creation of new, transnational rights falling under the encompassing principle of non-discrimination and protected by the CJEU (De Witte 2015). Non-discrimination has also involved extending national rights to non-national EU citizens as national welfare states have had to open up.

Despite being in some respects a source of opportunities for some individuals, liberalization has perhaps mostly been seen as a major challenge for social cohesion. This is because the objectives of market-making are primarily those of economic agents (profit-making) rather than those of society as a whole. Even when liberalization involves the expansion of services and rights, it undermines existing arrangements without providing sufficient regulation and resources at the EU level. To borrow Maurizio Ferrera's compelling book title, liberalization is bound to disrupt the established "boundaries of welfare" (Ferrera 2005). The crux of the matter is that social policy mostly happens at the national level, while the expansion of markets and liberalization is a transnational process by nature. A significant objective of EU social policy, especially through regulation, is to strike the right balance between opportunities created by liberalization and societies' needs for protective regulation. The ability of the EU to enact re-regulation at the supranational level is therefore key, but often insufficient. In this regard, subsidiarity can be an obstacle: the EU has neither the legitimacy nor the legal or practical means to re-regulate social matters with strong local and cultural roots. Ultimately, there can be a clash between two forms of solidarity: the ties binding the members of the national community anchored in the institutionalization of the welfare state, on the one hand, and the rights emerging from transnational EU citizenship, on the other. This chapter takes stock of and assesses the developments at stake in three areas highly illustrative of this tension, namely the free circulation of services, SGI and the opening of welfare states to non-national EU citizens.

The freedom to provide services and social dumping

From attempts to strike the balance between market freedom and labour law …

The posting of workers is at the centre of one of the greatest political and regulatory sagas in the history of the single market. A posted worker is sent by his or her company to another country to work for a limited period of time. The diversity in levels of remuneration and social protection within the single market carries risks of social dumping (i.e. competition between local workers and workers who may be posted from countries where wage levels and social protection are lower only because of their cheaper cost to employers). There were approximately 2 million posted workers in the EU in 2015, a 41 per cent increase since 2010. Some 36 per cent of postings are concentrated in the building sector, followed by industry and social services and healthcare sectors. It should be noted that 80 per cent of secondments take place between neighbouring countries. The main countries of origin are (in descending order) Poland, Germany, France, Slovenia and Spain. The main host countries are Germany, France, Belgium, Austria and the Netherlands. The successive episodes of contention surrounding the posting of workers show how politics have moved the cursor each time between the free circulation of services (or freedom to provide services) and tighter social regulation.

From the relaunch of the single market and the enlargements to the south in the 1980s, differences in remuneration and social protection between EEC member states raised fears of social dumping by countries sending workers to wealthier countries. Social dumping refers to the use by employers of lower labour costs as a comparative advantage in a context of economic competition. More broadly, it is "the practice of undermining or evading existing social regulations with the aim of gaining a competitive advantage" (Bernaciak 2014). In concrete terms, the cost of labour can be lower not only if wages are less, but also if the standards of social protection are weaker (leave, social security, safety, etc.), thus reducing the overall cost of production of goods or services.

In the European context, social dumping is made possible by the significant differences in living standards between European countries, a phenomenon that has been underpinned by the EU's continuous enlargement. From an economic point of view, social dumping hinders fair competition and prevents economic agents from enjoying a level playing field. From a social point of view, it strips some workers of their rights and leads to exploitative abuse. Furthermore, as Table 5.1 shows, several forms of fraud exist to challenge the established rules.

The CJEU's 1990 decision in *Rush Portuguesa* was the first move in what was going to become a continuous thorn in the side of the single market. In this decision, the CJEU ruled that governments could apply their own labour laws to posted workers. This position was, however, challenged by the European Commission, who considered it to be an obstacle to the freedom to provide services for foreign operators. A compromise was found in 1996 with the adoption of Directive 96/71/EC on the posting of workers. The directive establishes the laws of the country of origin as a rule, except for a core of critical rights (pay and leave). This was believed to facilitate the mobility of workers while ensuring the protection of their rights. Quickly, however, the directive was deemed insufficient by receiving states in western Europe and by trade unions who deplored social dumping. The situation

Table 5.1 Identified abuses to labour mobility

Working conditions/wages	*Social security abuses*
Business model based on evasion of pay and other wage components	Business model based on application of low social security contributions
Non-compliance with minimum pay, collectively agreed wages and working conditions	Falsification of A1-form/non-registration in the home country/underpay of contributions
Underpayment and/or too low scaling/ serious mismatch with skill level	Uninsured workforce/excessively low benefits/ pensions
Non-payment of overtime bonuses and other allowances; no overtime compensation	Contribution (in the country of registration) based on excessively low factual remuneration; overtime and other wage components not included
Unjustified deductions for lodging and transport	Unlawful deductions/double pay slips
Blurred labour relations	Bogus self-employment

Source: Cremers (2020: 24).

was exacerbated by the enlargements to central and eastern Europe in 2004 and 2007. A total of 12 countries with cheap labour and dramatically lower social protection levels compared with those of the older 15 member states then joined the EU. The provisions of the 1996 directive are unclear on many aspects of posted work, such as the payment of employers' contributions to social security (in the country of origin) or the issue of secondment via temporary work. And although posted workers are to be paid the minimum wage in the host country, they remain cheaper than local workers when the latter are paid above that minimum wage. Furthermore, the provisions of the directive were often violated because of a lack of effective controls in many countries. The setting up of "letterbox companies" in new member states has become common practice. In this way, western European companies can take advantage of local social regulations by making them the point of detachment for labour posted to "the West". Underpaid truck drivers coming from central and eastern Europe to work in the logistics sector in western Europe offers an appalling illustration of this mechanism.

… To a pro-market offensive

As several member states (essentially large receiving states in the West) were keen to regulate the posting of workers more strictly, the European Commission and the CJEU led a pro-market offensive in the mid-2000s to impose the primacy of the law of the country of origin.

In 2004, the European Commission, then under the chairmanship of the very liberal José Manuel Barroso, proposed a directive on services in the internal market, also known as the Services Directive. This directive aimed to horizontally liberalize the entire service sector, however diverse. The Commission's initiative was based on the observation that, unlike trade in goods and capital, the single market for services was still very fragmented, because of the multitude and diversity of national regulations in several sectors. To solve this problem, the main legal mechanism at the heart of the directive was the country-of-origin principle, according to which a company from an EU member state may provide services in another member state based on the regulations of its country of origin, that is the country where its headquarters are formally established. Although the directive was mainly aimed at administrative regulations (registration, etc.), it also touched on social regulations and the articulation with the 1996 directive on posted workers was unclear. The rebranded "Bolkestein Directive" triggered a broad campaign of opposition led by civil society organizations and trade unions (Crespy 2010; Crespy & Gajewska 2010). In France, the debate interfered with the referendum on the ratification of the European Constitutional Treaty and featured xenophobic claims by the far-right about "Polish plumbers" stealing French jobs. Eventually, the directive was extensively amended by the EP and the posting of workers arguably remained relatively unaffected by it.

The next stage of the saga strongly features the CJEU who, in 2007–08, issued four decisions[1] that dramatically reversed its earlier jurisprudence in *Rush Portuguesa*. In both the *Laval* (see Box 5.1) and *Viking* cases, the judges

---

BOX 5.1 THE *LAVAL* CASE IN WAXHOLM

In 2004, a struggle broke out between the Swedish construction trade union and Laval un partneri, the Latvian company hired by the Swedish town of Waxholm. The union demanded that the collective agreement regulating the remuneration of workers in the sector be applied to Latvian workers at Waxholm's worksite. When the negotiations failed, the Swedish union blocked the construction site to protest. This broke off the contract between Waxholm and Laval un partneri, which went bankrupt the following year. The situation created a political escalation between the Latvian and Swedish governments and threatened to jeopardize the adoption of the directive on services liberalization in the internal market (also known as "services" or the "Bolkestein" directive). For its part, Laval un partneri brought the case before a Swedish court, which in turn referred it to the CJEU. In its decision from December 2007, the CJEU ruled that union collective action constituted an illegitimate obstacle to the freedom to provide services. Alongside its *Viking* and *Rüffert* decisions, the CJEU ruling over the *Laval* case epitomized the court's pro-market offensive of the mid-2000s.

---

1. *Viking* (C-438/05), *Laval* (C-341/05), *Rüffert* (C-346/06) and *Luxembourg* (C-319/06).

found that collective action (such as a strike or site blockade) demanding that foreign providers abide by local collective agreements were unjustified in light of the free movement of services. The following year, in its *Rüffert* decision, the CJEU considered that the rules of public procurement in Lower Saxony, which require compliance with local collective agreements, was a barrier to the free movement of services. Finally, in the *Commission v Luxembourg* case, the CJEU considered that the state of Luxembourg was infringing on the principle of free movement of services as the government sought to impose national requirements and standards on companies posting workers in the Grand Duchy.

This jurisprudence hammered national traditions of industrial relations and provided leverage to employers to take advantage of wage competition. Depending on the structure of the domestic markets and propensity of employers to maintain social consensus, unions were more or less successful in preserving high levels of protection through collective bargaining, as shown in a study comparing the domestic impact of *Laval* and *Rüffert* in Denmark, Germany and Sweden (Seikel 2015). The effects have been most dramatic in Sweden where large companies have been happy to ignore national collective agreements when hiring an increasing number of foreign workers.

And back

When he took office at the head of the European Commission in 2014, Jean-Claude Juncker made this issue one of his priorities. After five years of economic recession and accusations of austeritarian policy, the new president of the Commission claimed he wanted to make the EU worthy of a "social triple A". In March 2016, the Commission proposed revising the 1996 directive on posting along three main lines: (a) posted workers should get equal pay for equal work in the same workplace – contrary to the prevailing situation so far, this means that collective agreements resulting from negotiations between social partners should therefore also apply to posted workers; (b) the duration of posting should be limited to two years; and (c) equal treatment will also apply to posted workers hired via temporary work agencies.

> In the preceding 2015 public consultation, a joint letter from Germany, France, Austria, the Benelux countries and Sweden demanded the introduction of the principle of "equal pay for equal work in the same place" and the adoption of clearer maximum posting duration. The Visegrad Group, as well as Bulgaria, Romania and the Baltic states, opposed the revision. (Lubow & Schmidt 2020: 9)

As expected, the struggle therefore crystallized around the host countries of receiving "the West" versus the countries of origin of workers from "the East" (spearheaded by Poland). In May 2016, the parliaments of ten central and eastern European countries (plus Denmark), opposing tighter regulation, raised a "yellow card" denouncing infringement on subsidiarity on the part of the Commission, an objection discarded by the latter. The negotiations were arduous in both the Council and the EP and climaxed when Emmanuel Macron was elected to the French presidency in May 2017. In line with his campaign pledge to tackle the ills of Europe, he disrupted the EU decision-making process by calling for even stricter regulation (regarding the duration of posting and "letter-box" companies) and travelled to central Europe to put pressure on reluctant leaders in the region. The act eventually agreed upon by the Council and EP in June 2018 established that all aspects relating to workers' remuneration and working conditions (including accommodation) should be regulated by the receiving country's laws based on equal treatment with local workers. The duration of posting is limited to 12 months (with a possible extension of 6 months upon justification) and cooperation for fighting abuse is reinforced. Importantly, these rules apply not only to intra-group posting, but also in cases involving contracting out or hiring out of labour through temporary work agencies.

As the revised directive on posted workers came into force in July 2020, ETUC issued a positive statement by claiming that "two million posted workers finally receive equal pay" and reckoning that

> in the landmark *Viking* and *Laval* cases in 2007, the ECJ [European Court of Justice] rejected equal treatment for local and posted workers in order to prioritise the freedom of movement for services. Those judgments, which drove down wages across Europe and gave the green light to employers to discriminate against foreign workers, have now effectively been overturned.[2]

However, most national trade unions as well as political parties articulating a social critique of the EU deplore that social dumping is still occurring due to legal gaps in implementation, transposition or enforcement and to the loosely coordinated (rather than harmonized) social security of workers.[3] A main issue remains that social security coverage and the related employers' contribution

---

2. "Two million posted workers finally receive equal pay", press release of ETUC, 30 July 2020, www.etuc.org (accessed 15 September 2021).
3. For example, "Sozialdumping in der Baubranche: Wir wollen endlich Veränderungen sehen", interview with Tom Deleu, the general secretary of the European Federation of Building and Woodworkers, *Euractiv*, 31 May 2021.

still depends on the workers' country of origin. This means that posted workers coming from countries with lower social standards still remain significantly cheaper than local workers in main recipient countries such as Belgium, France or Germany.

A major omission from the directive on posted workers was the regulation of the road transport sector. For years, and especially since the 2004–07 eastern enlargement of the EU, the sector has seen the rise of abusive practices of social dumping. As documented by the Belgian journalist Bryan Carter in his prize-winning documentary, western companies in the logistics sector have increasingly established subsidiaries in eastern countries with low pay and social protection standards to hire and exploit truck drivers (either from western or eastern countries) who would work and live on the road for months in deplorable conditions, leading notably to the death of two Polish drivers in a Belgian warehouse in 2012.[4] In July 2020, a set of three regulations dubbed the "mobility package" was further adopted to address a long-standing issue. Among other provisions, the package contains reinforced rules on access to the profession, maximum work and minimum rest times for drivers (controlled by means of tachometer), and it lays down rules on the posting of drivers; it also includes provisions concerning enforcement and control.

In this latter regard, a European labour authority was set up in Bratislava in 2019 in order to coordinate member states' action to guarantee the effectiveness of EU social regulation in practice. The deliberations leading to the decision to establish the authority proved contentious from the point of view of subsidiarity. The main task of the authority is to "assist member states and the Commission in their effective application and enforcement of Union law related to labour mobility across the Union and the coordination of social security systems within the Union".[5] This involves facilitating the exchange of information and coordination among the member states and their enforcement authorities. A key provision lies with the authority's capacity to coordinate and support concerted and joint inspections in the member states. It can also denounce frauds, including if it is alerted by the authorities of one member state or social partners organizations. The authority is conceived above all as a facilitator among national enforcement activities rather than as a European labour inspector. Many legal aspects of the authority's competences remain unsettled under the current regulation, notably

---

4. Bryan Carter's film *Inside Europe's Secret Truck War: Drivers Pay the Price for East–West Divide* was screened at numerous international documentary festivals and broadcasted by Euronews (short English version) and the Belgian national broadcaster RTBF (French extended version). In 2021, Carter was awarded the Louise Weiss Prize for European journalism. The extended English version is available at https://vimeo.com/462096862.

5. Regulation (EU) 2019/1149 of the European Parliament and of the Council of 20 June 2019 establishing a European Labour Authority.

with regard to the facilitation of joint inspections, sanctions and penalties, or the mediation of disputes among member states or stakeholders (Cremers 2020).

In conclusion, through its contentious pro-liberalization jurisprudence, the CJEU therefore played the role of an agenda-setter in the sense that it eventually prompted new legislative action to tighten the regulation of workers' mobility (Lubow & Schmidt 2019). Owing to growing political pressures to change the status quo, the Commission as well as the co-legislators (the Council and the EP) partly succeeded in breaking free from "over-constitutionalization" in the EU, namely the fact that policy-making is highly constrained by the CJEU's jurisprudence rooted in the authoritative interpretation of the EU treaties (Lubow & Schmidt 2019). From the point of view of regulation and law-making, the latest development tilts the balance and a new balance has therefore yet to be struck between market freedom in the area of services and labour law from the point a view of regulation. A future challenge will be to guarantee effective compliance with EU rules.

The marketization of welfare

From public service to competitive markets

Over the past three decades, the marketization of welfare has been a common trend across Europe and beyond. Under the postwar social consensus in the second half of the twentieth century, the provision of basic utilities (such as water, electricity, energy, telecommunications postal services) was carried out by public authorities. Similarly, healthcare, social assistance to people in need and, increasingly, childcare and elderly care (including income support in the form of pension), had been to various extents removed from the private sphere of the market or the family to be treated as a social risk and fall under the scope of welfare states. With the neoliberal restructuring of advanced capitalist economies from the late 1980s onwards, the provision of welfare services has been progressively removed from the realm of public service and displaced to the realm of the market. The UK has been at the forefront of such reforms (Taylor-Gooby 2012). In this new configuration, users are no longer seen as citizens entitled to equally enjoy quality services, but as customers who will afford different types of services with varying degrees of quality according to their purchasing power. As a result, welfare services have become "politically shaped, regulated and state supported markets providing social goods and services through the competitive activities of non-state actors" (Ledoux *et al.* 2020: 4). The role of states has shifted from that of a universal and mostly unique provider (through monopolistic structures) to that of a regulator among a variety of public and private providers competing with each other. As states retain key financial, regulatory and informational instruments, these markets are semi-public, semi-private. The (re)commodification of welfare has in turn reshaped relations between citizens and the state, between producers and the state, and between citizens and producers (Gingrich 2021). However, no systematic pattern in terms of political or distributional effects of marketization is emerging, as different sectors in different countries seem to follow largely particular trajectories (Gingrich 2011). This begs the question of the conditions under which citizens, elected representatives or bureaucrats will support or, on the contrary, attempt to resist welfare marketization.

Against this background, welfare services illustrate perfectly how the EU has acted as a catalyser reinforcing the national and global trends towards marketization. From the outset of the EEC, European policy-makers tried to strike a balance between the willingness to liberalize all service activities to build the single market, on the one hand, and the need to protect service activities that serve the public interest by accounting for their specificities that are at odds with a market logic (unprofitable activities aimed at disadvantaged populations or territories, management of costly network infrastructures, etc.), on the other. This dilemma is reflected in Article 90.2 of the EEC Treaty subjecting SGI to competition policy only if it "does not obstruct the performance, in law or in fact, of the particular tasks assigned to them".

The notion of services of general economic interest (SGEI) was forged in the Treaty of Rome to reflect the diversity of European institutional and legal traditions. Whereas in France, as well as in Belgium, public service is a universal notion anchored in state bureaucracy and public law, Germany has *öffentliche Daseinsvorsorge*, which are constitutionally recognized and strongly decentralized in the regions (*Länder*). For the British, public services embrace three concepts: the public sector itself (incorporated into government, such as health and education), utilities (distribution of basic services) and social services related to the welfare state. Multiple models and arrangements coexist in Europe and are often rooted in the postwar period: from public service directly provided by the state, to coexistence between public and private operators, public service concessions and public procurement. Therefore, the concept of SGI aims to recognize that some of these services can be provided in the context of competitive markets and thus be subject to the rules of European competition law. At the same time, the notion implies that exceptions must be acknowledged when the general interest may be threatened by the logic of competition.

Over the following decades, redefining the boundaries of this moving legal category has entailed political battles. Seized in multiple cases, the CJEU played a crucial role in the definition of the economic or non-economic nature of SGI, which conditions the application of the rules of competition. Case law has

Table 5.2 SGI and competition

Legal category	Sectors/activities involved	Impact of European competition law
Service of general economic interest	Network industries: telecommunications, energy, transport (rail, air, local urban transportation), water and sanitation	High
Social service of general interest (economic or non-economic)	Social housing, social security, healthcare, childcare, elderly care, family and indigent, support to families and the poor, higher education, non-mandatory education, training, culture	Moderate (sector-specific, case by case, at times contested)
Service of non-economic general interest	Army, police, judiciary, mandatory schooling	None

fluctuated, sometimes favouring the logic of competition, sometimes that of the general interest as the CJEU has proved unwilling to decide too definitively on a conflict of values that falls under the responsibility of the legislator (Hatzopoulos 2012; Prosser 2005; Szyszczak & Van de Gronden 2013). As shown in Table 5.2, the concept of SGI has progressively been defined and divided between different categories whose borders remain porous. In the area of social services, in particular, the extent to which competition rules should apply or not remains unclear and is defined on an ad hoc basis. Overall, in European law, competition is the rule, whereas the regulation and financial support of services by the state is an exception that must be duly justified.

At the point of friction between market and regulation, one finds a second conflict between those who want greater protective regulation at the European level and those who wish to avoid more EU interference in an area of competence strongly rooted in the history and legitimacy of national, regional and local institutions. The decade from the mid-1990s to the mid-2000s witnessed a political struggle led by a coalition of left-wing politicians, representatives of public companies within the platform of the European Centre of Employers and Enterprises Providing Public Services (CEEP) and French academics and high-ranking officials with support in a few other member states, notably Belgium and southern Europe. Their objective was not only the recognition of the specificity of SGI in the EU Treaty, which occurred when Article 16 EC was introduced in the Amsterdam Treaty, but also the establishment of a legal basis enabling the EU to enact regulation that would shelter SGI from competition policy. In this regard, the ten-year long campaign calling for an EU framework directive ensuring high levels of funding, quality, accessibility and affordability of SGI across Europe ended in a political deadlock. To this day, EU law pertaining to SGI remains ambiguous. A new Article 14 TFEU was introduced in the Lisbon

Treaty, which offers an explicit legal basis for the EU to legislate by regulation in the field of SGI, thereby finally meeting the demands for greater regulation to protect the missions of SGI at the European level. At the same time, however, protocol no. 26 on SGI, adopted at the request of member states (notably the Netherlands) anxious to limit new EU interference in the management of public services, places a strong emphasis on the diversity of SGI across Europe and the "discretionary power of national, regional and local authorities".[6]

One may conclude that market forces have largely had the upper hand, particularly because of a growing political resistance to subsidiarity. This has prevented the adoption of common European rules for protecting public services and the creation of specific tools to safeguard the principles of financing, accessibility to all, affordability and quality. The divergence of ideological and political positions, historical traditions and institutional arrangements across the continent remain, to this day, major obstacles to the development of policies tackling the problems facing public services throughout Europe.

Liberalizing welfare services through sectoral directives

After the Second World War, welfare services in Europe were isolated from market mechanisms and were provided essentially via public monopolies. Starting at the end of the 1980s, an increasing share of SGI – formerly public services – have been shifted to totally or partially competitive markets with public and private providers competing with each other. In this context, the consumer-choice paradigm implies that users are regarded as consumers making a choice between differentiated products rather than citizens enjoying a single universal and uniform service. Today, most SGI sectors are complex and combine the maintained existence of the former historical operator (rail), partial privatization of public enterprises (energy), semi-private or semi-public structures and the coexistence of public and private actors (hospitals); and the effective degree of competition is very variable as many markets tend to exhibit an oligopolistic structure with only two or three operators dominating.

To be sure, the marketization of public services in Europe reflects the global restructuring of advanced capitalist economies, which has happened in all western countries. But the European Commission (then the EU) has championed policies that accelerated the marketization of SGI. Representing 26 per cent of GDP and employing almost 30 per cent of the workforce in Europe, these

---

6. Consolidated version of the Treaty on the European Union – PROTOCOLS – protocol (no. 26) on services of general interest, http://data.europa.eu/eli/treaty/teu_2008/pro_26/oj (accessed 20 September 2021).

Table 5.3 European directives of liberalization in public services

Sector	First regulation	Latest act
Air transport	First air package Regulations 3975/87/EEC, 3976/87/EEC, Directive 87/601/EEC (1987)	Regulation 894/2002 on common rules for the allocation of slots at community airports (2002)
Telecommunications	First telecom package 88/301/EEC (1988)	Reform of the telecom package Directives 2009/136/EC and 2009/170/EC Regulation 1211/2009/EC (2009)
Audiovisual	Directive 89/552 EEC "Television without frontiers" (1989)	Amended "Television without frontiers" directive 2007/65/EC (2007)
Rail transport	First rail package 91/440/EEC (1991)	Fourth rail package Regulation 2016/796, Directives 2016/797 and 2016/798 (2016)
Electricity and gas	First energy package 96/92/EC and 98/30/EC (1996)	Third energy package Regulations 713/2009, 714/2009, 715/2009, Directives 2009/72/EC and 2009/73/EC (2009)
Postal services	First postal directive 97/67/EC (1997)	Third postal directive 2008/06/EC (2008)
Local urban transport	Regulation 1370/2007 on public passenger transport services (2007)	

services were not long left at the margins of the single market. The main EU tool in this instance is the adoption of liberalization directives in various sectors (see Table 5.3).

These directives carried deregulation measures (abolishing national rules) but also re-regulation ones (introducing new rules at the European level). EU rules focus particularly on the interoperability of networks across borders within a unified European space and on guaranteeing the universal service. The purpose of a universal service is to ensure that at least one operator, whether public or private, delivers services in the general interest by allowing all citizens access to basic services at an affordable price, even if this activity is not profitable. Universal service obligations exist in the areas of telecommunications, rail transport or postal service. However, the question of whether the universal service provisions are sufficient to ensure quality services at an affordable price in the context of a competitive market remains open.

Political debates over these texts have sometimes led to significant clashes between the European Commission who pushes for opening national sectors and reluctant member states, or between member states who wish to impose their model at the European level, as was the case in the energy sector. Some member states – the UK particularly under Margaret Thatcher and later the Scandinavian countries or the Netherlands – have outpaced the EU by liberalizing certain sectors, then having an interest in seeing this model extended to the whole of Europe. Technological changes (e.g. in telecommunications and audiovisual) have also facilitated the entry of private operators into these markets. It should be noted that the water distribution sector has so far not been the subject of any liberalization directive. This is because in the vast majority of European countries water is distributed locally without any cross-border interconnection. Despite many attempts by the European Commission to initiate liberalization in this sector, resistance among MEPs, member states and a number of interest groups have so far dissuaded it from submitting a directive proposal. Overall, the liberalization of SGI within the single market was strongly encouraged by the Commission (and often by the CJEU) and was never challenged by prevailing political forces within the member states.

Limiting public financing via the control of state aid

Another way in which EU policy affects welfare services is the prohibition of state aid within competition policy, an area in which the European Commission has exclusive competence. State aid may be understood as any kind of financial aid granted by public authorities to economic operators (public or private companies) and is considered as a cause of unfair competition in the EU single market. However, in the case of SGI it may be allowed if the Commission considers that the financial support provided to companies is proportionate to the financial burden of providing a public service (long hours of operation, coverage of the entire territory, prices adapted to users' income, etc.). If not, this is regarded as "overcompensation" and a distortion of competition between operators. Building on the *Altmark* case law of 2003,[7] the European Commission developed a complex set of rules in the so-called Monti-Kroes package[8] of 2005 to calculate whether aid for SGI is justified or not. More recently, the Commission has revised these rules in the face of criticisms. Regional and local authorities have often faced difficulties because of the complexity of European rules and there has been resentment over EU interference in the management of local services with no cross-border dimension whatsoever. Thus, the "Almunia package"[9] of 2011 contains clearer and more flexible rules, particularly for local services. A threshold has been set, below which public subsidies cannot be regarded as

---

7. *Altmark Trans GmbH* (C-280/00), 24 July 2003.
8. Named after the Competition Commissioners Mario Monti (1999–2004) and Nelly Kroes (2004–10).
9. Named after the Competition Commissioners Joaquín Almunia (2010–14).

state aid and therefore escape EU competition rules. Problems persist, however, particularly regarding the formal delegation of public service or the method for calculating the cost of compensation (Van de Gronden 2013).

The regulation of state aid has crucial implications for a whole range of public services. For example, in 2012, the Belgian postal service operator Bpost was obliged to reimburse €300 million to the Belgian state because of an overcompensation of public service obligations. Equally, in March 2015 the Commission authorized the UK government to grant £640 million to the Post Office Ltd network. It considered that this subsidy would support the operator in its public service missions, such as the payment of social allowances, basic banking services or the maintenance of its offices in rural areas. One case opposed public and private hospitals in Brussels between 2005 and 2016, the latter having lodged a complaint with the European Commission alleging that the former received unreasonable, and therefore illegal, state aid. The Commission concluded that the public funding granted to Brussels public hospitals since 1996 was justified in view of the public service obligations they meet, in particular their obligation to treat all patients in all circumstances, whether or not they are in a position to pay the costs of care.

Competition policy in matters of state aid can have structural effects on national social systems. The way in which the Dutch government has had to make significant changes to its social housing policy is a case in point (see Box 5.2).

BOX 5.2 COMPETITION POLICY AND SOCIAL HOUSING IN THE NETHERLANDS

In the Netherlands, the social housing sector is traditionally universal, meaning that the entire population can benefit from it in addition to the housing supply on the market. The bulk of the rental stock is managed by non-profit housing corporations (*woning corporaties*), while 17 per cent is managed by private lenders. The entire market is strongly regulated, particularly the rent levels.

The European Property Federation, which represents the private sector, lodged a complaint against the public funding of the *woning corporaties*. The claim was that they were using this aid to develop their commercial activities rather than for social housing. The European Commission considered that the situation distorted competition between the *woning corporaties* and private lenders and asked the Dutch government to change its social housing policy in July 2005. According to the Commission, a service of general economic interest must fulfil a specific public service mission, in this case access to housing for those who do not have the resources necessary to do so at market price.

The Dutch authorities engaged in a long controversy over the role of social housing and the risks of declining social diversity if it were to specifically target disadvantaged families. In 2009, a compromise was reached on introducing a ceiling of resources regulating access to social housing.

Since 2011, 90 per cent of social housing is allocated to households whose annual income is lower than €33,000 per year. Today, 41 per cent of households have access to social housing (compared to 100 per cent before 2011). The government has also introduced rent increases for high-income tenants to encourage them to leave the social housing sector.

In conclusion, through the powerful tools regulating services within the single market, the EU has had a major impact on welfare services. At the same time, however, European decision-makers have never had the will to develop a pro-active policy on the quality, financing or organization of public services, topics that remain the purview of states. Competition and the market are therefore the rule, while the regulatory and financial protection of SGI remains the exception.

The opening up of welfare states

The rampant liberalization of healthcare

Although the EU does not have regulatory powers in the area over healthcare (see Chapter 2), the regulation of services in the single market nonetheless has growing structural effects on the health sector.

As the EU fosters the emergence of a European health market, marketization raises many questions because of the crucial social importance of the sector. As previously shown with state aid, care structures are primarily regarded as com-mercial enterprises (some of which have public service obligations). Freedom of movement for health professionals depends in large part on the specifically regulated mutual recognition of qualifications. However, differences between the respective levels of training can be problematic in terms of quality of care. Furthermore, the EU supports the emergence of a unified insurance market as a growing number of Europeans voluntarily subscribe to private health insurance (complementary to public social security). The EU is therefore committed to the emergence of a unified European health area, in which a growing number of multinational firms operate. Profit-making does not only concern medicines, but also hospital care run by corporations such as the British group Apax and Nordic Capital, the German Fresenius or the Swedish

Medicover, which has become one of the main private operators in central and eastern Europe (André & Hermann 2009).

Another aspect of healthcare liberalization is increased patient mobility, a trend encouraged by EU law. As explained in Chapter 4, it is above all the jurisprudence of the CJEU that has gradually led national states to open their healthcare system to EU non-nationals, as case law made the reimbursement of health services incurred abroad an increasingly binding obligation. In a series of decisions in the 2000s, notably the *Müller-Fauré* decision of 2003, the judges strictly limited the possibility for social security organizations to require prior authorization for the reimbursement of patients having sought treatment in another EU country. Case law was then codified in Directive 2011/24/EU on the rights of patients in cross-border healthcare. Although quasi-automatic reimbursement has meant more freedom for patients, critics of liberalization, particularly political groups on the left in the EP, argued that such an approach reduces the ability of states to control their healthcare spending and promotes "medical tourism" where only the wealthiest will have the means to travel abroad to benefit from healthcare that they could not get at home. While today cross-border healthcare only accounts for 1 per cent of total care expenditure, the limited information available in Europe points to the existence of mobility from the west to the east of the continent with a rapid increase in the number of individuals seeking treatment abroad (Smith *et al.* 2012).

In short, the logic of the single market, based on the individual rights of patients, clashes with that of the national welfare state rooted in solidarity within national communities (Ferrera 2005). However, the idea that we are witnessing a de-territorialization of healthcare should be nuanced. Vollaard (2017) shows that Belgium and the Netherlands, for instance, have been able to develop effective strategies to resist liberalization, either by an extensive use of the possibilities of restricting the reimbursement of care provided abroad, or by establishing new control mechanisms at the European level.

The access of non-nationals to social benefits: a limited right

The free movement of workers and persons has led to the opening up of national welfare states, since the principle of non-discrimination on the basis of nationality means that member states must grant non-nationals a number of rights to social services enjoyed by nationals. However, a long-time perspective shows us that the CJEU does not make decisions in isolation from the prevailing political mood (Blauberger *et al.* 2018). When the judges must take a position on sensitive issues, they may fear the reaction of governments as well as public opinion. The long commitment of the CJEU to extending the rights of itinerant citizens, starting with workers and then, by extension, all Europeans (students, unemployed, retirees) has created an embryo of transnational social citizenship. More recently, however, the court has clearly bowed to governments by offering them more leeway to restrict the payment of such benefits. Directive 2004/38/ EC on the right of citizens of the EU and their family members to move and reside freely within the territory of the member states establishes that before claiming a permanent residence permit (after five years), every citizen of the EU shall enjoy the right of movement and establishment of residence if they have adequate health coverage and sufficient resources so as not to become a burden on the social benefits system of the host member state. This text was essentially based on the case law of the CJEU who, in 1998 and 2001,[10] had established the right of residency as a cornerstone of European citizenship.

In a political climate denouncing a supposed large-scale "benefits tourism" from eastern Europeans, case law reached a turning point in the second half of the 2000s. The underpinning idea is that of the need for a tangible link between the non-national resident and the host country to justify access to social benefits. In the *Brey* case from 2013 (C-140/12), the CJEU set out a list of criteria allowing national authorities to justify denial of access to benefits for inactive non-nationals. In the *Dano* case of 2014 involving a Romanian plaintiff and her son, as well as the *Leipzig Jobcenter* in Germany, the CJEU held that "a member state must therefore have the possibility of refusing to grant social benefits to economically inactive Union citizens who exercise their right to freedom of movement solely in order to obtain another member state's social assistance".[11]

In the *Jobcenter Berlin Neukölln v Oladele Alimanovic* case of 2015, which also involved the German government, the CJEU considered that job seekers no longer enjoy a right to social benefits beyond a period of six months of inactivity. In 2016, the judges ruled on infringement proceedings engaged by the European Commission against the British government after complaints from many non-nationals who had been denied access to family allowances and child tax credit in the UK. The British government had limited the access to these benefits for those not holding a residency permit. Although the court did acknowledge that this measure was discriminatory, it concluded that it was, however, justified by "the need to protect the finances of the host member state".[12] The fact that this decision was issued just a few days prior to the referendum on Brexit lends support to the claim that the Luxembourg judges have proved permeable to the politicization of this issue.

---

10. Decisions *Martinez Sala* (C-85/96) and *Grzelczyk* (C-184/99).
11. CJEU, Press release 146/14, 11 November 2014, www.curia.europa.eu (accessed 15 September 2021).
12. *European Commission v United Kingdom of Great Britain and Northern Ireland* (C-308-14), 14 June 2016.

Conclusion

As we have seen in this chapter, freedom of movement and the liberalization of markets entail social effects that have been only partially addressed by policy-makers. Labour mobility induced by the liberalization of services can be used to relieve the congestion of labour in some countries by meeting needs in particular sectors and allows companies to conquer new markets abroad. However, it also brings about social dumping and brain drain. Although states where the labour force is relatively expensive have constantly sought to regulate workers' mobility, political leaders in low-cost countries consider this position to be protectionist. This has led to intense political battles that are temporarily settled through rules.

On the matter of public services, liberalization has made it possible to reap the benefits of technological advances in certain sectors (telecommunications, audiovisual) and, to some extent, to better connect European infrastructure networks (energy, rail). However, competition policy and the logic of profit inherent to markets often impede continuity, accessibility, equality and quality. These are all the principles that safeguard the general interest in the provision of services that are essential to social cohesion. It is particularly difficult to assess the results of liberalization policies and of the privatization that often accompanies it. On the one hand, there is strong variation from one sector to another, and, on the other hand, the market structures and political trajectories remain highly contrasted from one country to another. That being said, several research projects (CIRIEC 2004; Flecker & Hermann 2012; Frangakis *et al.* 2008; Keune *et al.* 2008) have pointed out the problems that have emerged as common trends. These range from insufficient competition to high prices, worsening of working conditions and pay, and class bias in the ability to choose the most adequate service (Van Gyes 2009). Ultimately, a report assessing the liberalization of SGI for the European Commission concluded that "most of the positive effects expected did not materialize at all or were very minor ... these processes have had adverse effects on the European Social Models as they resulted in lower social cohesion in access to good-quality public services" (Loefler *et al.* 2012: 3). Despite all this, the marketization of welfare services has never been questioned by national or European leaders and continues undebated. In the field of healthcare, the EU has encouraged the unification of a pan-European healthcare market across which patients should be able to freely navigate. In turn, national governments have sought to contain such a de-territorialization of healthcare to prevent the negative financial effects of an excessive inflow of foreign patients.

Finally, the opening up of welfare states through the non-discrimination of non-national EU citizens has remained limited. Non-national EU citizens, especially when they do not work, have seen their entitlements to social benefits curtailed as the idea has gained ground among the public that some Europeans seek to take advantage of more generous social systems.

Overall, if liberalization has created opportunities for some economic agents and citizens, it has more often than not put social cohesion under strain. Remedies could be explored in two directions. First, there is a need to ensure that regulation does not get lost as markets expand beyond national borders. Because national authorities cannot control actors who operate Europe-wide, effective re-regulation at the EU level is necessary. This implies legislative battles but also effective administrative coordination to ensure the enforcement of rules on the ground. Another concern relates to the very nature of European citizenship. So far, it has essentially taken the shape of a market-focused citizenship whereby rights are attached to those who are economically productive in the single market. There is an obvious conceptual and political vagueness around European citizenship and its relation to national citizenship regarding cultural, political and fiscal bonds.

Further reading

- Amandine Crespy, *Welfare Markets in Europe: The Democratic Challenge of European Integration* (Basingstoke: Palgrave Macmillan, 2016).
- Maurizio Ferrera, *The Boundaries of Welfare: European Integration and the New Spatial Politics of Social Protection* (Oxford: Oxford University Press, 2005).
- Daniel Seikel, "Class struggle in the shadow of Luxembourg: the domestic impact of the European Court of Justice's case law on the regulation of working conditions". *Journal of European Public Policy* 22:8 (2015), 1166–85.

Questions to debate

- Is the posting of workers sufficiently regulated?
- Does the opening up of national welfare states enhance or undermine social rights?

6

DOES THE EUROPEAN SOCIAL DIALOGUE REALLY PROTECT EUROPEAN WORKERS?

The European social dialogue is arguably one of the most emblematic aspects of the EU's role in the field of socio-economic governance. Originally, in the late 1980s, the aim was to foster negotiations between employers and trade union organizations at the supranational level in an attempt to replicate the neo-corporatist logic shaping industrial relations in continental and northern Europe (see Box 6.1). In these countries, the regulation of working conditions through collective agreements concluded independently between employers and trade unions is the cornerstone of the social model. From a Polanyian perspective (see Chapter 1), therefore, the purpose of the European social dialogue is to re-embed the economy in social relations in a way that reconciles economic efficiency and social justice. As will be explained in this chapter, however, the European social dialogue is very different from neo-corporatism at the national level.

BOX 6.1 NEO-CORPORATISM

Corporatism refers to the grouping of trades, or occupational and social groups, in institutions in order to defend their interests, particularly vis-à-vis political authorities. Corporatism has a long European tradition with roots in the medieval trade guilds and the growth of capitalism.

Beginning in the late 1970s, neo-corporatism, theorized among others by Philippe Schmitter, aims to explain the structure of interest representation in contemporary democracies, specifically from a socio-economic viewpoint. Whereas pluralism assumes the competition between a multitude of interest groups and organizations attempting to influence public policies, neo-corporatism focuses on the core interests – workers and employers – and their relations with the state. Neo-corporatism is thus based on a monopoly of representation by a limited number of actors in specific fields of activity. Bipartite (between social partners) and tripartite relations (between employers, trade unions and the state) are institutionalized through concertation, negotiation and political trading mechanisms. These practices led to the regulation of working conditions and pay at the company, sectoral and cross-industry level.

Thus, neo-corporatism aims to regulate the conflicts between capital and labour and, by doing so, ensure the stability of the capitalist order and the performance of the production system in a context of international competition.

There is an overall consensus about the weakness of the European social dialogue not only in terms of the low number of binding norms it has generated over the course of the past 30 years (see Table 6.2), but also because of the limited talks between trade unions and employers at the EU level. Nevertheless, assessments diverge regarding the extent of and explanations for such weakness. First, when considering the big picture and the outcomes of the European social dialogue at a cross-industry level, it has mostly been argued that the process has waned since the early 2000s (Pochet 2016: 76; Prosser 2016: 86). In contrast, those looking at sectoral dynamics tend to be more positive about the effects of soft processes – as opposed to hard regulation – on the ground (Larsson *et al.* 2020; Perin & Léonard 2016). Then, there are disagreements about the ability of the labour movement to conduct unified, effective action on a European scale in order to advance the cause of workers. Some studies show that important forms of transnational mobilization have emerged (Gajewska 2008), while others stress the emergence of an "insider/outsider" divide at the European level and the potentially diverging interests of workers in different EU countries (Prosser 2017; see also Chapter 3). Finally, whereas many specialists call for an intensification of the European social dialogue, the most critical scholars have criticized its intrinsic nature. For them, the very notion of social dialogue replacing the concepts of industrial relations and collective bargaining is problematic because it conveys a technocratic culture of consensus whereby the expansion of markets is bound to prevail over workers' interests. In this perspective, the emergence of a European social dialogue epitomizes a "regime change", that is a shift towards a political culture of *partnership* that has "delegitimized the recognition and expression of the social conflict between labour and capital as a central element of democratic dynamics" (Dufresne & Gobin 2016: 32). This implies that the European social dialogue serves more to legitimize the EU institutions' policies rather than to effectively regulate industrial relations at the European level. In many respects, repeated calls for a more "social" Europe or a "fair Europe for workers" go hand in hand with the technocratic culture of Euro-unionism rooted in partnership with the EU institutions, instead of in an effective strategy rooted in power relations (Golden 2019). Remembering the lessons of Marxism leads to the realization that Euro-unionism has so far failed to "complement the force of their arguments with the argument of force" to restore unions' bargaining power (Jordan *et al.* 2020: 209; see also Bieler *et al.* 2019).

By exploring the historical developments, political dynamics, as well as the policy and institutional issues raised by the European social dialogue, this chapter will provide tools to understand why the embryonic form of neo-corporatism established at the European level now seems relatively sterile.

The labour movement and the EU: a complicated relationship

Trade unions between Europeanism and social critique in the early days

To understand the rise of European trade union cooperation, one must situate it against the double backdrop of the immediate postwar period and the Cold War, on the one hand, and the importance of the mining sector in the European industrial landscape, on the other. By the late 1940s, the international labour movement was divided between communist organizations and those who supported US financial aid for the reconstruction of Europe under the Marshall Plan. Eager to contain communism in Europe, an important part of the labour movement including social democratic and Christian unions actively supported the nascent project of European unification. This was particularly the case in Europeanist organizations such as the Socialist Movement for the United States of Europe founded in London in 1947. After the end of the war, the mining complexes of the Ruhr, in Germany, were supervised by the Allied forces because of their central role in the German war economy. This offered the opportunity for a first collaboration between French, Belgian, Luxembourgish and German trade unionists in the framework of the Ruhr interunion organization.

One year after the declaration by French foreign minister, Robert Schuman, the ECSC was created. The need for political leaders to secure support from the non-communist workers' movement motivated the inclusion of union representatives in the political structures of the ECSC. On the one hand, two trade unionists were members of the High Authority, the executive body of the ECSC, which can be regarded as the ancestor of the European Commission. On the other hand, the ECSC had an advisory committee composed of representatives of coal and steel consumers, producers and workers in the sector. In this advisory committee, the unions were represented by the "Committee of the 21" gathering representatives from the federations of the steel and mining sectors, from the national cross-sectoral confederations of the six ECSC member states, as well as from the corresponding international sectoral federations and the International Confederation of Free Trade Unions.

Almost from the start, the role trade unionists played in the European inte-gration process was ambivalent (Gobin 1997; Verschueren 2013). The support of the socialist and Christian unions for the ECSC served to legitimize the new supranational body. As Nicolas Verschueren (2013: 42) writes, "the idea was to make the European working class accept a form of more flexible economic lib-eralism in return for greater consideration for social progress through European collective agreements or the increase of low wages". The lack of effective coord-ination, however, granted the Committee of the 21 only a limited influence. At the same time, prominent personalities in the trade union world such as the Belgian André Renard, the German Franz Grosse or the Frenchman Nicolas Dethier were quickly critical of the weak social ambitions of the ECSC. But trade unionists were divided on whether to use mass mobilization to put pressure on the High Authority.

The transition from the ECSC to the EEC, with the adoption of the Treaty on Atomic Energy (Euratom) and above all the Treaty of Rome in 1957, brought about great disillusion among the labour movement. The ECSC was inspired by an inter-ventionist conception of economic policy based on industrial planning driven by a powerful supranational executive with the participation of trade unionists. In contrast, with the Treaty of Rome, European unification took both a liberal and intergovernmental turn. Its political philosophy was rooted in the liberalization of trade within a single market rather than in industrial cooperation. At the same time, the European Commission was a weakened version of the High Authority since the Council of Ministers was now the most powerful body in the new com-munity. Also, no trade unionists were included in the College of Commissioners. In this new set of institutions, both the importance of the concerns of the working class and the political role of trade unionists were marginalized.

The retirement of the trade unionists who had embraced European feder-alism after the war, the resurgence of claims of sovereignty (particularly under Charles De Gaulle's presidency in France), along with the economic boom of the 1960s all led union organizations to withdraw to social struggles at the national level (Degryse 2006: 32–3; Verschueren (2013: 54–8). Nevertheless, practices of consultation within cross-sectoral tripartite committees developed and issues such as the free movement of workers, continuing education and ESF actions were discussed. In the 1970s, an embryo of bipartite consultation between social partners developed, supported by governments and the EU institutions. The oil shocks occurring in that decade meant that all European countries were faced with rising unemployment. Thus, employment policy began to emerge as a common issue at the European level but discussions did not lead to new initiatives, policies or procedures for a true social dialogue (Degryse 2006: 34–5).

In the decades that followed, union action coordinated at the European level mainly pursued three goals: recognition as a legitimate partner by the institutions of the EEC, bringing employers to accept the development of contractual relations at the European level and unifying the labour movement at the European scale (Gobin 1997: 31). In 1973, trade unions of the six EEC member states agreed on the creation of ETUC, a permanent European organization backed up by a secretariat based in Brussels. After the wave of social protests in the late 1960s, employers went on an ideological offensive deploring the excessive increase in wages; a message echoed at the European level by the Union of Industrial and Employers' Confederations of Europe (UNICE, today BusinessEurope). Unable to use an allied political party as a bulwark, ETUC persistently tried to find legitimacy by joining the technocratic apparatus that developed around the European institutions (Gobin 1997: 31). By the mid-1980s it abandoned its Keynesian programme and converted to the liberal ethos of the market underpinning European integration. It engaged in a social dialogue that features a managerial concertation style rather than a political confrontation with employers.

The rise and fall of the European social dialogue

The second half of the 1980s and the beginning of the 1990s saw a gradual institutionalization of social dialogue at the European level. After the relative inertia of the 1970s, European leaders agreed to revise the Treaty of Rome and adopted the Single European Act in 1986, which aimed to deepen the integration of the single market. A few years later, amid an unstable international context marked by the fall of the Berlin Wall and the disintegration of the USSR, Europeans decided to strengthen the cohesion of the European bloc by converting the EEC into a political union bolstered by a common currency. Jacques Delors, a French socialist with close ties to the Christian trade union movement, chaired the European Commission from 1985 to 1995. He was convinced that deepening economic integration through the single market ought to be accompanied by social integration and he was proactive in ensuring the unions' support for the pursuit of European unification.

As soon as he took office at the head of the European Commission in 1985, Delors brought together representatives of the European labour and employers' organizations (ETUC, UNICE and CEEP) at the Château of Val Duchesse outside Brussels. He hoped to circumvent the obstacles to social legislation in the Council (particularly obstruction by the British government of Margaret Thatcher) by forging agreements between social partners at the European level (Falkner 1998: 72; Mias 2004: 664). However, this strategy was only relatively successful, in particular because of UNICE's refusal to enter into binding collective agreements (Falkner 1998). In addition, as early as 1985, ETUC had expressed its opposition to the 1985 European Commission White Paper on the completion of the internal market by 1992. Nevertheless, the European Commission encouraged experimental forms of tripartite consultations from which "joint opinions" on topics such as continuing education or workers' mobility emanated in the second half of the 1980s.

When the negotiations on the Maastricht Treaty started, the European Commission promoted the flanking of the envisaged political and monetary union with new social provisions. As early as 1988, the Delors Commission had pleaded for the procedural strengthening of the European social dialogue but faced political resistance. During the intergovernmental negotiations, and much to their surprise, the Dutch presidency of the Council accepted inclusion of the provisions proposed by the social partners to institutionalize the European social dialogue in the treaty without any change (Falkner 1998: 89–95). However, because of the British government's refusal to endorse the new social provisions, they formed a protocol on social policy appended to the Treaty of Maastricht.

Thus, while governments were perhaps only wishing to endorse declarative formulas in favour of the European social dialogue, they in fact agreed to give social partners a quasi-legislative competence (see Box 6.2). This paved the way for the most dynamic period of the European social dialogue, which saw the conclusion of sectoral and cross-sectoral agreements (see Table 6.2). During this time, the structural weakness of the unions in the face of the employers was compensated, to a certain extent, by the voluntarism of certain actors within the European Commission, ready to wield the threat of legislative action to push employers to negotiate with ETUC (Degryse 2006: 40). This dynamic nevertheless stalled in the 2000s.

BOX 6.2 THE SOCIAL PARTNERS AT EU LEVEL

Employers

BusinessEurope (formerly UNICE)

European Centre of Employers and Enterprises Providing Public Services (known under its French acronym CEEP)

SMEunited: European Association of Craft, Small and Medium-Sized Enterprises (formerly UAPME, recognized as a social partner since 1998)

Workers

European Trade Union Confederation (ETUC)

The breakdown of the social dialogue takes place against the background of a decline in legislative activity as all political actors at the EU level promote the non-binding coordination of European policies. In 2000, the Lisbon Strategy adopted by the heads of state and governments aimed to stimulate Europe's competitiveness through the promotion of the knowledge economy and the reform of the welfare state. The policy measures aimed at achieving these common objectives were to be decided and implemented at the national level and to be monitored and discussed at the European level via the OMC. In this context, the European Commission has considered that the social partners' role is to facilitate labour market reforms in order to promote the adaptability of companies and ensure their competitiveness (Degryse 2006: 41). At the same time, social partners demanded greater autonomy. Unable to forge binding agreements through the procedure established by the Maastricht Treaty, they fostered so-called autonomous agreements, concluded independently of the European Commission and implemented by different (often non-binding) channels at the national level. As the recession caused by the financial and debt crisis of 2008–10 hit, employers only made more radical claims for increased competitiveness, in particular the deregulation of labour markets. The decentralization of collective bargaining has led to an overall weakening of workers' protection and unions' role (Leonardi & Pedersini 2018).

The Great Recession and the further weakening of neo-corporatism

Since 2014, the efforts deployed by the European Commission to revive the European social dialogue seem to have produced barely any tangible results. According to Pochet and Degryse (2016), the current dead end is due partly to the Commission's limited commitment to the European social dialogue and partly to the inability of the unions to assert themselves in a transnational fashion. Most importantly, it is the consequence of the hardening of BusinessEurope's positions. With the redeployment of capital and production outside Europe, international competitiveness through wage moderation, the lowering of taxation on labour and the easing of social norms have become the priority of employers.

Furthermore, while the EU institutions were pledging to revive the European social dialogue, the rise of the post-crisis economic governance has had major effects on industrial relations at the national level. In the aftermath of the financial and debt crisis of 2008–10, both the EU institutions and national governments have consistently advocated for the decentralization of collective bargaining as a means to enhance the competitiveness of European economies; an idea that is textbook neoliberal economics rather than an established policy diagnosis. The underlying assumption is that agreements found at the company level, instead of at a sectoral or cross-sectoral level, can better accommodate management's specific needs in terms of contracts, pay and working hours. Germany initiated a powerful movement of decentralization starting in the 1990s and more decidedly with the support of unions in the mid-2000s. The need to go down this path became one of the key mantras of the EU's ECFIN political constellation including the ECB, the ECOFIN (and its committees) and DG ECFIN within the European Commission. It has featured as a key demand in MoUs agreed with over-indebted EU countries, as well as in the country-specific recommendations of the European Semester more generally. The recommodifying push has proved greater as member states were economically vulnerable and thus covered by procedurally more coercive (or perceived as such) EU procedures like, for instance, in Ireland, Italy or Romania (Jordan *et al.* 2020). Furthermore, union resistance, institutional and sectoral specificities have served to filter and, to a certain extent, tame the "declarations, pledges and elaborative normative processes instigated by national governments, often retranslating and redefining commitments of European origin" (Carrieri *et al.* 2018: 41).Thus, a general trend towards "neoliberal decentralization" (Baccaro & Howell 2011) of collective bargaining under the impulse of the EU has been observed, but with various forms and extents across countries.

For now, it seems difficult to envisage the European social dialogue being reignited in a way that would be conducive to substantial progress in terms of workers' protection and social cohesion. With institutional provisions unchanged since the Maastricht Treaty, and power relations between workers and employers still unbalanced, practices are not likely to change in the current political constellation (Prosser 2016). The recent directive proposal on "fair minimum wages" put forward by the European Commission in 2020 is a case in point. When the Commission launched the mandatory consultation phase in January of that year, neither BusinessEurope, opposed by principle to the initiative, nor ETUC, mildly enthusiastic about the issue, were willing to engage in social dialogue negotiations.

The European social dialogue in practice: a toothless bite?

An awkward delegation of legislative powers

The institutional innovations inaugurated by the Maastricht Treaty's Social Protocol are today enshrined in articles Article 154–5 TFEU. These provisions compel the European Commission to consult social partners on all social policy legislative initiatives (for all policy issues falling in the domain of the shared competence in social policy). The key innovation lies with the possibility for social partners to enjoy a delegation of legislative powers. Whether they negotiate over

---

BOX 6.3 PROCEDURE ON AGREEMENTS ACCORDING TO ARTICLES 154 AND 155 TFEU

1. The Commission consults the social partners to announce a social policy legislative initiative.
2. In the case when social partners do not wish to negotiate among themselves, the Commission consults them a second time on the content of the envisaged proposal and then submits it to be adopted according to the ordinary legislative procedure.
3. The social partners may express their desire to negotiate on the same topic.
4. If they do not reach an agreement within a period of nine months, the Commission can take back the initiative and proceed with a legislative proposal.
5. If they do reach an agreement, and upon requests from both parties, the agreement can be implemented through a decision of the Council who adopts it without modifying its terms. Alternatively, they may opt for an autonomous agreement to be implemented by the social partners at the national level.

---

a Commission proposal (Article 154 TFUE) or decide on their own to open negotiations on a topic (Article 155 TFEU), the agreements negotiated by them can be turned into a binding regulation by the Council (see Box 6.3).

The fact that the Commission can take back the initiative if negotiations fail means that no party is able to completely block the process. This has been particularly important considering that, more often than not, employers have shown little interest in the development of social legislation at the European level (Dufresne & Gobin 2016: 37). As a matter of fact, negotiations have almost always happened on the basis of a Commission proposal showing that the social dialogue has mainly existed "in the shadow of hierarchy" (Smismans 2008). Only three so-called framework agreements with a cross-sectoral scope were adopted using this procedure in the late 1990s, and nine at the sectoral level (see Table 6.2).

The peculiar procedure whereby binding agreements take the form of Council regulations has raised a number of legal controversies. Although it allows the CJEU to sanction the lack of implementation, it holds the EP at bay, thus undermining the representative nature of EU law-making (Weiss 2011). Furthermore, the representativeness of the social partners at the EU level (see Box 6.2) was challenged by SMEUnited (formerly UAPME), who was then also involved as a social partner. More importantly, the automaticity of extending autonomous agreements into legislation has recently been dramatically called into question. Since 2012, the European Commission has opposed the implementation of the framework agreement on health and safety in the hairdressing sector signed by the social partners through an EU regulation (see Box 6.4). Similarly, the European Commission refused to make a proposal to the Council allowing the implementation of the agreement on information and consultation rights signed by the European Public Services Union (EPSU) and the employer organization for central government administrations in December 2015. This led the EPSU to start an action against the Commission before the CJEU in order to gain recognition that there was a breach of Treaty rules on the European social dialogue. Yet, in September 2021, the CJEU ruled that the European Commission had the right to decide on whether or not to submit collective agreements for the approval of the Council. Thus, taken together, the hairdressing case and the EPSU case seriously undermine future prospects for binding rules, thus recasting the European social dialogue as soft law altogether.

BOX 6.4 THE DISPUTE OVER HEALTH AND SAFETY IN THE HAIRDRESSING/BEAUTICIAN SECTOR

Building on previous agreements and a history of negotiations, the European Confederation of Professional Beauticians and Cosmeticians and UNI Europa Hair and Beauty concluded a framework agreement on health and safety issues in 2012 and demanded, in tune with treaty provisions on the European social dialogue, that the agreement be implemented via an EU directive. The agreement aims at protecting workers from a wide range of risks, involving the use of chemicals causing asthma and skin pathologies, musculoskeletal disorders, etc.

Under the presidency of José Manuel Barroso, the European Commission launched a programme called "Better Regulation" with the objective of decreasing the administrative and regulatory burden on businesses ("cutting red tape"), meaning that the Commission would regulate on a minimal basis. In spite of its vivid rhetoric about the relaunch of the European social dialogue, the Juncker Commission remained committed to "Better Regulation", which provided the motive for opposing that the framework agreement in the hairdressing sector be turned into EU law. Laurent Vogel (2018) suggested that the fact that hairdressing is typically a female occupational sector has played a role in EU officials not considering the issue significant enough to pass the political hurdle.

In 2016, the signatories revised the agreement to improve the formulation in the eyes of the European Commission who nevertheless remained hostile to making it a legislative proposal. In 2018, it proposed an autonomous (i.e. non-binding) implementation of the agreement, which the signatories refused, leading to a formal rejection of their demand by the Commission, an unprecedented move with regard to the established institutional practice of the European social dialogue provisions.

The final settlement of the case remains open.

Sources: Vogel (2018) and Tricard (2020).

The patchy implementation of autonomous agreements

From 2000s onwards, the regulatory thrust of social dialogue ran out of steam and the social partners sought to emancipate themselves from the European Commission's supervision. They turned to autonomous agreements, which are started and negotiated autonomously and can then be implemented either through the binding European legal route (see Box 6.3), or "in accordance with the procedures and practices specific to management and labour and the member states" (Article 155 TFEU). As of 2003, social partners also started developing autonomous multi-year work programmes that serve as the basis for joint actions on broad themes, lifelong development of competences and qualification in 2002 or actions on gender equality of 2005.

Since it is left to the goodwill of national organizations, the implementation of autonomous agreements proves to be, more often than not, problematic. From a political and substantial point of view, national affiliates may not share the objectives of the European agreements, or disagreements may emerge between employers and workers on the interpretation of such agreements (Smismans 2008: 175). From an institutional and procedural point of view, several member states (notably the UK or the countries of central and eastern Europe) do not have a mechanism to automatically extend the provisions contained in national or European agreements to the whole country (creating an *erga omnes* binding effect). Therefore, there is a very large disparity in the extent to which these agreements are implemented in the different member states. As shown in Table 6.1, the instruments chosen to implement a European agreement at the national level can be legally binding (collective agreement, legislation) or amount to mere joint declarations. The agreement may even not be implemented at all. Thus, rather than a top-down logic implying the homogeneous implementation of agreements concluded at the European level, autonomous agreements rely on a bottom-up logic whereby national affiliates have to be convinced of the relevance of the solutions or rules included in a European agreement (Weiss 2011: 161).

Table 6.1 Tools chosen for the implementation of the 2002 framework agreement on teleworking

National collective agreement	*Interprofessional*	Extended through legislation, *erga omnes* binding	FR, BE, LU, GR, IS*
		Binding for the signing parties and their members	IT
	Sectoral		DK
Legislation		Based on an agreement between social partners	PL
		After consulting social partners	HU, SK, CZ
		Little or no implication of social partners	PT, SI
Agreements between social partners		Recommendations to the lower levels of negotiation	FI, ES
Guidelines		Sent to the lower levels of negotiation, to companies and teleworkers	NK, SE, UK, IE, AT, IE
Joint declarations			DE
Model agreements suggested by social partners			DE, IE
No implementation, no information			CY, EE, LT, MT, BG, RO

*See country codes glossary by Eurostat at https://ec.europa.eu/eurostat/statistics-explained/index.php?title=Glossary:Country_codes (accessed 15 September 2021).

Today, the bulk of the social dialogue output is made of joint opinions, recommendations (frameworks of actions, guidelines, codes of conduct, policy orientations) and exchange of information. In that sense, the "softening" of the European social dialogue – from binding to non-binding instruments – has followed the broader trend of EU governance towards voluntary coordination.

The sectoral European social dialogue

The procedures applicable to the European social dialogue at the cross-industry level were expanded to the sectoral level after 1998. However, sectoral industrial relations have a much older history, dating back to pioneer cooperation in the coal and steel sector. As explained by Anne Dufresne (2006), two generations of sectoral structures preceded the sectoral European social dialogue as we know it today. From the 1960s to the 1980s, joint bipartite committees (employers and workers) were formed in areas of EEC common policies (transport, agriculture, fisheries). Many of them were created at the request of the European Commission who relied on these committees to gather expertise. The second generation of committees emerged in the 1980s and 1990s in the areas affected by liberalization policies, namely maritime transport, civil aviation, telecommunications and post. These committees were aimed at helping employers and workers face the threats posed by the opening to competition, whether it was a loss of competitiveness, for employers, or cuts in jobs for workers.

The European Commission formally recognized sectoral social dialogue committees in its decision of 20 May 1998 (98/500/EC) and there are 43 in existence today. They are composed of up to 66 members representing employers and employees at parity and cover the main sectors of the economy (transport, energy, agriculture, construction, trade, chemistry, etc.). Sectoral committees may adopt all instruments ranging from legally binding agreements to soft tools such as studies or recommendations. Since 1998, nine binding sectoral framework agreements have been adopted by Council decision (see Table 6.2), with four of them concerning working time in specific sectors that had been left out of the scope of the 1993 Working Time Directive. Once again, the results of social dialogue are therefore closely linked to political and regulatory dynamics.

Although a few agreements have also been reached at the sectoral level, most of the committees' work has led to the adoption of joint opinions, frameworks for action, codes of conduct, declarations, instruments, political guidelines, follow-up reports or procedural texts. And the overwhelming majority of those documents aim to lobby the EU institutions rather than establish mutual commitments between employers and workers (Degryse & Pochet 2011). Furthermore, a recent study of the sectoral dialogue in the hospital and metal sector shows that some national unions have a clear preference for soft instruments over regulatory involvement from the EU. In that sense, there is an effectiveness trade-off between the nature of the instruments used and the ability for unions to create consensus on what should be done at the European level (Larsson *et al.* 2020).

European works councils

European works councils can either represent workers alone or workers and management jointly, depending on national and local traditions in industrial relations. They usually meet once a year and deal with various topics such as research, environment, investment, health and safety and equal opportunities. The Directive 94/95/EC European works councils adopted in 1994 was adopted in the wake of the Hoover case, a prime example of how companies can instrumentally use the lack of common rules on workers' information across Europe. Back in 1993, the American multinational's management took advantage of the distinct procedures

Table 6.2 Agreements concluded in the framework of European social dialogue

Agreements implemented by Council directive	Cross-sectoral	Framework agreement on parental leave (1995, revised in 2009)
		Framework agreement on part-time work (1997)
		Framework agreement on fixed-term contracts (1999)
	Sectoral	Agreement on the organization of working time of seafarers (1998)
		Agreement on the organization of working time of mobile workers in civil aviation (2000)
		Agreement on certain aspects of the working conditions of mobile workers engaged in interoperable cross-border services (2004)
		Framework agreement on prevention from sharp injuries in the hospital and healthcare sector (2009)
		Framework agreement on the protection of occupational health and safety in the hairdressing sector (2012)
		Agreement concerning certain aspects of the organization of working time in inland waterway transport (2012, 2016, adoption of Council directive pending)
		Agreement on the work in fishing (2012)
		General framework for informing and consulting civil servants and employees of central government (2016)
		Social partner agreement on the maritime labour convention (2016)
Autonomous agreements implemented by the social partners at national level	Cross-sectoral	Framework agreement on telework (2002)
		Framework agreement on work-related stress (2004)
		Framework agreement on harassment and violence at work (2007)
		Framework agreement on inclusive labour markets (2010)
		Framework agreement in active ageing and an intergenerational approach (2017)
		Framework agreement on digitalization (2020)
	Sectoral level	Agreement on the European licence for drivers carrying out a cross-border interoperability service (2004)
		Agreement on workers health protection through the good handling and use of crystalline silica and products containing it (2006)
		European agreement on the implementation of the European hairdressing certificates (2009)
		Agreement regarding the minimum requirements for standard player contracts in the professional football sector in the EU and in the rest of the UEFA territory (2012)

Source: Social dialogue texts database, www.europa.ec.eu (accessed 15 September 2021).

and lack of communication between its French and Scottish sites as it pushed Scottish workers' representatives to accept a downgrading of their working conditions and pay in exchange for maintaining production. The talks eventually led to lowering salary costs in Scotland and the closure of the French site. Thus, under the European works council directive, all companies with over 1,000 workers, at least 150 of which are in two (or more) countries of the EU, have the obligation to establish a European works council. The purpose is to guarantee the rights of workers in sites located in different member states to meet, dialogue with management and to defend their rights (or possibly to make strategic counterproposals) during the restructuring of production activities at the European level (relocation, site closure, collective redundancies, etc.).

At the end of the 1990s, there were four types of European works councils: most of them are purely symbolic, some essentially provide information, others develop autonomous projects and a minority have real influence on the company's strategic decisions (Gumbrell-McCormick & Hyman 2015: 6).

Nevertheless, in some cases, negotiations in the framework of European works councils have led to unconventional agreements such as those reached at Ford and General Motors in 2004 and 2005. These aimed at insuring that restructuring and downsizing affect all production sites in Germany, Belgium, the UK, Poland and Sweden equitably and guarantee a workers' solidarity clause (Weiss 2011: 164).

Trade unions and many observers rapidly came to see the directive as insufficient to guarantee workers' rights to information and consultation. In the mid-2000s, a decade after the directive was adopted in 1994, only one-third of the companies concerned had set up a European works council. They did, however, cover 64 per cent of European workers.[1] Also, the ways in which existing committees operated could not counter the strategies deployed by management in large groups, such as information retention or muddling useful information, or even manipulating the information asymmetry. In the 2000s, ETUC as well as the European Commission and the EP called for a revision of the 1994 directive. After having refused to reopen negotiations for a long period of time, in 2009 BusinessEurope finally agreed to a minimal revision (Morin 2014: 30). The new measures focus on the temporality of the dialogue and insist on the fact that information about potential restructurings be shared "in due time" to allow a genuine consultation and involvement of workers in strategic reorientations. But ETUC's proposals to implement the directive through control or sanction mechanisms,

---

1. See ETUC, www.etuc.org/fr/les-comitper centC3per centA9s-dentreprise-europper centC3per centA9ens-cee (accessed 15 September 2021).

on the one hand, and to lower the threshold of representation from 1,000 to 500 employees, on the other hand, were rejected, thus leading to little substantial change (Morin 2014: 30). Research carried out on the agreements that led to the creation of some 1,100 European works councils shows that the revised directive has made it possible to extend and strengthen practices acquired with the first directive, in particular through "learning effects". Indeed, these allowed workers to take inspiration from councils based elsewhere and secure a precise definition of information and consultation, the right to training for representatives on European works councils and to carry out their missions without loss of salary, better communication of the decisions of European works council at the national level, access for representatives of the European works council to sites and employees to assemble the necessary information for adequate representation, the creation of a select committee for better operational functioning and an increased presence of union representatives within the European works council (De Spiegelaere & Waddington 2017).

To sum up, the European social dialogue appears to a large extent to be toothless regarding industrial relations regulations through binding norms. Additionally, EU politics have seen the principle of incorporating social partners agreements into EU law undermined in recent years. That being said, sectoral dialogue or European works councils certainly help – albeit to a limited extent – the world of labour to cope with the realities of the single market, especially in large sectors and companies.

The trade unions' role beyond the social dialogue: *vox clamantis in deserto?*

Institutionalized forms of participation

Workers' unions are involved in a series of discussions that do not strictly relate to industrial relations but rather to a broader political dimension. Since 1999, the so-called macroeconomic dialogue has been based on a biannual meeting between the ECB, the Council, the Commission and all the social partners in which they discuss the main budgetary, fiscal and salary guidelines. This forum was created under the impetus of the Social Democrats wishing to involve social partners in the discussions over the major socio-economic issues within the EMU. ETUC wants to use the macroeconomic dialogue for a closer coordination of wages. It has proposed a "European framework formula" that would base wage trends on an inflation offset plus compensation for increased productivity. However, employers, the ECB and some member states have so far opposed such a policy. Until today, the macroeconomic dialogue mainly remains an informal forum in which the different actors exchange political views.

The creation of a tripartite Social Summit for growth and employment was formalized by a Council decision in 2002 and then recognized by Article 152 TFEU. It brings together the president of the European Council, the president of the European Commission, the head of state holding the rotating presidency of the Council of the EU and all the social partners. The aim of this summit is to see how, through social dialogue, these actors can help reach the objectives set out by European macro strategies such as the Lisbon Strategy and its successor Europe 2020. The Social Summit is therefore a broad framework for dialogue on the European social agenda. At the Gothenburg summit in October 2017, discussions focused on the social dimension of Europe, the involvement of social partners in national reforms and investment in the digital economy. In addition, the summit has seen the heads of states and governments endorse the Commission's initiative to create an EPSR (see Chapter 7 and Box 7.4, p. 156). The last Social Summit held in Porto in May 2021 was staged by the Portuguese Council Presidency as a display of the social dimension of the recovery agenda. However, no significant leap towards enhanced EU action occurred as 11 member states clearly expressed their will to maintain social policy's centre of gravity at the national level in a political statement issued just a few days before the summit. The so-called Porto Social Commitment signed by the EU institutions, the European social partners and civil society representatives[2] merely endorses the European Pillar of Social Rights Action Plan put forward by the European Commission, including the definition of more specific targets and proposals for both national and European implementation tools (see Box 7.4, p. 156).

Finally, the social partners are now involved in the governance of the European Semester (see Chapter 7 and Table 7.2). In 2015, the European Semester was reformed to enhance the "ownership" of reforms by various national actors, including the social partners. In particular, social partners should be involved in the drafting of national reform programmes. However, their actual involvement remains very uneven between member states (Sabato *et al.* 2017). In most cases the unions' influence remains limited and their involvement is restricted to top-down communication or to consultations in which unions are heard but not necessarily listened to. Social dialogue traditions and the resources available to trade unions are decisive in explaining their degree of involvement and influence. In any event, the European Semester remains a bureaucratic process steered by national governments and administrations. Its paradoxical intention is to create more political ownership while staying removed from national politics to avoid problematic contention over its very objectives. However, the unions

---

2. "Porto Social Commitment", website of the Portuguese Presidency of the Council of the European Union, www.2021portugal.eu/en/porto-social-summit/porto-social-commitment (accessed 15 September 2021).

are precisely the national actors whose political commitment to the object-ives of the European Semester (in terms of, for example, reforms in the labour market, pensions, wage moderation or even fiscal discipline) is the weakest (Vanheuverzwijn & Crespy 2018).

Advocacy and protest

Trade unions also participate in European political life outside the institutional realm. On its own, ETUC regularly conducts advocacy campaigns on a range of issues such as wages, decent work and social rights, the fight against tax havens or the protection of whistle-blowers. These campaigns are aimed at ensuring the visibility of specific social issues and keeping them on the agenda. Campaigns are organized through petitions, communication or public events. At the national and European level, trade unions can also play an important role in launching European citizen initiatives. In 2012, for example, ETUC actively participated in the Right2water initiative under the motto: "Water and sanitation are a human right! Water is a public good, not a commodity!" This campaign demanded that European institutions guarantee access to water for all, notably by prohibiting the liberalization of water distribution. In 2013, Right2water became the first European citizens' initiative to collect 1.8 million signatures, well beyond the threshold of 1 million required by regulation for a petition to be validated and considered by the European Commission. Despite a large mobilization, it did not spur the Commission to address the substantial issues raised by the initiative. In 2015, the European Transport Federation launched the Fair Transport Europe European citizens' initiative to combat social dumping and the deterioration of working conditions in the transportation sector.

A more protest-based repertoire of action comes occasionally into play. According to Dufresne and Pernot (2013: 18),

> European trade unionism distinguishes three types of euro-actions: euro-demonstrations, concentrated in a given place (mostly Brussels or Strasbourg), euro-strikes, stoppages of work which take place in several countries simultaneously, and finally, European action days, with events organized in all EU countries on the same day.

In the 1990s, trade unions mobilized against the European directives on the lib-eralization of public services. In the transport sector, for example, the European Transport Federation started the first actions of transnational coordination: two marches in Brussels in 1996 and 1998, a Euro-strike in 1998, a "train of cooper-ation and solidarity" from Brussels to Turin in 2001, and transnational events, including one in Lille in 2004 (Hilal 2007). In the mid-2000s, ETUC strategically converged with organizations within civil society that were protesting the liberalization of public services found in international free trade agreements. From 2000 to 2007, a campaign was led in global and European networks against the General Agreement on Trade in Services reached within the World Trade Organization. The watchword was the defence of the public interest against the private interests and profit pursued by multinational companies. The most significant protest episode of the first decade of the century was undoubtedly the mobilization campaign against the Services Directive (also known as the "Bolkestein Directive") (Crespy 2016; Parks 2015). Although initially reluctant in the face of the virulent campaign launched in 2004 by Belgian trade unions and members of the radical left, ETUC then fully endorsed the mobilization under the common motto of the defence of "Social Europe".

The 2008 financial crisis opened a new, difficult era for trade unions. As mentioned earlier, unions have had to face domestically multiple political and legislative pressures for wage freezes and the decentralization of collective bargaining. In the broader arena of contentious politics, Euro-unionism proved mostly unable to provide an efficient and coordinated response to austerity. The social and economic crisis hit European countries with varying strength and, in doing so, worsened the divergence in views (and interests) between workers from northern and southern, western and eastern European countries (Gumbrell-McCormick & Hyman 2015: 10–11). In the countries of continental and southern Europe, and in the UK, trade unions have often used radical actions at the company level (general strikes, damages to the work site, kidnapping bosses) to limit job losses. In continental and northern Europe, more consensual measures such as partial redundancy or furloughs, and the increased use of short-term contracts were partially offset by public authorities.

In the aftermath of the financial and debt crisis, ETUC denounced the "totally unacceptable" direction taken with austerity policies enforced in the name of stability and competitiveness, and it put forward alternative neo-Keynesian proposals in its "Social Contract for Europe" in 2012.[3] The discourse of ETUC, traditionally articulated around a broad claim for a more social Europe, has to a certain extent refocused on the historical key claim for higher wages. On the mobilization front, three to four euro-actions were initiated every year. On 14 November 2014, ETUC coordinated the first transnational cross-trade strike in the history of European unionism, an action called "14N". Whereas the work stoppage was general in Spain, Greece, Italy and Portugal, workers in Belgium and Lithuania were less involved, and softer types of action were carried out

---

3. European Trade Union Confederation, "A social contract for Europe", www.etuc.org/fr/un-contrat-social-pour-lper centE2per cent80per cent99europe (accessed 15 September 2021).

in some 20 EU countries at the same time. Yet, overall, ETUC has struggled to coordinate an effective strategy at the European level with most instances of mobilization being driven by domestic agendas only. More recently, ETUC has returned – yet again – to a more conciliatory stance pursuing "social partnership" with the EU institutions (Golden 2019). For instance, it seems to embrace the idea that the European Semester has become much more "social" over time and seems to be placing hopes in the EPSR (see Chapter 8).

As a matter of fact, anti-austerity protest was driven by movements of a novel kind marking the start of a new protest cycle radically different from the global justice movement of the previous decades. Occupying squares in the public space, struggling against evictions and creating local fora for horizontal deliberation, those movements only rarely addressed the EU institutions directly or articulated demands for a more "Social Europe" (Pianta & Gerbaudo 2016). Instead, they showed "deep disappointment, not only with representative institutions and political parties, but also with unions or associations of various types, which [were] stigmatized as unwilling or unable to address the financial crisis" (Della Porta 2017: 28). A main explanation for the lack of genuinely transnational anti-austerity protest has to be found in the EU's responses to the crisis and how it changed the structure of political opportunities for civil society mobilization. The intergovernmental turn of economic governance and the marginalization of the EP, in particular, amounted to closing keys channels used by former movements for the transmission of grievances to the EU political realm (Crespy & Parks 2017; Della Porta & Parks 2018). In conjunction with a national instead of transnational framing of the sovereign debt crises, this led to a mobilization pattern where somewhat similar, yet distinctively national, movements developed in which unions only played a marginal role when they were not seen as antagonists.

Conclusion

In the field of European social dialogue, as in other areas relating to social policy, a "glass half-full, glass half-empty" approach should be avoided in order to understand the qualitative aspect of the changes at play. This chapter has shown that the European social dialogue is profoundly different from the forms of neo-corporatism and industrial relations inherited from Europe's history. The European social dialogue was promoted to legitimize market integration beyond national boundaries through the creation of a single market affecting not only goods and capital but also workers. At the end of the 1980s and early 1990s, the European Commission fostered supranational concertation to side-step political resistance to the adoption of social regulation in the Council. This strategy quickly showed its limits, especially when, amid the rise of neoliberalism in the 1990s, the Commission itself stopped applying strong pressure on employers.

Although it certainly lacks scope, the European social dialogue serves the cause of workers in various ways. The agreements reached so far respond to one-off problems affecting workers across Europe. The sectoral dialogue committees and the European works councils all help to foster consultation among social partners and to create channels to transmit grievances. At the political level, the various arenas for consultation allow workers' interests to be taken into consideration in the European political process. They have also helped strengthen coordination between trade union organizations cross-nationally.

However, the European social dialogue cannot be considered as an effective neo-corporatist mode of governance that regulates industrial relations. Its networks remain embryonic, both the vertical ones (i.e. the channels of representation of social partners from the local to the European level) and the horizontal ones (i.e. the dialogue between social partners). The small number of binding agreements adopted since the 1990s makes the European social dialogue a soft process and ETUC is rather committed to a logic of managerial partnership with the EU institutions. Therefore, because of its nature, the relevance of the European social dialogue can be called into question at a time when we are witnessing antagonized social relations, important retrenchment of rights and a clear re-commodification of labour and of social life in general. Through the socio-economic governance brought about by the 2008–10 crisis, the EU has even contributed to accelerating the decline of workers' representation.

That being said, it is hard to put the blame on the EU alone. In fact, the weakness of the European social dialogue reflects the long structural trend leading to the weakening of labour forces. The discredit of Keynesianism and the supremacy of neoliberal theories, the declining representativeness of trade unions along with the marginalization of their role in socio-economic governance and divisions between national organizations are all evils that affect national movements and translate into powerlessness at the European level. The hopes of many observers and actors who wished for a European corporatism in the 1990s (Falkner 1998) were disappointed. EU integration has not allowed the deficits of national trade unionism to be overcome nor has it brought about renewed practices for industrial democracy. The rise and fall of the European social dialogue thus seems to confirm the predictions made by Wolfgang Streeck in the 1990s (Streeck 1994), when he claimed that the success of a possible European corporatism would depend above all on employers' organizations. According to him, if those representing the interests of the capital were not given clear incentives to promote European social regulations, they would hinder the process as a whole, as neither the unions nor the European Commission would have the power to influence their strategic calculations or counter their structural power.

This outlook seems to account for the current deadlock faced by the European social dialogue. At the same time, "big questions" related to work have made their way back on to the European agenda, for instance the issue of minimum wages and in-work poverty. In the face of the important transformations currently facing the labour world in Europe (erosion of conventional employment relations and the rise of self-entrepreneurship, digitalization and robotization, labour shortages in public services, ageing of the activist trade union base, integration of immigrants, etc.), the future of neo-corporatism will depend to a large extent on the unions' capacity to come up with new ways of making their voices heard.

Further reading

- Christophe Degryse, "The relaunch of European social dialogue: what has been achieved up to now?" In Bart Vanhercke, Sebastiano Sabato and Denis Bouget (eds), *Social Policy in the European Union: State of Play 2017* (Brussels: ETUI/OS, 2017), 115–32.
- Jamie Jordan, Vincenzo Maccarrone and Roland Erne, "Towards a socialization of the EU's new economic governance regime? EU labour policy interventions in Germany, Ireland, Italy and Romania (2009–2019)". *British Journal of Industrial Relations* 59:1 (2021), 191–213.
- Joanne Kiess and Martin Seeliger (eds), *Trade Unions and European Integration: A Question of Optimism and Pessimism?* (Abingdon: Routledge, 2019).

Questions to debate

- Has the labour movement been mainly supportive or critical of European integration?
- Has the European sectoral social dialogue been more fruitful than the interprofessional European social dialogue?

7

DOES SOFT COORDINATION SUPPORT WELFARE STATES?

After four decades of European integration, the coordination of national social policies emerged in the late 1990s as an alternative to EU-binding regulation. In several areas (labour markets, social protection, healthcare, elderly care and the fight against poverty and exclusion) European leaders felt the need for coordinated responses without transferring new competencies to the EU institutions. Voluntary non-legally binding coordination thus emerged as an alternative to regulation. Inspired by the broad economic policy guidelines established in the run-up to the monetary union, soft coordination was then applied to employment policy and progressively formalized and extended to a larger range of public policies under the so-called open method of coordination (OMC). The OMC is therefore based on the willingness of national governments to implement policies aimed at reaching objectives that have been defined at the European level. The implementation of these policies is also monitored on the basis of indicators set out by national civil servants who meet in Council working groups and committees in Brussels. Coordination occurs through a forum aimed at forging a shared consensus on policy problems and adequate solutions or policy recipes. This environment creates incentives and pressures that can potentially be exploited by domestic governments to implement reforms. In the aftermath of the 2008–10 financial and debt crisis, existing OMC processes were consolidated into the European Semester, an all-encompassing governance framework combining binding regulation and soft coordination. The European Semester serves as the basis for the review of national budgets, the control of fiscal discipline (the Stability and Growth Pact), the monitoring of macroeconomic imbalances and monitoring issues around social cohesion.

At its inception, the OMC triggered great interest and enthusiasm from academia. Many specialists of social policy saw it as a means to tackle common problems while preserving national sovereignty in the social realm. Since member states could not agree on transferring competences to the EU, nor on a single policy model for addressing social cohesion, monitoring and benchmarking, a system of ongoing dialogue was set up to resolve disagreements (Radaelli & Borras 2010: 24). The OMC was also depicted as a form of "experimental governance" (Sabel & Zeitlin 2008), epitomizing a modern way to tackle the difficult dilemmas involved with welfare state reform based on learning (Dunlop & Radaelli 2016) and peer review. Politically, the implementation of the Lisbon Strategy through the OMC was designed as a third-way compromise between neoliberals and regulators, allowing for a knowledge-based economy to flourish by reconciling competitiveness along with social cohesion (Rodrigues 2002). According to Vanhercke (2020: 118), 20 years after its inception, the many forms of soft coordination have proven their added value in their conduciveness to more binding forms of integration. It is used by domestic policy-makers as a "selective amplifier of reforms strategies" and allows "the creative appropriation and leverage by European, national and subnational stakeholders".

However, scholars have increasingly become sceptical of the OMC and have formulated three main criticisms (Goetschy 2005). First, they argue that the OMC has accentuated the subordination of social policy objectives to the double imperative of competitiveness (resulting from competition in the context of the Europeanization and globalization of markets) and fiscal discipline (resulting both from the ideology and the governance at the basis of the EMU). In other words, the OMC has accentuated the "displacement" of Social Europe (Garben 2018) into the realm of economic policy. Second, soft coordination does not provide a satisfactory alternative to the community method: the lack of legal constraints jeopardizes implementation, whereas the lines between hard and soft law are blurred, without clear political benefits for the EU (Hatzopoulos 2007). Third, the OMC has fallen short of expectations in terms of democratic legitimacy (De la Porte & Nanz 2011). The absence of parliamentary legitimation is in no way compensated for by bureaucratic governance involving essentially administrations and a limited number of stakeholders. The absence of public debate in domestic arenas reflects the absence of real alternative agendas, with available policy options situated in a narrow spectrum underpinned by a centrist (social) liberal *doxa* (Copeland 2020).

In the past few years, this controversy has extended to the nature and effects of the European Semester. Zeitlin and Vanhercke (2014, 2017), followed by others (Bekker 2018, 2020; Verdun & Zeitlin 2017), have argued that the European Semester has undergone a "socialization" process from 2013 onwards. Starting from a marked bias for fiscal discipline, there is evidence that both the involvement of social policy actors and the visibility of social issues in the European Semester have improved over time. However, other scholars have not – or only partly – agreed with that thesis, as they emphasize that the European Semester had mainly served to accentuate the subordination of social policy to economic imperatives (Crespy & Menz 2015c), leading to major welfare state retrench-ment (De la Porte & Heins 2016) and the further weakening of corporatist indus-trial relations (Jordan *et al.* 2020). Insofar as social policy actors have become more involved, they have been "captured" into the logic of the Semester (Dawson 2018) and have never been in a position to initiate a shift from a commodifying to a de-commodifying paradigm (Copeland 2020; Copeland & Daly 2018; Crespy & Vanheuverzwijn 2017).

To what extent does soft coordination at the EU level serve to support welfare states? To address this question, this chapter presents the functioning of soft coordination and the underlying politics over two time frames: from the early days in the 1990s until the 2008–10 crisis and from the inception of the European Semester in 2011 to its coupling with NextGenerationEU. It argues that soft – and then hybrid – coordination has considerably enhanced the capacity of the EU to not simply support but in fact *reshape* welfare states. By promoting ambiguous and contested policy concepts such as activation (see Box 7.1), social invest-ment or structural reforms, the EU has sometimes spurred progressive mod-ernization. However, it has also often provided incentives, legitimacy and even exerted pressure on national decision-makers to enforce retrenchment. The emphasis was consistently on supply-side policy, (labour) market imperatives and the cost-efficiency of public services without a coherent agenda for tackling inequality and generate social cohesion. The set-up of NextGenerationEU and its coupling with the European Semester has opened a new era. The association of reform recommendations with EU resources is a major opportunity to actually strengthen welfare states. Whether and along which lines this will materialize remains an open question.

A new economic and governance philosophy for welfare state modernization

Soft coordination is not a means to "Europeanize" areas in which the EU has no role in a top-down fashion. Rather, it reflects the profound change in the way European political leaders have approached social policies from the 1980s onwards and their attempt to formulate "solutions" that could be shared at the EU level. From an economics perspective, EU coordination has accompanied – if not encouraged – the shift from a Keynesian demand-side policy towards a liberal supply-side policy (see Box 7.1) as a solution to the endemic unemploy-ment affecting Europe. From a governance perspective, it allows for non-legally binding voluntary coordination between national governments who thus retain their full prerogatives in the areas that are less affected by interdependency stemming from the single market, namely employment and social protection.

BOX 7.1 SUPPLY-SIDE POLICY AND EMPLOYMENT POLICY

Supply-side policy is based on the liberal theory that weak economic growth (and unemployment) results from the bad environment in which companies operate to create a supply of goods and services. This policy aims thus to lower corporate taxes, favour profit over wage increases and deregulate markets. It is often contrasted with the Keynesian policy of stimulating demand from households by maintaining or increasing their purchasing power.

Regarding employment, supply-side policies entail measures that aim at ensuring the quantity, quality and limited cost of labour. These include increasing the employment rate of all categories of the active population; ameliorating education and training; increasing the flexibility of working hours, as well as that of hiring and firing rules; limiting the share of social protection in labour costs; and wage moderation (wage stagnation or wage reduction).

Policies of so-called employment activation are the continuation of a supply-side policy. They make social welfare conditional upon the active attitude of job seekers in terms of job training, job seeking and even accepting jobs that are unrelated to their qualifications. Financial incentives make work more attractive than welfare benefits.

From the outset, the European Employment Strategy (EES) was grounded in four essential aspects of supply-side policy: the development of labour supply, activation and training, labour market flexibility and containing labour costs (Conter 2007). The EES can also be seen as the inception of a social investment logic seeking to reconcile economic and social objectives by focusing on "social protection as a productive factor" and individuals' "employability" (De la Porte & Palier 2021).

The European Employment Strategy and the turn to "activation"

A European employment agenda slowly emerged in the 1970s, with the European Commission giving it a significant boost in the early 1990s, at a time when the unemployment rate in Europe increased from 7.7 per cent in 1990 to 11.1 per cent in 1994, in contrast with both the United States and Japan, which had much lower rates of unemployment (Goetschy 1999). Jacques Delors, the Commission president at the time, was proactive in putting forward a strategy that could enjoy broad support from the centre left and right. The purpose was to legitimize the EMU decided at Maastricht and offset its expected negative social effects by expanding the action of the EU in the area of employment and social inclusion. In its White Paper on growth, competitiveness and employment of 1993 (European Commission 1993), the Commission drew the outlines of a new approach to employment anchored in supply-side policy. The main objectives were mainly the optimization of human capital through training, wage moderation to encourage investment and job creation, labour markets efficiency and an approach to "equal opportunities" focusing on access to work for young people, women and long-term job seekers. Endorsed by the heads of state and government at the Essen summit in 1994, the strategy was in tune with the turn away from Keynesianism and towards neoliberalism of the 1980s. Championed by Thatcher in the UK (and Reagan in the United States), this shift occurred at a varying pace across European countries.

Regarding governance, the European Council considered that because of the "institutional, legislative or contractual specificities of each member state, the Community should focus on setting objectives and leave member states [to] choose the means adequate for their situation within a commonly determined broad framework" (Browne 2004: 59). The aim was to find a flexible form of coordination inspired by what existed in the area of economic policy. In order to be able to join the common currency, member states had to meet the so-called Maastricht criteria – setting targets on levels of inflation, deficit, debt, the exchange rate and interest rate – and to do so would follow the broad economic policy guidelines set up after the adoption of the Maastricht Treaty (Hodson & Mahler 2001). Similarly, the EES would materialize as member states transposed the guidelines for employment into action plans and wrote annual progress reports on their implementation. These were then reviewed and summarized by the Commission and the Council (ECOFIN and EPSCO), and finally presented to the European Council, which was charged with adopting the new guidelines.

The formalization of this new approach into an EES during the Employment Summit of Luxembourg in 1997 was the result of a period of intense mobilization in which the European Commission (under the presidency of Jacques Santer between 1995 and 1999) "succeeded in mobilising its traditional allies in social affairs: the EP, the Economic and Social Committee (ECOSOC), the Committee of the Regions, the Standing Employment Committee and the ETUC" (Goetschy 1999: 121). An important political change also occurred in the run-up to the intergovernmental conference on the Treaty of Amsterdam. Austria, Finland and Sweden (who joined the EU in 1995) actively supported the EES. The Nordic model was then perceived as very successful and provided inspiration. Allan Larsson, former leader of the Swedish Social Democratic Party and finance minister, published an influential report entitled *Put Europe to Work* in 1993 (see De la Porte 2011). Then appointed the head of the European Commission's DG EMPL in 1995, he made an important contribution to the Amsterdam Intergovernmental Conference (De la Porte 2011). The newcomers were therefore strengthening the positions of the Benelux countries, Denmark and France. In addition, shortly before the intergovernmental conference, the electoral victories of the Labour Party led by Tony Blair in the UK and the Socialists under Lionel Jospin in France gave the Social Democrats a clear political majority, isolating the Germans who were critical of the European employment initiative (Goetschy 1999).

While employment was not on the agenda in Amsterdam, the treaty did end up including a new chapter on employment (Articles 125–30 EC, today Articles 145–50 TFEU). This new chapter defines employment as a common challenge, asks member states to develop a "coordinated strategy for employment", defines the method of implementation following the guidelines from the Essen Summit and constitutionalizes the existence of EMCO within the Council and its collaboration with social partners. When Gerhard Schröder became the German chancellor in 1998, the Social Democrats were in government in 11 out of 15 EU member states. Tony Blair and Gerhard Schröder championed an ideological revision of social democracy, dubbed the "Third Way" or *"neue Mitte"*. This constituted the political momentum that would usher in the Lisbon Strategy to promote an Anglo-Nordic policy model "emphasizing social rights and responsibility for all to contribute to the labor market" (De la Porte & Palier forthcoming).

The Lisbon Strategy as an ambiguous modernization project

The European Council of Lisbon in March 2000 took place in a broader context in which European leaders feared Europe's loss of competitiveness in a globalized and digitized economy. Following proposals by Belgium, France, Sweden and Finland in the 1990s, the heads of state and government adopted a long-term strategy aimed at making the EU "become the most competitive and dynamic knowledge-based economy in the world, capable of sustainable economic growth with more and better jobs and greater social cohesion" by 2010 (European Council 2000). The "Lisbon Strategy" was meant to be a balanced, centrist vision of Europe's future in which the willingness to boost economic growth and employment through technology and innovation was coupled with greater social cohesion (Goetschy 2004). The activism of the Portuguese presidency of the Council took strength from the work of academics seeking to theorize the necessary modernization of the European social model (but also its specificity) in the framework of a knowledge-based economy that safeguards competitiveness along with social cohesion (Rodrigues 2002). From the outset, the Lisbon Strategy represented an ambiguous and unworkable compromise between Social Democrats and neoliberals.

In addition to quantified objectives (average annual growth at 3 per cent, female average employment rate between 60 and 70 per cent), the Lisbon Council endorsed the expansion of soft coordination on the model of the EES to various fields including pensions, social protection and training under the label of the OMC. Based on guidelines defined at the European level, member states would voluntarily adopt policies that would then regularly be evaluated in Brussels and feedback for future recommendations and new guidelines would be provided. At the Lisbon Council, the Commission proposed a first set of six indicators to evaluate and compare national performances, with an additional 18 specific indicators a year later. As suggested by Kenneth Armstrong, discussions around the nature of indicators reflected from the outset a lack of political consensus and the "unstable institutionalization of three (competing) paradigms": the (neoliberal) paradigm of activation, the (Social Democrat) paradigm of redistribution and the (libertarian) paradigm of social citizenship (Armstrong 2010: 94–5).

The initial fragile equilibrium between competitiveness and social cohesion rapidly shifted in favour of the former. In 2005, the mid-term evaluation of the Lisbon Strategy revealed weak implementation results as the ambitious goals set out in Lisbon were clearly out of reach. Early on, the EES exhibited the fundamental problem of soft coordination, namely that domestic policy-makers only follow European guidelines when they are consistent with their own political priorities (Anderson 2015; Copeland & Ter Haar 2013: 120–1). Two high-level groups of experts, the first led by the economist André Sapir and the other by former Social Democratic prime minister of the Netherlands Wim Kok, submitted reports reaching convergent conclusions (European Commission 2004; Sapir 2004). They criticized the "Christmas tree" effect caused by the multiple goals of the Lisbon Strategy and asked to refocus the Lisbon Strategy on growth and employment in a narrower way. Social cohesion was then no longer seen as an objective in and of itself but rather as the result of having a more dynamic economy. Anti-poverty and anti-exclusion policies were diluted and subordinated to the imperative of public-spending reduction, while emphasis was placed on job seekers' "activation" and flexicurity (see Box 7.2).

Whereas the Lisbon Strategy had initially been backed by a series of European NGOs active in the social field (notably the European Anti-Poverty Network), its neoliberal reboot under the leadership of the new Commission president José Manuel Barroso gave rise to criticisms and resistance from organized civil society. Although the goals set out in Lisbon in matters of public policy remained largely unmet, the codification and legitimizing of the OMC as a new mode of governance in the EU survived the Lisbon Strategy and continued to be put into practice.

BOX 7.2 FLEXICURITY AND EUROPEAN COORDINATION

Pioneered by Denmark and the Netherlands in the 1990s, the concept of flexicurity flourished in European policy debates in the 2000s. The underlying idea was to reconcile the social principles of the continental welfare model with the tenet of competitiveness dominating the Anglo-Saxon liberal model. Flexicurity implies labour market reforms conducive to relaxed regulation of employment rules (working hours, hiring and firing conditions, type of working contract, etc.) as demanded by employers. At the same time, greater flexibility should be combined with more security for workers as they benefit from generous social protection and effective (re)training in order to rapidly find a new job when they are made redundant.

Within the European Commission, DG EMPL builds on research from international experts over the virtues of the Danish model. The purpose was both to present flexicurity as an alternative to the neoliberal activation so as to overcome resistance from the unions and to depoliticize policy debates and supersede the ideas promoted by DG ECFIN.

At the national level, the concept of flexicurity served as a frame of reference for the labour law reforms undertaken by numerous governments. The ability of trade unions to resist regressive reforms was sometimes impeded by their political divisions, as was the case in Portugal in 2003 and 2009. Furthermore, unions were not equally successful in proposing national "translations" of the flexicurity concept. The French Confédération française démocratique du travail (CFDT), for instance, put forward the notion of "securitizing career paths".

While the use of the term "flexicurity" faded away from political discourses over the past few years, the related ideas have underpinned all labour market reforms implemented across Europe over the past 20 years or so.

Source: Caune, 2014.

The OMC: a problematic soft touch in EU governance

Soft coordination through the OMC differs from the simple adoption of *soft law* in at least two respects. On the one hand, it is based on procedures that institutionalize a decentralized multilateral surveillance between member states in the Council, and on the other hand, it sets up a bilateral dialogue between national governments and European institutions. It also relies on the emulation of "good practices" – a process of learning built on peer evaluation of national performance through benchmarking. One must not view the OMC as a stable and unified mode of governance. Rather, it is a moving target that has been used

Table 7.1 Uses of OMC in socio-economic policy areas

Policy area	Change over time
Fiscal and economic policy	Created in 1993 (Treaty of Maastricht)
	2006: integrated in the broad economic policy guidelines of the Lisbon Strategy
	2011: integrated in the European Semester
European Employment Strategy	Created in 1997 (European Council of Luxembourg)
	2006: integrated in the broad economic policy guidelines (growth and employment) of the Lisbon Strategy
	2011: integrated in the European Semester
Social protection and social inclusion	Created in 2000 (European Council of Lisbon)
	2006: integrated in the social OMC
Pensions	Created in 2001 (European Council of Laeken)
	2006: integrated in the social OMC
Health and long-term care	Practical aspects discussed during a Council meeting in 2004 but there never has been a formal launch of a specific OMC
	2006: integrated in the social OMC

at different times in different policy fields for different purposes, using different legal bases (see Table 7.1) (Zeitlin 2005b). Some practices such as the naming and shaming of the worst performing member states have been dropped due to reticence from governments. In 2006, the review of the Lisbon Strategy brought about rationalization of the OMCs in the socio-economic field. The guidelines for employment were merged with broad economic policy guidelines within the so-called integrated economic and employment guidelines and the OMCs within the social policy field were recast under the umbrella of a single social OMC. These procedural changes reflect the new focus of the Lisbon Strategy on competitiveness and the relative marginalization of social cohesion objectives (Barcevicius *et al.* 2014b).

Although the OMC became a mode of governance particularly *en vogue* in the 2000s, its codification in the treaties remained very limited. The Convention on the future of Europe, which drafted the Constitutional Treaty between 2001 and 2004, showed a willingness to give the OMC constitutional recognition (Zeitlin 2005b). However, this readiness came up against the inability to standardize a method that is by nature multifaceted, and the fundamental incompatibility of the OMC with the legal standard of competence allocation in the treaties (Armstrong 2010: 100–1). In the end, the Treaty of Lisbon refers indirectly to the OMC in its Article 5 (TFEU), which stipulates the following:

1. The member states shall coordinate their economic policies within the EU. To this end, the Council shall adopt measures, in particular broad guidelines for these policies.

   Specific provisions shall apply to those member states whose currency is the euro.

2. The EU shall take measures to ensure coordination of the employment policies of the member states, in particular by defining guidelines for these policies.
3. The EU may take initiatives to ensure coordination of member states' social policies.

Furthermore, the treaty mentions the coordination of policies in areas of economic governance (Broad Guidelines for Economic Policy, Article 121 TFEU), budgetary discipline (Stability and Growth Pact, Article 126 TFEU and Eurozone, Article 136), employment (Article 148 TFEU), social policy (Article 156) and research (Article 181). It is striking that Article 156 TFEU on social policy encourages coordination in fields that are *not* those where the OMC is already institutionalized. It focuses on employment and working conditions,[1] whereas social inclusion and poverty are not even mentioned. In matters of governance of social policy, the Lisbon treaty therefore fails to provide a coherent constitutional framework.

Looking at the constellation of actors, the Council is undeniably at the heart of the OMC, since experts from national administrations sit in the committees and working groups (ECOFIN, EMCO and the Political and Security Committee [PSC]) that conduct the peer review. The evaluation of national reports and the formulation of indicators is carried out in conjunction with the services of the Commission and joint reports are drafted by the two institutions. The European Council also plays a leading role in formulating the integrated economic and employment guidelines. The EP is largely marginalized in this mode of governance,[2] just as the lack of legally binding norms excludes the CJEU. However, the *open* aspect of the OMC reveals the ambition to include multiple actors in the definition as well as the implementation of the national reform programmes (local authorities, economic actors, civil society, social partners, etc.). The OMC is therefore anchored in a logic of governance that echoes the European Commission's 2001 White Paper on governance, rather than a representative conception of government.

---

1. This includes areas where the EU has regulatory competence, thereby creating some confusion. These areas are employment, labour law and working conditions; vocational training and development; social security; health and safety at work; the right to organize and carry out collective bargaining between employers and workers.
2. Article 148 TFEU on employment states that the Council must consult the EP before mapping out the guidelines. Article 156 TFEU on the coordination of social policies states that the EP is "fully informed".

From its early days, assessments of the OMC have been conflicting. For some, it provides an innovative form of governance establishing a dialogue at the European level in policy areas where the transfer of competences to the EU is neither possible nor desirable (Goetschy 2005; Sabel & Zeitlin 2008). For others, it reinforces the subordination of EU social policy to the economic imperative epitomized by the Lisbon Strategy, contributing to hollow out national welfare states (Daly 2006; Offe 2003). Moreover, although implementation is often problematic, the lines between hard and soft law are increasingly blurred, without clear political benefits for the EU (Hatzopoulos 2007).

As suggested by Jonathan Zeitlin, it is useful to distinguish between substantial effects and procedural effects (Zeitlin 2009). The authors who evaluated the OMC in terms of legislative initiatives or national policy reforms most often concluded that European coordination was mostly limited to good intentions, while the goals defined in Brussels were very seldom reached. Instead, the effects of the OMC are mainly to be found in ideas and narratives (Radaelli & Borras 2010: 30–7). Far from being only "cheap talk", substantial effects include "agenda shifts" and "cognitive shifts", leading national political and social actors to change their preferences on the effectiveness and desirability of certain public policy choices (Barcevicius et al. 2014a; Zeitlin 2005a). Whether EU soft coordination leads to progressive modernization or to the regressive retrenchment of welfare states depends not only on European compromises, which are often ambiguous and short-lived. Most importantly, EU guidelines are strategically taken on board by national actors in a political, institutional and historical trajectory specific to domestic arenas. Willingness to reform, the role of the opposition in party politics, resistance from the social partners and civil society or weak administrative capacity are all relevant factors explaining the effectiveness of European soft coordination in social policy. As such, the OMC should be seen above all as a "selective amplifier" of national reform processes (Vanhercke 2009).

Turning to procedural effects, major debates have unfolded about the democratic legitimacy of soft coordination. On one hand, the OMC has strengthened horizontal coordination between areas of public policy as well as vertical coordination between territorial levels of governance. However, the OMC has hardly fulfilled its democratic promises (De la Porte & Nanz 2004; Kröger 2007). While it has served to enhance the administrative capacity of member states, as well as the involvement of non-state actors in policy-making, this has often been restricted to the EU level where participation of NGOs such as the European-level European Anti-Poverty Network or the Social Platform has been tangible. In contrast, social partners or grassroots participation in the elaboration or implementation of national reform programmes has remained weak, although there is a lot of variation between member states (Radaelli & Borras 2010: 42–7). Broadly speaking, soft coordination is essentially populated by networks of bureaucrats and experts within government administrations and the EU institutions and has not penetrated debate arenas in the national public spheres.

In its first two decades of existence in the social policy realm, soft coordination has proved not to be a panacea, but rather an imperfect complement to regulation. Conceived as a way to instil welfare-state reform in a context of heightened global economic competition, its policy direction has oscillated between social-liberal recalibration and neoliberal retrenchment. This can be explained by the rise of the "Third Way" social democracy, followed by its electoral demise (combined with the eastern enlargement of the EU) from the mid-2000s onwards. The OMC developed neither as a top-down process of European policy implementation, nor as a tool for bottom-up democratic debates over social policies. Rather, it has created a space for dialogue and surveillance between national administrations and EU institutions in which policy solutions (often ambiguous political compromises) were found and then used or ignored by national decision-makers. The euro crisis of 2008–10 profoundly transformed the nature of coordination.

The European Semester: the rise of a Leviathan from one crisis to another?

Created in 2011, the European Semester is the institutional response to the destabilization of the eurozone by the financial crisis of 2008 and the ensuing sovereign debt crisis. The European Semester arose as a very broad, encompassing framework of governance that brings under a single umbrella the three areas where EU decision-makers used soft coordination, namely fiscal policy (with the Stability and Growth Pact, see Box 7.3), macroeconomic policy (with broad economic policy guidelines) and social policy (the OMC on social inclusion). Structurally dominated by economic actors and biased towards fiscal discipline, the European Semester has further weakened social policy's "semi-autonomy" vis-à-vis economic policy (Streeck 2019: 133). Far from becoming an irrelevant white elephant, it has become a central political process in the post-Covid-19 environment. Not only will the EPSR be streamlined into it, but the Semester recommendations will also serve to assess the national plans for spending the money originating from the Recovery and Resilience Facility – the €672.5 billion-endowed key financial instrument under the recovery agenda dubbed "NextGenerationEU". In this new political constellation, the very nature of the European Semester is changing, while its relation to the Stability and Growth Pact as well its democratic credentials remain problematic.

BOX 7.3 THE STABILITY AND GROWTH PACT

In its chapter on the EMU, the 1992 Treaty of Maastricht included Article 140c, stating that the "member states shall avoid excessive government deficits" setting a limit to deficit and debt levels at respectively 3 per cent and 60 per cent of GDP.

In 1997, the German finance minister Theo Waigel proposed to strengthen the monitoring and coordination of national fiscal policies in order to enforce the deficit and debt levels. This was seen as a way to preserve and continue the German ordoliberal model of monetary policy (i.e. the low-inflation, low-deficit policy underpinning the Deutschmark) in the run-up to the common currency. This set of rules, called the Stability and Growth Pact, was adopted. In 1999, a corrective arm foreseeing sanctions for non-compliant states was included in the pact.

The Stability and Growth Pact was nevertheless the object of continuous criticism, especially from southern member states, including France. Although some have deplored its lack of effectiveness (because the sanctions were never applied), others found that the blind application of such arbitrary thresholds would only exacerbate recessions in times of economic downturn. In 2002, the Commission president Romano Prodi famously called the pact "stupid". In 2005, both France and Germany failed to comply with the rules of the pact. Under their impetus, the rules were relaxed to take economic cycles into account in the monitoring of deficit levels. For many observers, however, this harmed the credibility of the Stability and Growth Pact and constituted an original sin, encouraging non-compliance by other member states.

In the aftermath of the financial and sovereign debt crisis in 2010, the Stability and Growth Pact became more stringent, both from a legal and a political point of view. However, the flexibility around the interpretation of "the rules and the numbers" has not ceased fuelling political conflicts over the legitimacy of European fiscal coordination (Schmidt 2020).

Social policy subsumed by economic policy

While the ECB progressively became the "hero" of the euro crisis with its pro-active monetary policy, awareness grew among EU leaders that monetary policy alone could not fix all the problems of the eurozone. Creditor states – led by Germany – therefore advocated for making fiscal coordination more stringent. A sort of OMC before the letter, the 1997 Stability and Growth Pact had defined rules for states to curtail their budget deficit and debt level. Since the 1990s it was regularly ignored by member states. The first goal of the European Semester was to strengthen the flexible coordination on budgetary and fiscal matters. That said, potential macroeconomic imbalances (e.g. regarding the balance of payments, interest rates, investments, employment, housing markets, credit, etc.) or social problems (unemployment, lack of equal access to the labour market, excessive poverty, poorly performing education and training systems, etc.) were also seen as potential causes of destabilization in the eurozone, thus necessitating reinforced monitoring as well. Compared to the previous era of soft coordination under the OMC and the Lisbon Strategy, the European Semester operates a triple hybridization: on the policy level, it accentuates the imbrication of economic and social objectives; on the legal level, it blurs the boundary between hard and soft law; in governance matters, it redefines the roles and distorts the distinctions between intergovernmentalism and supranationalism (see Table 7.2).

Table 7.2 The European Semester (2011–20)

Field	Legal basis	Instruments	Level of constraint on national policy-making
Fiscal policy	Stability and Growth Pact "Six-pack", "two-pack" Treaty on stability coordination and governance	Midterm objectives Excessive deficit procedure (sanction up to 0.3 per cent of GDP)	High Has the potential to trigger politicization and contentious debates either within domestic arenas or between national governments and the European Commission
Macroeconomic policy	"Six-pack" Integrated guidelines (broad economic policy guidelines + EES)	Macroeconomic imbalance procedure (score board, sanctions up to 0.1 per cent GDP)	Relatively low Legal grey area and low public salience
Social policy	Europe 2020 EES Social OMC	Joint employment report Social scoreboard	Low
	Annual growth survey (fall) Country reports (winter) Country-specific recommendations (spring)		Differentiated implementation of "structural reforms", depending on: – national reforms, agendas and electoral cycles – economic and political weight of member state – budgetary position in terms of deficit and debt

First, the European Semester integrated fiscal policy, macroeconomic policy and social policy under one annual cycle of back and forth between the EU institutions and member states. At the end of the year (November), the Commission publishes its annual growth survey, which contains an overview of the economic situation of the EU, gives recommendations for the eurozone and shares its opinion on the budget proposals made by the governments of member states. Based on this, the Council discusses and adopts suggested recommendations and priorities. In the beginning of the year, the Commission carries out bilateral discussions with national governments and administrations who share their national reform programmes on economic policy, as well as their stability programmes (for eurozone members) or their convergence programmes (for non-members of the eurozone) on budgetary policy, on the basis of which the Commission drafts its country-specific reports. In the spring, country-specific recommendations – suggesting orientations and reforms that governments should adopt in the fiscal, economic and social fields – are sent out. These recommendations are adopted (and possibly slightly modified) by the Council in early summer. Member states are then responsible for the implementation of policies aimed at meeting the recommendations during the second half of the year.

One must not consider the European Semester as a unified governance mechanism, because the nature of the tools as well as the level of (legal) constraint is variable from one field to another. In the area of fiscal policy, the rules of the Stability and Growth Pact have undergone a process of "hardening", whereby soft law was turned into binding regulation. In 2011, through ordinary legislative process, the EU adopted six regulations (the "six-pack") setting budgetary goals for curbing public spending; it also included the excessive deficit procedure, which outlined financial sanctions for eurozone countries in case of repeated breaches. In 2013, two regulations (the "two-pack") established a common calendar for the drafting of national budgets that are reviewed by the Commission and the Council and potentially revised before their adoption by national parliaments. Going further into the constitutional realm, 25 of 28 heads of state and governments signed the Treaty on Stability, Coordination and Governance (also known as the fiscal compact) in 2012, which included a provision requiring member states to introduce a "golden rule" in their national constitutions, prohibiting deficits (except those linked to economic downturns) and requiring the maintenance of their annual budget at a point of structural equilibrium. This sequence shows a string reversal of the 2005 revision of the Stability and Growth Pact, when a French–German coalition argued for a softening of the rules against the EU institutions and a number of member states (Terpan & Saurugger 2021).

One must, however, put the constraining power of fiscal rules into perspective. Faced with stagnant growth and the rise of social inequalities brought about by austerity policies, in 2014, the European Commission progressively became more flexible in its evaluation of member states' compliance with the regulations on fiscal discipline. The EU's ambition to "govern by rules and rule by numbers" met increasing resistance, thus feeding into a broader crisis of legitimacy (Schmidt 2020). Failing to take effective action to comply with the pact's rules, France and Italy were granted two years extension without facing sanctions in 2013 and again in 2015. The discretion enjoyed by the Commission nevertheless triggered criticism from northern creditor countries and the advocates of fiscal discipline within the European Commission (e.g. from the commissioner for economic and monetary affairs, Olli Rehn). In early 2014, the more flexible approach to the rules was therefore clarified and so-called flexibility clauses introduced, under pressure from, notably, French president François Hollande and Italian prime minister Matteo Renzi.[3] In 2016, a controversy arose as the Commission used the clauses to grant Italy an unprecedented flexibility, while decisions regarding Spain's and Portugal's excessive deficits were postponed until after the Spanish elections in June to then give way to a symbolic decision with no financial sanction. The legal hardening versus political softening of the EU rules on deficit and debt have been the symbol of political disagreements between creditor and debtor states over fiscal governance.

This shows that the European Semester has led to a blurring of the boundaries between hard and soft law. In this regard, macroeconomic policy within the Semester finds itself in a grey area. On one hand, the macroeconomic imbalance procedure, similar to the excessive deficit procedure, was included in the "six-pack". States' performances are measured with a scoreboard, including around 30 indicators, and an alert mechanism, which can also lead to sanctions as high as 0.1 per cent of GDP. However, this mechanism has never been used and it seems politically very unlikely that the Commission would suggest punishing a state because of poor economic performance. Leverage in this area therefore builds mainly on the integrated economic and employment guidelines and the EES.

The social strand within the European Semester remains based on soft coordination as no new regulation or enforceable procedure has been set up despite the acute social consequences of the recession. In fact, the impact of the financial crisis collided with the EU's reflections on Europe 2020, the successor to the Lisbon Strategy. Endorsed by the European Council in June 2010, Europe 2020 aimed at improving the productivity and competitiveness of the EU while reasserting a commitment towards a *social* market economy. It would help member states to coordinate their reforms in the areas of employment, research

---

3. According to the clauses, (1) investment spending, (2) the costs of structural reforms recommended by the EU and (3) economic cycles impeding the reduction of budgetary deficit could be factored into the calculation of deficits.

and development, climate change and energy, education, and poverty and social exclusion. Monitoring and peer review would happen on the basis of a score-board featuring 42 indicators. Key benchmarks included raising the employment rate in the 20–64 age group to 75 per cent, and lift at least 20 million people out of poverty and social exclusion by 2020. The adoption of such a "poverty target" reflected the will of a coalition of member states to address social issues (Copeland 2020: 77). At the same time, EU politics came to focus on bailouts and fiscal issues and "as such, policy entrepreneurs in DG ECFIN seized control of the drafting process of Europe 2020 and the reforms of EU economic governance" (Copeland 2020: 76). As a result, social policy objectives became secondary. The hardening of budgetary rules gave European institutions an access point to indirectly exercise constraint over employment and social policies for better or worse, as will be discussed later in the chapter.

Third, the European Semester has led to a hybridization of governance as it exhibits power dynamics between supranationalism, intergovernmentalism and parliamentarism, which differs from the community method and the OMC (Coman & Ponjaert 2016; Schmidt 2018). The European Council and the Council of the European Union play a major role in defining the agenda and the broad social and economic guidelines, as was the case in the first phase of crisis management in 2009–12. In the years that followed, the European Commission was gradually granted broader oversight powers over national reforms and recommendations, via continuous bilateral dialogue with member states' governments and administrations. As for the EP, largely marginalized in the early stages of the process, it slowly carved out a place for itself as an observer and as a place for discussing and politicizing socio-economic governance goals, but without having any real capacity to participate or make decisions. The absence of parliamentary legitimation and of democratic debate therefore constitutes a continuous feature of EU socio-economic coordination.

Political schizophrenia between austerity and social investment

The crisis of sovereign debt in Greece, Portugal and Ireland revealed how much European political economies were interdependent, especially within the Euro-area – a monetary union without a state, with a centralized monetary policy but highly decentralized and non-binding macroeconomic coordination. Although the flare-up of sovereign debt in these countries was largely caused by the accumulation of private debt and the crisis of the banking sector, European leaders framed it in terms of public spending. The way in which bailouts were designed and implemented have given rise to a large body of literature to which it is not possible to do justice here, and I will only point out two important aspects. First, the bailouts provided by the Troika (see Box 3.1, p. 51) made the loans dependent on the implementation of reforms aimed at reducing public spending, a mechanism known as social conditionality. This led to dramatic cuts in wages (or freezing at best) and to the debasing of public services, especially education and healthcare, which are two labour-intensive services – and therefore costly. In Greece, this resulted in a humanitarian disaster. In Spain, home evictions triggered vivid protest and became a national issue. In Portugal (as in Greece) the MoU with the Troika foresaw a far-reaching plan of privatization of all remaining publicly owned companies across energy and water distribution, the media and communications, air and railway transport, and naval construction and mining.

In all EU countries, these cuts disproportionately affected individuals at the bottom of the social ladder. Thus, EU crisis management contributed to the acceleration of inequalities both among and within member states. Second, one should not buy into a simplified reading, whereby the EU would have enforced top-down domination on bailed-out countries. Not only did the Troika and EU institutions frame the crisis in terms of domestic failures of policy-making in the southern periphery, calling for a neoliberal cure (Moreira Ramalho 2020), but domestic elites also participated actively in legitimizing the reforms and persuading constituencies that there was "no alternative" to austerity (Borriello 2017). Moury *et al.* (2021) also argue that bailouts should not be seen as diktats from the Troika. Depending on partisan preferences and countries' bargaining power, executive elites in Cyprus, Greece, Ireland, Portugal and Spain had leeway to resist, design or sometimes reverse reforms. More often than not, they "capitalized on external constraints" to pass reforms they deemed necessary, while being unwilling to bear the political costs thereof (Moury *et al.* 2021). The MoUs between bailed-out countries and their creditors nevertheless constitute a separate arena of politics. After the "adjustment programmes" were ended, countries would reintegrate into the more routine procedures of the European Semester.

The first cycle between 2011 and 2013 of the European Semester was very focused on fiscal discipline and the reduction of public spending. However, soon, actors from the social policy field such as DG EMPL – representatives within the Council committees for employment and social policy – supported by ETUC and social NGOs mobilized and were relatively proactive in fighting their way into the European Semester. This led to the inclusion of social indicators in the scoreboards used, the involvement of DG EMPL in drafting the country-specific recommendations and an overall increased visibility of social issues. However, attempts to define thresholds that would trigger alerts or recommendations (as in economic and budgetary affairs) were countered by a majority of member states and the DG ECFIN. This led Zeitlin and Vanhercke to argue that from 2013 onwards, the European Semester had undergone a process of "socialization" (Zeitlin & Vanhercke 2014, 2017). However, a number of scholars (Copeland & Daly 2018; Crespy & Schmidt 2017) have pointed out that this thesis needs to be (strongly) qualified.

It is true that, after an initially "austeritarian" (Hyman 2015) focus, the Juncker Commission from 2014 in particular shifted the emphasis away from fiscal discipline towards investment. In fact, the EU institutions have traded fiscal flexibility for more commitment from the member states towards the implementation of structural reforms. Historically, structural reforms stem from the "adjustment programmes" conceived in the 1980s and 1990s by the IMF and the World Bank in Asia, Latin America and Africa. In spite of a fuzzy meaning, structural reforms refer to a core of standard neoliberal policies, that is the liberalization of goods and services markets, the deregulation of labour markets, the "rationalization" of welfare states and public administration. In EU politics, structural reforms have acquired a more ambiguous meaning, reflecting an ideological battle of ideas. A close look at the Semester country-specific recommendations shows that structural reforms have from the outset encompassed calls for social investment *as well as* welfare retrenchment (Crespy & Vanheuverzwijn 2017). And even though the importance of progressive social investment has increased over time, they were always secondary vis-à-vis fiscal recommendations grounded in a hard-law basis with the threat of possible sanctions. In spite of some social actors' activism, in particular the commissioner for employment and social affairs Lazslo Andor, who pushed forward a communication on a "social investment package", social investment was never at the centre of a coherent and sustained agenda at EU level. In the framework of the European Semester, governments found themselves facing contradictory injunctions to save (fiscal discipline) and to spend (social investment).

With many member states under excessive deficit procedures and without a major breakthrough in social investment, country-specific recommendations have been at best partially implemented at the national level. The most emblematic and tangible set of reforms promoted through the European Semester has concerned labour markets. Between 2011 and 2018, they represented the largest share of all the country-specific recommendations (between 18 and 30 per cent), followed by reforms in pension and health spending (between 9 and 16 per cent) (Crespy & Vanheuverzwijn 2017). The proposed reforms hinge on the idea that creating financial incentives and/or constraints would be sufficient to "activate" job seekers and combat unemployment. Furthermore, in line with the paradigm of social investment in human capital (see Box 7.5), recommendations encouraged governments to modernize their education and training systems. Although labour market reforms started long before the crisis, the EU's pressure in favour of continued reforms particularly influenced those countries who have faced resistance – notably from unions – in the past. Italy's 2015 "Job Act" and the "Lois Travail" adopted in France in 2016 and 2018 are illustrative of this. Operating a

Table 7.3 Labour market reforms in 11 member states since 2000

Country	Total reform effort per year		
	2000–07	2008–09	2009–14
Greece	2.3	9.5	12.0
Italy	3.4	7.5	14.6
France	4.8	11.5	7.6
Germany	6.0	8.0	3.4
The Netherlands	4.1	4.0	7.2
Sweden	5.5	5.0	5.2
Ireland	3.0	7.5	7.6
United Kingdom	3.9	13.0	9.0
Czech Republic	5.0	3.0	4.8
Slovakia	2.8	3.0	7.6
Slovenia	1.5	4.0	6.6

Source: Theodoropoulou (2018).
Note: The table shows the reform indicator elaborated by Theodoropoulou by dividing, for each given period considered, the total number of reforms by the number of years.

breakthrough on "flexibilizing" the labour market in the interest of employers, these reforms only offer limited results regarding new rights, increased security for workers, significant progressive reforms of education systems or of public services to assist job seekers. Theodoroupoulou's study on 11 EU countries (see Table 7.3) shows a clear acceleration of labour market reforms from 2008 onwards (Theodoropoulou 2018). Her "reform effort" index shows that deregulation and retrenchment have been most intense in Italy, Greece and the UK.

Rather than a proper convergence towards a single model, she detects a common direction towards recommodification to various extents. The early movers in implementing labour market reforms with robust welfare states (Czechia, Germany, the Netherlands, Sweden) were more prone to preserve an overall balance reached in the early 2000s, whereas those who had often met resistance from unions in the past (France, Italy, Slovenia) proceeded to significant readjustment of welfare benefits and flexibilization. Governments under the constraints of bailouts (Greece, Ireland), as well as the UK, enforced outright retrenchment. Overall, reforms rooted in the prism of "activation" and flexicurity have mainly undermined the security of insiders in the labour market, rather than improved pay and working conditions for outsiders (Arpe *et al.* 2015). Social investment constitutes a prism for the reforms only in a group of eight countries in continental Europe and Scandinavia with historically more robust welfare states and who have fared better through the great recession of the 2010s (Bouget *et al.* 2015).

Instead, inequalities have been on the rise in most EU countries and the proportion of working poor has reached 9.4 per cent of the labour force on average in the EU in 2020. This is largely due to part-time work, the precarious nature of newly created jobs in the services sector and the rise of poorly remunerated independent work in a decade where Europeans are enduring two successive recessions (the euro crisis and the current health crisis as a result of Covid-19) (ETUI 2020). Overall, EU coordination through the European Semester has created a diffuse pressure to comply with fiscal discipline and revise social regulation in a way supposedly conducive of growth and competitiveness; but there has been considerable variation in the pace and nature of implementation of structural reforms (Agostini *et al.* 2017: 109–10).

The European Semester in flux in the era of resilience and recovery

When Jean-Claude Juncker took office in 2014 as president of the European Commission, he stated that he wanted the EU to have a "triple A" on social issues. In this regard, the main proposition – and as a matter of fact the main trademark for the Commission's social ambition – has been the EPSR (see Box 7.4). Essentially a catalogue of rights, the nature of the EPSR as a policy instrument of the EU was as new as it was unclear. Just like the European Semester, it relies on both hard and soft law. Although the notion of social rights seems to refer to a legal concept, none of the provisions included in the EPSR are formulated as rights, let alone enforceable rights in front of courts (De Schutter 2021; Sabato & Vanhercke 2017). NGOs consulted pointed out the risk of discrepancy between high expectations and insurmountable limitations linked to the weakness of the EU's competences in social policy and the lack of political will for these rights to materialize through national policy (Sabato & Vanhercke 2017; De Schutter 2021). The EPSR was nevertheless proclaimed and endorsed by 28 EU heads of state and government at the Gothenburg Social Summit in November 2017. This was, however, essentially symbolic and did not lift the reluctance of many member-state leaders to see the EU play a greater role in social policy. Debates over the EP resolution in the assembly revealed clear conflict lines on European social policy. The rapporteur from the Socialists and Democrats Group, Maria João Rodrigues, was supported by the Radical Left and the Greens in putting forward an ambitious vision of the EPSR conducive to binding instruments, for instance a guarantee to tackle child poverty (see Chapter 8). Coupled with opposition from Eurosceptic groups, it was striking to see how the large groups of Liberals (the Alliance of Liberals and Democrats for Europe [ALDE]) and the Conservatives (EPP) split over the vote. Within

BOX 7.4 THE EUROPEAN PILLAR OF SOCIAL RIGHTS

The European Pillar of Social Rights (EPSR) is a catalogue of 20 principles assembled in three chapters: (a) equal opportunities and access to the labour market, (b) equitable working conditions and (c) adequate and sustainable social protection. It was put forward by the European Commission in April 2017 and then proclaimed by heads of states and governments at the Gothenburg Social Summit of November 2017.

Like social rights in the European Charter of Fundamental Rights, these principles are not directly enforceable. The EPSR relies on two routes to make these rights effective: European hard law, as the EU adopts social regulation; and soft law, whereby member states commit to take action through soft coordination. So far, the EPSR has yielded four regulatory initiatives at European level:

- a directive (2019/1152) on transparent and predictable working conditions, obliging employers to provide more information to workers over their working contract;
- a directive on work–life balance for parents and carers that extends the rights to maternal and paternal leave and creates rights to leave for those who care for dependent relatives (2019/1158);
- a Council recommendation (non-legally binding) on access to social protection for workers and the self-employed in order to improve the social coverage of workers who have an atypical employment contract or who are self-employed (2019/C 387/01); and
- a directive proposal on adequate minimum wages aiming to introduce a clear framework for setting minimum wages at the national level – deliberations are ongoing at the time of writing.

Considering the soft-law implementation strand, the objectives of the EPSR are supposed to guide the monitoring and recommendations in the European Semester. In 2021, the European Commission submitted an "Action Plan" for ensuring the implementation of the EPSR. The plan, endorsed at the 2021 Social Summit in Porto, sets three targets:

- reaching an employment rate of 78 per cent by 2030;
- having 60 per cent of Europeans participating annually in training and promoting access to basic digital skills for at least 80 per cent of people aged 16–74; and
- reducing the number of people living in poverty or social exclusion by at least 15 million (compared to 2019 figures), including 5 million children, by 2030.

The plan also includes a range of national and EU policy instruments and resources to be used to achieve the objectives of the EPSR.

them, the delegations from the northern member states including Austria, Germany and the Netherlands, from the Visegrad countries, and to a lesser extent the Baltic countries, rebelled against the party line and voted against the resolution (Vesan & Corti 2019).

Besides the Commission's regulatory initiatives (See Box 7.4), the main route envisaged for the implementation of the EPSR has been its combination with the European Semester, however it remains unclear how. Studies show that the EPSR has been used as a compass to further strengthen the salience of social issues in the European Semester. However, this has occurred in a partial and sometimes distorted manner, as indicators on the social scoreboard do not fully overlap with the rights mentioned in the EPSR (Sabato & Corti 2018). Moreover, if the EPSR is very present in the analytical documents of the Semester (the annual growth survey, the employment guidelines and the country reports), it tends to disappear at the political stage when country-specific recommendations are adopted (Adranghi *et al.* 2019). So far, the EPSR has mainly had a "symbolic" value for relaunching the EU social policy agenda, combining and attempting to bring all EU social policy initiatives under one roof; as in the past, the inspiration seems to come from the Nordic model, which combines a universal tax-financed strong welfare protection with social partners' autonomy and competitiveness in global capitalism (De la Porte 2019a). The ongoing Covid-19 pandemic and the ensuing recovery agenda of the EU institutions have brought about a new constellation and both the 2020 German presidency and the 2021 Portuguese presidency have pledged to make the EPSR's implementation a priority. In March 2021, the European Commission put forward the European Pillar of Social Rights Action Plan (European Commission 2021), which consists essentially of four components. First, it sets three overarching specific policy goals in the form of targets to be met by 2030 (see Box 7.4); second, it specifies the actions that the EU institutions and national governments should undertake to reach the objectives of the EPSR; third, it explains which EU resources (i.e. funds ranging from cohesion policy to the ESF and the Recovery and Resilience Facility) can be used to support these actions; fourth, it includes a revised social scoreboard to allow the monitoring of progress in the EPS implementation in the framework of the European Semester. Time will tell whether the EPSR can serve to address the entrenched asymmetry in the EU's action away from market-making and in favour of market correction and social cohesion.

To be sure, the coming of age of NextGenerationEU – a recovery package of €750 billion coupled with the EU budget for 2021–27 – opens a historic window of opportunity for strengthening fiscal solidarity, redistribution (see Chapter 8) and European social policy. The belief that the EU should give a new impetus for social cohesion was largely embraced by the Von der Leyen Commission in office since October 2019. Furthermore, social issues have only become more acute with the outbreak of the Covid-19 pandemic and its socio-economic consequences. Along with the ECB's pandemic emergency purchase programme, the European Semester has been at the centre of the EU's reaction to the recession in many ways.

A first dimension concerns the turn from fiscal discipline to fiscal stimulus. As the coronavirus pandemic brought European economies to a halt in the spring of 2020, an immediate consequence has been the suspension of the rules of the Stability and Growth Pact. As employment was almost instantly hit, governments released large-scale fiscal stimulus packages, causing public expenditure to skyrocket. On 20 March 2020, Ursula von der Leyen proposed to invoke the Stability and Growth Pact's general escape clause. Owing to the protracted pandemic, the fiscal strand of the European Semester has therefore been frozen in 2020 and 2021. Yet, soon enough political discussions about whether the pact needs to be reactivated and how to reactivate it will be resumed and old conflict lines within the Commission and the Council alike are very likely to resurface. Even before the outbreak of the pandemic, there had been many calls to revise the EU framework for fiscal coordination, notably from the Socialists and the Democrats. The idea had been embraced by the Commission under the aegis of the commissioner for economic and financial affairs, Paolo Gentiloni, an Italian from the Partito Democratico. In the face of a skyrocketing deficit, at 5.8 per cent of GDP, and an average debt level at 89.8 per cent of GDP,[4] it remains uncertain whether one can expect a major overhaul of the Stability and Growth Pact to bring it in line with the recovery and investment turn taken by the EU as a whole. At the time of writing, contentious debates between fiscal "hawks" and advocates of a deep reform of the EU fiscal rules are still ongoing.

A second point of intersection between the recovery agenda and the European Semester stems from the fact that the grants distributed through the Recovery and Resilience Facility – the main financial instrument within NextGenerationEU – will occur through the Semester. In fact, the 2021 cycle of the European Semester is undergoing a drastic change. Neither country reports nor specific recommendations will be adopted; instead, its highlight will be the adoption of the national recovery and resilience plans that have been intensively discussed with the Commission and outline how the recovery funds will be spent. This distributive metamorphosis of the Semester is nevertheless a double-edged sword as the established fiscal and macroeconomic surveillance are not suppressed. On the contrary, Article 10 of the regulation on the Recovery and Resilience Facility (European Union 2021) introduces macroeconomic conditionality. Clearly it links the facility with compliance to the rules on deficit and

---

4. The respective figures for the eurozone are 5.8 and 97.3 per cent, see https://ec.europa.eu/ eurostat/documents/portlet_file_entry/2995521/2-21012021-AP-EN.pdf/a3748b22-e96e-7f62- ba05-11c7192e32f3 (accessed 15 June 2021).

debt, and the Council – on the recommendation of the Commission – can decide to suspend the payment of the funds. Moreover, Article 19 stipulates that the national resilience and recovery plans shall "contribute to effectively addressing all or a significant subset of challenges identified in the relevant country-specific recommendations" (European Union 2021). This seems to establish a new kind of structural-reform conditionality (see Chapter 8). The European Semester will, therefore, further shape social policy by determining the fiscal conditions and the political direction of its implementation at the national level.

Finally, there are grounds for concerns relating to democratic legitimacy. Reproducing the bias of the OMC, the Semester has remained, to a large extent, a bureaucratic exercise serving to consolidate a European administrative space (through intense dialogue between the EU Commission and national administrations). Over the years, it has gained almost no salience in national political arenas (Papadopoulos & Piattoni 2019; Vanheuverzwijn & Crespy 2018), with overall little ownership among national parliaments, the social partners and the grassroots within civil society. The fact that both the EP and national parliaments were held at bay by fiscal and socio-economic coordination had already been problematic in the past. Christina Fasone, for instance, argued that the European Semester encroaches massively on the powers of the EP to control the expenditure of the EU, hence undermining the idea that there should be "no taxation without parliamentary representation" (Fasone 2014: 172). Before the onset of the pandemic, there had been reflections within the EU institutions over a major overhaul aiming at making the Semester more legitimate (Leino-Sandberg & Losada Fraga 2020). In this regard, the governance of the Recovery and Resilience Facility is highly problematic. Crudely put, the EP is only given the role of a "talking shop". In the name of transparency, the MEPs will have access to all relevant documents and they "may invite the Commission every two months to discuss" all stages of the procedure in the framework of the established "recovery and resilience dialogue" (Article 26) (European Union 2021). But nowhere is a formal role for the EP in actual decision-making foreseen: it is the Commission and the Council who remain in the driving seat. This is all the more problematic as NextGenerationEU implies key collective redistributive choices with a major impact on welfare states in a significant number of member states (Crum 2020). As it stands, those choices will have no parliamentary democratic basis.

Conclusion

By tracing its development since its origins in the 1990s, this chapter has shown that European socio-economic coordination has always been instrumental in reshaping welfare states in ways that were necessarily politically loaded. In the time of non-binding coordination with the EES and the OMC, the EU served as a laboratory of policy recipes. Unavoidably, the arena of soft coordination became a field of ideological conflict between the advocates of reforms inspired by neoliberal retrenchment (the Anglo-liberal model), on one hand, and those of social-democratic modernization (the Nordic model), on the other, and everything in-between (the Dutch and German models). Whether national leaders strategically used Europe to pursue their own reformist agenda or whether they were (or felt) genuinely constrained by the *"vincolo esterno"* remains an object for investigation. The overall direction for reforms, however, led to the recommodification of labour and societies.

With the inception of the European Semester in 2011, social policy was largely subsumed into fiscal and economic coordination. Instead of addressing the "displacement" of social policy to the fiscal and economic field, the European Semester accentuated it (Dawson 2018), thereby further curtailing its "semi-autonomy" vis-à-vis the market imperative (Streeck 2019). Stubborn austerity and the social disaster orchestrated by the Troika in bailout countries after 2009 will remain a dark page of the EU's recent history. Across the EU more broadly, ambiguous "structural reforms" have served to recalibrate welfare states in a way that was compatible with the lack of fiscal revenue faced by governments. The coming of age of NextGenerationEU is altering the very nature of socio-economic coordination profoundly. The European Semester is no longer only – or primarily – a regulatory instrument for ensuring fiscal discipline: it has now become a distributive instrument for guiding investment. This new mechanism for fiscal solidarity also means more European/multilateral constraint on national social policy, as creditors' countries will aim to ensure that EU money is spent "responsibly" by recipients in the southern and eastern periphery. From a policy point of view, this raises the question of whether the policy reforms encouraged will actually bring about a green modernization of sluggish economies. From a democratic point of view, NextGenerationEU reproduces and accentuates the lack of representative legitimizing basis, with neither national parliaments nor the EP being conferred substantial decision-making powers. Considering that coordination through the European Semester will now rely on European common fiscal resources (and debt!), it seems to contradict the notion inherited from the American Revolution that there should be "no taxation without representation". Finally, leading us to the redistributive issues addressed in the following chapter, the ability of the recovery funds to effectively foster social cohesion within and between societies will certainly have an influence on whether or not the resources from the recovery package will be made continuously available after 2027.

Further reading

- Paul Copeland, *Governance and the European Social Dimension* (Abingdon: Routledge, 2020).
- Caroline de la Porte and Bruno Palier, "The politics of European Union social investment initiatives". In Julian L. Garritzmann, Silja Hausermann and Bruno Palier (eds), *The World Politics of Social Investment* (Oxford: Oxford University Press, 2021).
- Bart Vanhercke, "From the Lisbon Strategy to the European Pillar of Social Rights: the many lives of the social open method of coordination". In Bart Vanhercke *et al.* (eds), *Social Policy in the European Union 1999–2019: The Long and Winding Road* (Brussels: ETUI, 2020), 99–123.

Questions to debate

- Has the OMC had an effective impact on welfare states?
- Has the European Semester become more "social" over time?

8

IS REDISTRIBUTION UNCONDITIONAL?

Contrary to national welfare states, social policy at the EU level focuses primarily on regulation rather than redistribution. However, the EU does pursue a redistributive policy in the form of EU funds, notably the European Social Fund (ESF). Generally, a redistributive policy consists of transferring resources from the wealthiest territories, social groups or individuals to those who are the least well-off, with the aim of reducing inequalities and ensuring a sufficient level of social and territorial cohesion. Typically, this occurs as fiscal revenue is being collected in a central budget, which can then be redistributed in different ways. In the case of the EU, with a budget capped at around 1 per cent of the GDP over recent decades, its redistributive capacity has nevertheless remained very limited. This reflects the fact that, unlike national states, the EU does not enjoy strong legitimacy to act as a redistributive authority.

As early as 1957, Article 123 of the Treaty of Rome establishing the EEC had forecast the creation of an ESF that "shall have the task of promoting within the Community employment facilities and the geographical and occupational mobility of workers", particularly for those from the poorest regions of the six member states.[1] Today an integral part of European "cohesion policy", the ESF is enshrined in Title XI TFEU. It has been the main social policy instrument of the EU, amounting to approximately 10 per cent of the total EU budget since the 1990s. Along with four other funds,[2] the ESF has been integrated into the European structural and investment funds, thus underlining that it should serve as a tool to implement a broad socio-economic strategy rather than as an instrument of unconditional redistributive solidarity. Two smaller funds with social objectives deserve to be mentioned here. The European Globalization Adjustment Fund (EGF), created in 2006, provides support to people who lose their jobs as a result of firms relocating

---

1. Treaty Establishing the European Economic Community (Rome, 25 March 1957), www.cvce.eu (accessed 15 September 2021).
2. The European Regional Development Fund, the Cohesion Fund, the European Agricultural Fund for Rural Development, and the European Maritime and Fisheries Fund.

production activities outside the EU. Since 2014, the Fund for European Aid to the Most Deprived supports national programmes providing food and material assistance to people in need. All three funds have undergone recent reforms, and they have seen their resources increased and their missions enlarged to help alleviate the social consequences of the coronavirus pandemic.

With a few exceptions (Bachtler & Mendez 2020), there is little literature jointly addressing the issues of redistribution and conditionality or raising broader normative debates in relation to EU social funds. Scholarship on cohesion policy tends to be rather praxis-oriented and studies on the ESF focus predominantly on implementation and effectiveness, often through a Europeanization lens (e.g. Bussi *et al.* 2019; Van Gerven *et al.* 2014; Zimmermann 2016). This chapter shifts the focus by asking whether redistribution in the EU has become conditional. Is financial solidarity a condition *sine qua non* of integration or is it at threat due to lack of results and political disagreements? The objectives underlying political ideas and governance arrangements of EU cohesion policy are examined with a particular focus on the ESF. It is argued that, despite the elusive nature of socio-economic convergence, redistribution is here to stay. Yet, it has come under increased political and institutional pressure. By incentivizing partnership, evaluation and various forms of conditionality through a multi-level bureaucracy, the transformation of the ESF over time has aimed to generate the support of all involved actors – from governments to local project holders – for a common unified socio-economic strategy, from the Lisbon Strategy to Europe 2020 (see Chapter 7) and now the recovery and green agenda. On one hand, ensuring that the funds target certain policy areas can help increase policy coherence and effective implementation. On the other hand, using the funds (and their possible suspension) as a stick to ensure compliance with principles exogenous to cohesion policy has proved a divisive and largely ineffective strategy. In that regard, the EU budget for 2021–27, which features the historical deal on an additional €750 billion recovery package dubbed "NextGenerationEU", confirms the trend whereby more financial solidarity is accompanied by more conditionality regarding, for instance, the implementation of "structural reforms" or compliance with the rule of law.

From regional convergence to investment and resilience

Economic transformations and elusive convergence

The idea that convergence and cohesion should be fostered through redistribution dates back to the origins of European unification. However, this was never meant to be unconditional redistribution. Like the other funds established later, the ESF has been reshaped over time to respond to economic transformations and challenges, on the one hand, and to the successive enlargements of the EEC (and then the EU), which only increased the necessity of redistribution, on the other.

From the outset, the ESF was conceived as a tool for adapting human capital to changes in the productive structure at the regional scale. Regulation 9/EEC/ 1960, which sets out the criteria and conditions for the operational functioning of the ESF, aimed at achieving the "vocational rehabilitation" of workers who were unemployed as a result of industrial modernization that, more often than not, led to redundancies. After the postwar reconstruction boom and until the 1980s, the function of the ESF was therefore twofold. First, it was to control and ensure the mobility of the workforce from the poorest areas with high unemployment rates to the wealthier industrial regions in need of labour force. Second, the fund aimed at facilitating the (re)-qualification of workers in order to accompany economic modernization through a policy of vocational training at the scale of the single market. At the beginning of the EEC,

> the European social fund was mostly aimed at reducing unemployment in the Mezzogiorno and at providing vocational training to Italian workers in Germany, France and Belgium. Between 1961 and 1973, more than 1,700,000 workers benefited from the social fund. Italy was the largest beneficiary (65 per cent) along with Germany (25.5 per cent).
> (Leboutte 2008: 655–6)

In 1973, enlargement to the north (the UK, Ireland, Denmark) increased the needs of the ESF with the conversion of industrial regions in the north of England. The two oil shocks of the 1970s reinforced the crisis of the manufacturing sector and further widened the scope of the ESF's action. Back then, the ESF was both anchored in the logic of state intervention and in the redistributive logic of convergence between European territories. In the 1980s, the southern enlargement to Greece (1981), Spain and Portugal (1986) significantly increased the demand for such policies. The accession of regions with much lower levels of development meant increased flows of workers from the south to the north of Europe. Alongside other structural funds, the ESF then had to help offset the negative effects of increased competition within the common market on the poorer regions.

Starting at the end of the 1980s, the ESF entered a new era amid effects of globalization coupled with the launch of the EMU at the European level. French socialist president Mitterrand relinquishing a radically Keynesian policy and the Thatcher era in the UK (along with Reagan in the United States) paved the way for Europe's gradual conversion to neoliberalism. The European Single Act of 1986 and then the Maastricht Treaty accelerated the deepening of the single market, based on a far-reaching liberalization not only of goods but also of capital and financial services. In the 1990s, all European countries faced the relocation of productive and industrial activities to regions with cheap labour, mainly outside of Europe, and the mass unemployment that came with it. Among other regions, the East German *Länder*, which joined the EEC following German reunification, received massive aid to cope with the necessary conversion of their industry and high unemployment rate.[3] In 2000, the Lisbon Strategy promoted by the EU aimed at maintaining the competitiveness of the old continent in the face of globalization by accelerating the European conversion to the knowledge economy based on information and communication technologies.

Rather than a redistributive policy, or an instrument of regional convergence driven by Brussels, the ESF progressively developed into the financial arm of the coordination of national employment policies. This was made clear in 1997 with the EES, which inspired the OMC and subsequently the Lisbon Strategy. In parallel, the move towards the single currency increased pressure on certain member states, especially those in the south, to reform their welfare state in order to meet the convergence criteria on debt and public deficit for membership in the EMU. In this respect, transfers via the ESF aimed at alleviating the effects of convergence on public finances rather than facilitating socio-economic convergence as such. The enlargements to central and eastern Europe, and the Baltics, in 2004 and 2007 respectively, put regional convergence further out of reach because of the accession of regions whose average per capita income was significantly lower than the European average.

The 2008–10 financial and debt crisis and the ensuing recession accentuated the challenges faced by the EU. Not only did unemployment and inequalities rise across the board, but imbalances in welfare also increased between the countries of Europe's wealthy core in the centre and north of the continent and the peripheries of the southern, Baltic, central and eastern parts. With the exception of Ireland, the crisis also revealed that the peripheries' convergence in socio-economic development had only been moderate. In spite of the EU's structural funds amounting to over 1.5 per cent of southern and eastern member states' GDP, EU cohesion funds "have not reached their objectives of reducing the gap to poorer and richer regions. This is due in part because the funds are not targeted at the least developed regions in the peripheries" (Makszin *et al.* 2020: 343). On a different note, Thomas Piketty, for instance, has questioned

---

3. Bundesministerium für Arbeit und Soziales, *Le Fonds social européen a 60 ans – Des investissements dans le capital humain*, www.bmas.de/SharedDocs/Downloads/DE/Publikationen/37850-le-fonds-social-europeen-a-60-ans.pdf;jsessionid=9D6ED394EA1A283F43D45776E925BCA2. delivery1-replication?__blob=publicationFile&v=2 (accessed 15 September 2021).

the redistributive nature of the East–West relationship by pointing to the fact that amounts of capital flowing out of central and eastern Europe because of profit-making by foreign (read "western") companies were by far exceeding the benefits of cohesion policy (Makszin *et al.* 2020: 350). Furthermore, the harsh social conditionality attached to both the EU's and the IMF's financial assistance to over-indebted countries aggravated rather than alleviated the social impact of the recession, with especially concerning outcomes in southern Europe facing skyrocketing levels of youth unemployment, among other problems.

In the context of broad economic transformations and the challenges Europe has consequentially been confronted with, the policy objectives of the ESF have become increasingly dependent on a cohesion strategy focused on performing labour markets rather than inequality as such.

From regional policy to employment policy

The 60-year history of the ESF reflects an evolution from a regional cohesion approach to the fund becoming an instrument of employment policy and social investment, even if its redistributive logic means targeting the most economically challenged regions. The operational functioning of the ESF became increasingly subordinate to the overall socio-economic strategy of the EU through synergies with other European funds and soft law, particularly after 2000.

The origins of the ESF were purely intergovernmental, with states contributing directly to the fund (rather than through the European Commission's budget) and the fund reimbursing retroactively the expenditures made by governments in the three areas defined by the 1960 regulation: industrial conversion, resettlement and requalification of workers. This procedure favoured a logic of fair return by which member states tried first and foremost to recover the sums they had contributed, while European institutions had no power to define the objectives or the use of the fund. Gradually, the regional approach was supplanted by an approach of employment policy directed primarily at individuals (Leboutte 2008: 663). The most significant reform of the ESF occurred in 1988 under the impulse of then European Commission president Jacques Delors and put the ESF under the banner of the structural funds all co-managed by the European Commission, in charge of programming and control, and regional authorities responsible for implementation. At that time, the resources of the ESF were significantly increased from just over 4 per cent of the European Commission budget in the 1960s to 8–10 per cent in the 1990s (Leboutte 2008: 661).

In terms of policy objectives, the paradigm of equal opportunities and inclusion in relation to labour markets became prominent, with specific programmes such as NOW or EQUAL aiming respectively at integrating women in the labour market or fighting discrimination based on gender, ethnic origin, religion, dis-ability, age or sexual orientation. The ESF was thus used to promote the ambi-tious European policy for gender equality started in the 1970s. From the 1990s onwards, however, the strategy of "gender mainstreaming", emphasizing the inclusion of gender-related concerns horizontally through all policy initiatives, contributed to diluting the objectives and the resources that had made European Commission policy successful in this realm (Jacquot 2015; Pochet 2019: 104–7). Since 2007, anti-discrimination programmes have been separated from social policies and connected to fundamental rights policies under the tutelage of the European Commission's DG Justice. In the period from 2014 to 2020, the Rights, Equality and Citizenship programme funded projects previously funded by programmes such as EQUAL. According to Sophie Jacquot, the transition of the European gender equality policy from a model based on discrimination (particularly in relation to the labour market) to a model focused on fundamental rights has further continued to weaken the EU's policy of equality between men and women in the EU (Jacquot 2015).

A main trend characterizing the 2007–13 as well as the 2014–20 ESF pro-gramming periods has been the subordination of the ESF to the Lisbon Strategy (later Europe 2020) around the core objective of investment (Sbaraglia 2018: 89). Structural funds, including the ESF, became the EU's financial instrument aimed at assisting member states to achieve the quantified targets on employment rates (75 per cent), investment in research and development (3 per cent), climate change (20 per cent of renewable energy), education (10 per cent reduction in school system exit rate) and poverty alleviation (20 million fewer people affected or threatened).

Redistribution in times of crises

Against the background of the great recession after 2010, the ESF became key in encouraging policies of social investment (see Box 8.1) in line with the recommendations for reforms formulated in the framework of the European Semester (see Chapter 7). Since the mid-2000s, social investment had been promoted within European policy circles by a group of experts and academics who saw it as a progressive strategy for welfare state reform in Europe. Embracing this approach, then commissioner for employment and social affairs within the Barroso II Commission, László Andor, pushed for the publication of the "Social Investment Package" (European Commission 2013) in 2013 in an attempt to balance the EU's response to the crisis. In this package, the Commission proposed that 25 per cent of structural funds be used by member states to finance social investment in human capital and identified the ESF budget lines that may be

BOX 8.1 SOCIAL INVESTMENT

The paradigm of social investment appeared towards the end of the 1990s, based on a shared diagnosis among social policy specialists not only concerning long-term unemployment, increasing inequalities and the rising number of poor workers, but also the lack of adequate qualifications among the population and effective social services in many countries. This situation is explained by the fact that welfare states designed in the twentieth century fail to address adequately new social risks such as an ageing population, an increasing number of single-parent families, insecure employment contracts and rapid skill depletion in the face of technological change.

Social investment therefore aims to operate a social policy shift from a logic of *ex post* compensation through cash transfers to a logic of *ex ante* individuals' adaptation to new social risks. This is only possible with adequate investment in services helping individuals to improve their capabilities. Social investment is based on valuing human development (through education, early childhood policies and continuing education) and the effective use of human capital in labour markets (through measures supporting, for example, women and single parents, through so-called job-seeker activation policies). It also implies fostering the inclusion of disadvantaged or discriminated groups.

The concept of social investment has been irrigated by different theoretical and ideological traditions ranging from the neoliberal approach of Anthony Giddens stressing individual responsibility, to the leftist libertarian approach of Len Doyal and Ian Gough, emphasizing individuals' needs for health, freedom and autonomy, to the mid-way Rawlsian, social-democratic conception of Gosta Esping-Andersen focused on equal opportunities. Overall, social investment has failed to be acknowledged as a new alternative paradigm replacing the classical Keynesian–Beveridgean welfare state and the succeeding neoliberal critique (Hemerijck 2016).

At EU level, the promotion of social investment has remained elusive and it has relied on ambiguous and changing political motivations over time (De la Porte 2019b). Rather than serving progressive paradigmatic change, it has arguably been absorbed into the broader EU social-liberal agenda focusing on the "activation" of workers and adapting society to the requirements of global capitalism, notably a highly skilled labour force coping with flexible labour markets.

Since the mid-2010s, however, the need to invest in children and young people is making its way on to the EU political agenda.

used to this end. Recommended targeted investments should be aimed at three objectives: ensuring an adequate level of income; combatting inequalities and gender discrimination; and ensuring the effectiveness of social services, with a special emphasis placed on investments targeting children and young people. It is, however, not clear whether EU policy could make a difference in spurring on social investment. A report from 2015 shows that social investment policies are only implemented in a group of nine northern and continental European countries that have historically robust welfare states (AT, BE, DE, DK, FI, FR, NL, SE, SI). Nine EU countries (CY, ES, HU, IE, LU, MT, PL, PT, UK) exhibit an increased awareness but only piecemeal reforms towards social investment, whereas in the last group of ten member states, no tangible social investment policy can be detected (BG, CZ, EE, EL, HR, IT, LT, LV, RO, SK).[4]

A second important initiative spurred on by the European Commission amid the recession is the introduction of the Youth Guarantee through a Council recommendation (on the Commission's initiative) in 2013 (see Box 8.2). The Youth Guarantee was set up to tackle the high youth unemployment rate, which had increased from 15.9 per cent in 2007 to 22.2 per cent in 2012 with record peaks in southern European countries. In line with social investment, the purpose was to pour public resources into training and education rather than into unemployment benefits. More specifically, its purpose is to ensure that all young people under the age of 25 receive an offer of employment, continuing education, apprenticeship or internship less than four months after they have left school or their jobs. In other words, the aim is to reduce the number of young people not in education, employment or training (called NEETs). The guarantee revolves around three types of actions: (a) a partnership between public authorities, public and private unemployment service agencies, institutions in the field of education and training and youth and social partners; (b) creating structures for reaching out to young people and ensuring their inclusion in the Youth Guarantee programme and personalized guidance; and (c) facilitating the integration of young people into the labour market by targeting those who have dropped out of school and creating tax incentives for the hiring of young people.

Looking at the big picture, three critiques can be levelled at the EU's social investment strategy. First, the resources clearly earmarked for social investment have remained too limited to address the needs. Second, while there have been scattered means and initiatives, the EU institutions have not made social investment a main priority articulated in a coherent discourse or programme. Third, the vision of social investment promoted by the EU has been

---

4. See Eurostat glossary for country codes, https://ec.europa.eu/eurostat/statistics-explained/index.php?title=Glossary:Country_codes (accessed 15 September 2021)

BOX 8.2 THE YOUTH GUARANTEE

The Youth Guarantee is a hybrid instrument that combines financial resources through the ESF with the soft coordination of national policies. The initiative was adopted by a Council recommendation that, unlike directives and regulations, is not legally binding but relies on a commitment by member states to implement the policy. The funding comes mainly from national resources but the EU budget has provided non-negligible support through both the ESF and a specific financial instrument, the youth employment initiative, which was created to support regions with a youth unemployment rate above 25 per cent. Taken together, both sources of funding have provided €15.1 billion to support implementation in regions most in need.

Evaluations show that, along with a re-start of economic growth, the Youth Guarantee has contributed to a decline in the number of young people who are not in employment, education or training from 13.2 per cent in 2012 to 10.9 per cent in 2017. Yet the Commission pointed to a slow and uneven implementation across member states and ETUC, together with some MEPs, deplored that it failed to address the magnitude of the problem. Before the outbreak of the coronavirus pandemic, youth unemployment was still above 20 per cent in seven member states, peaking above 40 per cent in Spain and Greece. One of the main problems is the sustainability of the jobs on offer, since many young people are offered a temporary contract, having then to return to the Youth Guarantee programme.

In the face of the new recession caused by the coronavirus pandemic, in October 2020, the Council adopted a new recommendation for a "reinforced Youth Guarantee", extending the mechanism to the 15–29 age group. EU-level financial support will stem from the ESF+ (within the 2021–27 budget), as well as from the additional funds under the recovery plan NextGenerationEU.

a narrow one, focusing on labour market participation and efficiency gains in a context where the resources available for social policy have shrunk. In recent years, however, policy debates on equality and poverty have gained ground across EU institutions. In-work poverty has been increasingly addressed by the European Commission and since 2015 the EP, under the impetus of the Socialists and Democrats Group, has pushed for the establishment of a child guarantee. Following the diagnosis that one in five children in Europe suffers from poverty, the guarantee would ensure that all children have access to free, quality healthcare, education and childcare, decent housing and adequate nutrition. In fact, a Council recommendation called "Investing in Children" was adopted in 2013 but – as might be expected of the combination of a non-binding instrument with no actual resources – it bore little fruit. MEPs therefore asked that a new financial instrument – modelled on the Youth Guarantee – be established; a demand that was endorsed by Ursula von der Leyen and included in the work programme of the European Commission with a proposal expected for 2021.

The adoption of the 2021–27 budget together with the €750 billion in response to the Covid-19 pandemic opens a new era under the motto of "recovery and resilience". In that framework, the ESF is redeployed under the label ESF+ to encompass all previously existing social funds.[5] In addition, REACT-EU (Recovery Assistance for Cohesion and the Territories of Europe), a fund set up in 2020 and endowed with €47.5 billion, will channel further resources to all cohesion funds, including the ESF. Its aim is to alleviate the impact of the recession caused by the Covid-19 pandemic through support to job maintenance, short-term work schemes, support to the self-employed, the fight against youth unemployment or support to vulnerable people. The final set up of the ESF+ was highly disputed between the Council and the EP. The latter was successful in its endeavours to preserve a significant amount of resources and secure the earmarking of money towards certain priorities, particularly youth unemployment and child poverty, thereby prefiguring the adoption of the above-mentioned child guarantee supported by EU funds.

Thus, in the current turbulent context in which Europe is facing social challenges more acute than ever, the ESF seems to be chasing three sets of policy goals at the same time in pursuing its long-standing agenda centred on "skills" and social inclusion, tackling the effects of the current recession in terms of job losses and poverty rise and substantiating the EPSR. It remains to be seen whether these three agendas can fully overlap and be conducive for coherent, effective policy outcomes.

In a nutshell, cohesion policy and the ESF in particular were never envisaged as being mere redistribution tools towards poorer individuals and territories. Rather, the ESF was from the outset focused on the functioning of labour markets and human capital. Redistribution through the EU budget always depended on the EU's response to broader economic transformations. The next section explains how the governance of the ESF was conceived to ensure member states' compliance with the policy objectives promoted by the EU institutions.

---

5. The ESF, the Youth Employment Initiative, the Fund for European Aid to the Most Deprived, the Employment and Social Innovation Programme.

Planning redistribution through multi-level governance

Budgetary programming and broad operational principles

The implementation of ESF-funded social policies is one of the most illustrative examples of European multi-level governance. In such an arrangement, financial solidarity must respond to careful planning to make sure that the money spent serves policy objectives commonly agreed. The life cycle of the ESF extends from financial programming decided by European institutions to implementation at the local level, through to the partnership between the European Commission, the states and the regions around action programmes. The purpose is to ensure that actors at all levels of governance gear towards the policy objectives defined within the framework of EU cohesion policy, and hence in the way they employ EU funds.

Making decisions on EU funds is part of the EU's multi-annual financial framework, negotiated every six years. The policy objectives and operational principles for the spending of funds are defined in a general regulation as well as fund-specific regulations. The Commission and EP generally request more ambitious financial commitments, whereas member states try to limit their financial contribution to the EU budget. This was especially the case after the 2008 financial crisis. For the period 2014–20, €325 billion was allocated to cohesion policy (23 per cent of which went to the ESF), which represented a 9 per cent decrease compared to the previous period 2007–13. This was owing to an exacerbated tension between creditor states of the north and west looking to limit their contribution and ensure the budgetary discipline of recipients, and the southern and eastern states with more acute needs for financial support as a result of the recession (Baun & Marek 2014: 95–6). In 2020, negotiations over the multi-annual financial framework included the adoption of an exceptional recovery plan, effectively increasing the total EU budget for 2021–27 to €1.8 trillion. The heated negotiations between the Council and the EP discussions concluded in November resulted in almost €88 billion for the ESF+, which is approximately 8.2 per cent of the overall EU budget for 2021–27 and 23 per cent of all EU cohesion policy funds.

All structural and investment funds rely on a set of common principles. First, the redistributive aspect of cohesion policy is reflected by the fact that allocation formulae aim to direct the bulk of the money to regions most in need by distinguishing three categories: (a) the less developed regions with a GDP per capita below 75 per cent of the European average, which are located in the countries of central and eastern Europe, including Latvia, as well as Greece, Portugal, southern Italy and southern Spain; (b) transition regions with a GDP per capita between 75 and 90 per cent of the EU average, which are essentially located in France, East Germany, Spain, Italy, the Baltic region, Finland, the Czech Republic, Slovenia and Cyprus; and (c) the more developed regions in continental Europe and Scandinavia with a GDP per capita over 90 per cent of the EU average (2019). For 2021–27, allocation will also take into consideration further criteria such as levels of youth unemployment, education, greenhouse gas emissions or the reception and integration of migrants. ESF+ resources will also be more important for regions with a greater number of young people not in education, employment or training, or with more people at risk of poverty and social exclusion.

Furthermore, the distribution and use of the funds are regulated by a series of operational principles:

1. States must set up a *partnership* with the representatives of regional, local and urban or other competent authorities along with the economic and social partners, as well as relevant bodies representing civil society (including environmental partners, NGOs and organizations promoting social inclusion, gender equality and non-discrimination), while ensuring that the most representative actors are involved.
2. The principle of *additionality* means that projects cannot be financed entirely by European funds. These come in addition to sources of national funding, the proportion of which varies depending on the level of socio-economic development of the target regions (a maximum of 50 per cent for more developed regions, 60 per cent for regions in transition and 80 per cent for less developed regions; although some states, such as France for its overseas territories, complement this co-financing rate to 85 per cent with own resources).
3. *Complementarity* aims at eliminated duplication between the various funds and sources of funding.
4. *Subsidiarity* states that policies must be implemented at the territorial level closest to citizens and that the competencies of local, regional and national authorities must be fully respected.
5. According to the *programming* principle, the use of funds must be decided by multi-annual programmes of action defined by member states in accordance with the objectives and strategic priorities of the EU.
6. The *concentration* principle implies funnelling funds to the regions that are most in need. *Thematic concentration* means that in 2014–20, 20 per cent of all ESF money had to be directed at fighting poverty and social exclusion.
7. The *proportionality* principle means that the EU must not do more than is necessary to meet its objectives. This entails using the means that are least constraining for the other levels of governance and being mindful of not creating undue bureaucratic or regulatory overload.

A bureaucratic partnership between multiple authorities

The principle of partnership that exemplifies multi-level governance comes with a series of institutional arrangements that fix the obligations and responsibilities of the authorities and actors in charge, from the negotiation of the budget to implementation and evaluation (see Table 8.1). The European Commission plays a key role in laying down a common strategic framework defining investment priorities. In the current programme, the emphasis is put on the green transition of the economy, the digitization of economic activities and tackling social issues relating to employment and inclusion. As explained above, the EU funds have increasingly been attached to macroeconomic coordination through soft law. The new period confirms this trend as the allocation of funds will be closely related to country-specific recommendations and national reform programmes made in the framework of the European Semester.

Once the priorities are set at EU level, member states adopt a *partnership agreement* negotiated with all regional actors and with the European Commission. The partnership agreement includes provisions relating to the strategy and modalities of the use of funds in line with the priorities for action, as well as more detailed elements relating to implementation. States must also establish an *operational programme* at the regional level, which defines priority areas for investment and/or thematic axes, as well as the target regions. These choices must be justified and supported by specific information on expected outcomes, the type of actions supported, implementation indicators, implementation phases and tables detailing the financing of the measures under consideration. The operational programme is discussed (or negotiated) between the regional authorities and the responsible DGs of the European Commission (mainly EMPL, the Department for Regional and Urban Policy [REGIO] and ENVI) (Sbaraglia 2018: 204) and is eventually approved by the Commission.

Table 8.1 Political cycle of the ESF

Process phase	Institutional arrangements
Budgetary programming	Intergovernmental negotiations + EP deliberation
Determining the strategic objectives	Vote on the regulations on the structural funds: community method (ordinary legislative procedure)
	Partnership agreement between the European Commission and each member state
Implementation	Negotiation and adoption of the operational programme
	Call for projects and selection of projects
	Actions on the ground by operators (or holders of recipient projects)
Evaluation and control	European Commission report on cohesion
Financial audit	By the European Court of Auditors and the competent regional authorities

The implementation of the ESF is supervised by a managing authority or agency, which represents public authorities. Depending on states' territorial organization, these agencies are run by central and/or regional authorities. At a more local level, *intermediary bodies* are charged with the management of global envelopes of ESF funds. In order to unlock the funds allocated to the regions, public, semi-public or private bodies are called on to submit projects. In the area of social policy (employment, training, early childhood services, elderly services, anti-discrimination, etc.) implementation is therefore mostly delegated to semi-public or private structures and civil society organizations. ESF money can be a heavy burden for project carriers at the local level who must dedicate an important share of their resources to mastering the managerial and bureaucratic process linked to setting up and implementing projects (Sbaraglia 2016).

When the European Commission carried out its evaluation for 2014–20, many stakeholders and consulted parties complained about the excessive burden of bureaucracy and overlap between different instruments leading to multiple applications and demands. In response, simplification was a main objective for the new programming period.

Does it work?

Effectiveness is a key question in the literature about cohesion policy. In spite of a clear trend towards carrying out ever-more policy evaluation both from within and outside the EU institutions, various studies and strands of scholarship are inconclusive as to the extent to which the EU funds produce the desired policy outcomes in terms of convergence and social cohesion.

Since 1996, for every financial programming period, the European Commission has conducted systematic *ex post* reviews of projects through its report on the cohesion policy. For the past two periods of programming, these evaluations consist of the verification that the use of funds has been efficient in reaching the objectives of the Europe 2020 strategy for lasting and inclusive growth. Overall, these reports detect a slow convergence in terms of GDP/capita, a trend interrupted by the financial crisis of 2008 and ensuing recession. Other studies have shown that the disparities between poor and rich regions within member states are growing. It is in fact extremely difficult to unravel the effectiveness of the structural funds from other more global factors such as the European economic situation or local political and economic conditions. A case in point is the exceptional socio-economic catch-up of Ireland, which is, to a large extent, the result of foreign investment (notably from America) and an aggressive fiscal policy rather than the product of EU cohesion policy. Along with broader socio-economic variables, the quality of governance at the national and local level is decisive. If anything, experts agree that the outcomes of cohesion policy depend significantly on the national and local contexts, and how specific institutional arrangements affect the implementation of the funds. This is not only about the capacity of local public administrations, but also about the existence of organizations within civil society that have the capacity to propose and obtain funding for projects. A key issue has been the absorption capacity, which measures the ratio between the sums made available to the regions and the amounts actually spent. As of December 2020, Romania, Croatia and Italy had only spent about 40 per cent and Spain 35 per cent of all the allocated EU funds for 2014–20.[6] Since 2014, a so-called performance reserve, consisting of 6 per cent of the funds allocated, is withheld by member states and only paid if predefined objectives set in regional and national programmes have been met.

Research dealing specifically with the ESF is equally unable to draw causal relationships between ESF implementation and policy outcomes. Some studies find that the positive effects of social funds are clearer at the local level, in matters such as youth unemployment or gender equality, rather than global effects on growth (Bachtler *et al.* 2017: 2–3). For example, a higher absorption rate of the ESF and European Regional Development Fund funds targeting young people has had a positive influence by reducing or slowing the growth of youth unemployment between 2000 and 2006 (Tosun *et al.* 2017). Yet, other studies show that the ESF failed to have a decisive impact on the development of human capital in the small and medium-sized enterprise sector in Poland (Dubel 2019), to boost firms' competitiveness through training in the Czech Republic (Pelucha *et al.* 2019) or to foster active labour market policies in Spain (González-Alegre 2018). The literature inspired by a Europeanization framework emphasizes the role of the strategic use of funds or the cognitive use of policy concepts by local actors. Studying the use of the ESF for employment policy in 18 cities across six member states, Zimmermann (2016) finds very different patterns of outcomes, ranging from important change and usage by local actors, to a complete refusal to engage with the ESF objectives and resources. She concludes that "that money alone apparently does not drive change, nor do programmatic or procedural conditions. While usage can be explained well by individual motivation or high incentives, change is more complex" (Zimmermann 2016: 1473). More generally, the implementation of the ESF is a bottom-up rather than top-down process, whereby the local actors of social policy learn strategically how to apply for EU money by using the

---

6. See European Commission website, "Structural and investment funds", https://cohesiondata. ec.europa.eu/overview (accessed 15 September 2021).

policy concepts promoted by the EU to sustain funding for their established tasks and collaborations (Sbaraglia 2016).

The issue of effectiveness will be crucial with regard to the €312.5 million in grants that will be distributed to member states through the Recovery and Resilience Facility from 2021 onwards. To receive the funds, national governments have to draft their national reform plan to be approved by the European Commission in April 2021. However, there are already concerns that the precipitated preparation of such plans will lead to misspending. With the three main recipients being Italy, France and Spain, the purpose of the facility is clearly to dampen the effects of the pandemic-induced recession on already fragile economies and prevent the southern periphery from drifting further from the wealthier northern core of the continent. After the euro crisis doomed young southern Europeans to social downgrading, the impoverishment of a whole generation of children, students and young professionals across the continent may well prove to become Europe's political time bomb.

To conclude, the governance surrounding cohesion policy and the ESF has become increasingly institutionalized and stringent over time. A multitude of policy instruments underpinning a multi-level *partnership* aims at generating policy actors' adherence and ensuring that the redistribution of EU money actually supports the EU's strategy for cohesion and convergence in an effective manner. Although the very existence of redistribution through funds was never really questioned, the scant evidence of policy effectiveness might have contributed to undermine the legitimacy of cohesion policy and hence fed into the rise of multiple forms of conditionality.

The rise of conditionality, between bureaucracy and politics

Since the turn of the century, and even more so since 2014, cohesion policy has seen a remarkable rise in the conditionality principle that is making the allocation of funds dependent on compliance with a range of institutional and political constraints. There is an important distinction between two different forms of conditionality: the endogenous form aimed at improving the implementation of cohesion policy, on the one hand, and the exogenous form trying to use EU funds to achieve other political goals, on the other. In both cases, however, the effectiveness of conditionality can be questioned but, in addition, the latter raises serious legitimacy concerns.[7]

---

7. This section draws extensively from Bachtler and Mendez (2020).

Endogenous conditionality: improving policy implementation

Ex ante conditionality was introduced in 2014 and aims at ensuring that the right conditions are in place for the funds to be spent effectively in three particular respects: first, the existence of broader *strategic frameworks* allowing for a coherent implementation of polices (see Box 8.3); second, the *regulatory conditions* referring mainly to compliance with EU law, for example, as far as public procurement or state aid are concerned; third, the *institutional dimension* aiming to ensure that public authorities have sufficient administrative capacity

---

BOX 8.3 EXAMPLES OF *EX ANTE* CONDITIONALITY CRITERIA FOR ESF (2014–20)

Thematic goal

Promote social inclusion, fight poverty and all forms of discrimination ("fighting poverty" goal).

Investment priorities

Improving access to affordable, durable and quality services, including healthcare costs and social SGI.

***Ex ante* condition**

Health: presence of a national or regional healthcare strategic framework within the TFEU guarantying economic viability.

Criteria used to verify that conditions have been met

Presence of a national or regional healthcare framework to implement and monitor:

- coordinated measures aiming at improving access to healthcare services;
- measures aimed at stimulating the efficiency of the healthcare sector by deploying models of service provision and infrastructures; and
- a system of follow-up and re-examination;

A member state or a region thereof has adopted a framework with an indicative description of the available budgetary resources and an economically advantageous concentration of resources on the priority areas of healthcare needs.

Source: Annex XI, Regulation 1303/2013 from 20 December 2013.

---

to allow the actual spending and monitoring of the funds, which can imply requirements for further capacity-building measures.

The European Commission has claimed that *ex ante* conditionality helped improve consistency across policies as well as the framework in which the funds operate. In contrast, some observers have pointed to a lack of accuracy and enforcement (Bachtler & Mendez 2020: 134).

Performance conditionality was introduced in 2000 to link funding to the achievement of policy objectives. On the basis of monitoring, money from the performance reserve consisting of 6 per cent of all funds can be distributed as a reward to those who implement on time or, on the contrary, be reallocated from programmes that have not achieved their goals to those who have. The specificity here is that conditionality does not act as a constraint or a stick to punish poor performers, but rather as a carrot for incentivizing practices conducive of effective implementation.

Finally, the practice called *earmarking* comes close to thematic conditionality since it imposes a constraint upon regions as to how EU money can be spent. Practically, earmarking consists of allocating in advance a given amount of the funds to certain categories of spending or policies. Under the budget period 2021–27 earmarking of ESF+ money has proved a means to settle political compromises and make certain priorities visible. The share that each member state should allocate for social inclusion was increased from 20 to 25 per cent compared to 2014–20, including a new allocation of 3 per cent to food and basic material assistance for the most deprived. Similarly, at least 12.5 per cent of the ESF+ resources should be devoted to help young people find a job or a training scheme (in line with the Youth Guarantee). Moreover, member states with a level of child poverty above the EU average should use at least 5 per cent of their ESF+ money to address this issue. Across the entire multi-annual budget, including the additional NextGenerationEU package, 30 per cent of all EU resources will be directed to the transition towards a green economy. By using earmarking, the EU seeks to reinforce its grip on implementation and lead national governments to address the priorities identified at European level.

Exogenous conditionality: using the funds as a stick

Unlike previous forms of conditionality, a set of three further mechanisms introduced into the 2014 regulation link the distribution of cohesion funds to broader considerations that find their rationale outside of the objectives of cohesion policy.

Structural reform conditionality requires that member states implement "structural reforms" spelled out in the so-called country-specific recommendations issued by the Commission and the Council in the framework of the European Semester (see Chapter 7). However, there is little evidence so far that this connection has actually taken place, neither at the stage of programming and designing of the partnership agreements, nor at the stage of implementation. Whereas the recommendations of the European Semester tend to focus on the national level and on fiscal and macroeconomic issues, the use of the funds concerns regional projects. More broadly, there is a serious risk that some political orientations of the European Semester, for instance its initial focus on fiscal discipline and cutting public expenditure in the first years, may directly contradict the objective of tackling cross-regional disparities. The will to "de facto transform cohesion policy into the primary enforcement tool for EU economic governance" (Vica 2018: 43) has not vanished in the post-coronavirus political constellation, it has, on the contrary, been reinforced. Under the new EU budget augmented by NextGenerationEU for 2021–27, the national plans motivating the distribution of funds have to be in line with the country-specific recommendations of the European Semester, and the European Commission is tasked with verifying that "the criteria of consistency with the country-specific recommendations ... shall need the highest score of the assessment" (European Union 2021: recital 42). Yet, the methodology for assessing said consistency remains unknown (as of February 2021). Furthermore, it seems that the loans within NextGenerationEU (€360 billion out of the total €750 billion) will be subjected to stronger conditionality as the Commission specifies that loans "are to be proposed in exchange of additional reforms and investments beyond those that already benefit from the non-repayable financial support" (European Union 2021: n.p.). It is worth noting that the EP has secured its involvement in the monitoring of the spending of the recovery facility together with the Council and the Commission.

Macroeconomic conditionality appeared in its first form in 1994, when the cohesion fund was created to help southern European countries fulfil the so-called Maastricht criteria. These criteria were targets to be met in order to foster convergence among the future members of the EMU; they covered a number of indicators including the inflation rate, levels of deficit and debt and thus can be regarded as the predecessor of the Stability and Growth Pact of 1998. The negotiations on the multi-annual financial framework 2014–20 saw the net contributors to the EU budget from the west and north of Europe (particularly Germany, the Netherlands, but also France under Nicolas Sarkozy) attempt to increasingly constrain the recipients to an efficient use of funds in conformity with the common objectives (Coman & Sbaraglia 2018). Under the presidency of José Manuel Barroso, the Commission backed this coalition and introduced a macroeconomic *ex ante* conditionality that would tie the structural funds to the criteria of budgetary discipline of the Stability and Growth Pact (level of debt and of budgetary deficit) in the regulation on structural funds. This punitive use of structural funds created a strong backlash within the EP during negotiations on the 2013 regulation, which led to a weakening of the automaticity of sanctions. In the end, Article 10 of the regulation on "measures linking effectiveness of the European structural and investment funds to sound economic governance" states that "the Commission shall make a proposal to the Council to suspend part or all of the commitments or payments for the programmes of a member state" (European Union 2021: n.p.) that would not have implemented sufficient measures to remedy a situation of excessive debt or macroeconomic imbalance. This form of conditionality had become politically very salient in the initial austeritarian response to the eurozone crisis, but was subsequently approached more prudently (Coman & Sbaraglia 2018). The only instance of actual suspension was enforced against Hungary in 2012, but was only effective for a few months until the country brought its deficit back to under the 3 per cent threshold. In 2014–15, the economic grounds were not deemed solid enough to decide sanctions against France or Italy. In 2016, when the issue of sanctioning Spain and Portugal with an excessive debt procedure arose, Jean-Claude Juncker decided not to recommend the adoption of sanctions against these countries that were politically and economically weakened by austerity policies. In fact, the rationale behind the sanctions was from the outset highly contentious with a coalition of southern states (as well as Belgium and the UK) rejecting the sanctions. Over the years, the legitimacy of the Stability and Growth Pact itself eroded, including within the European Commission where the (French) commissioner for economic affairs Pierre Moscovici (2014–19), for instance, led the camp of those advocating a more flexible approach to deficit and debt.

Macroeconomic conditionality has been maintained in the new 2021–27 framework and can lead both to reprogramming or the suspension of funds. However, an "escape clause" was introduced to prevent depriving regions of funds when they need them most, for example when faced with severe economic problems. This specific form of conditionality will largely depend on the political fate (still uncertain at the time of writing) of the Stability and Growth Pact itself in the years to come.

Finally, the Commission proposal to include a *rule of law conditionality* in the regulation over the 2021–27 EU budget has triggered a major political struggle. The purpose is to use the funds to foster compliance of recipient states to the broader democratic values of the EU and basic requirements for the rule of law. Main arguments supporting this measure have been that the goals of cohesion policy could not be achieved without guarantees that funds would be managed in a financially sound and lawful environment as well as to prevent waste and misspending. Supported by most creditor countries, the provision was fought vividly by the Hungarian and Polish governments who denounced an attempt to politicize cohesion policy and threatened to veto the agreement over the 2021–27 budget, including NextGenerationEU. Besides political concerns, many observers noted that this type of value conditionality is highly problematic in many respects. A main concern relates to the clarity of the criteria that indicate an actual infraction of the rule of law. In that sense, the Commission proposal of 2018 lacked clarity and accuracy to be effectively enforceable. Moreover, EU institutions should make sure that the interests of the individual beneficiaries (farmers, students, researchers, civil society organizations) should be protected. Finally, to avoid the risk of bias and political meltdown, procedures should be transparent and all member states should be placed on an equal footing. However, the suspension of funds as a "stick" to foster compliance with the rule of law only makes sense for a very limited set of EU countries where these funds account for a significant share (above 2 per cent) of their GDP. Even then, it is doubtful whether suspending EU payments would have any effect whatsoever on decisions made on primarily political rather than economic grounds. After months of heated debates and a dramatic climax delaying the adoption of a historic budgetary package, the European Council founded a political agreement on 10 December 2020 that, if cumbersome, could rally Viktor Orbán and Mateusz Morawiecki. In fact, the Council merely issued a political statement asserting that all member states will be treated equally. To that end, the Commission needs to develop a methodology on how the mechanism will be implemented in consultation with the member states and refrain from taking any action until then. Yet, claims have been raised in the EP and elsewhere that the Council statement had no legally binding character and Commission president Von der Leyen claimed that the mechanism effectively entered into force on 1 January 2021. All this confirms that the rule of law conditionality has indeed become a "political time bomb" (Bachtler & Mendez 2020: 135) for the EU.

Conclusion

The ESF and subsequent funds were established with the aim of fostering social cohesion within as well as across European member states. A main goal has been to bring about upward convergence in levels of socio-economic development across Europe. The aim of this chapter was to assess whether the corresponding policy instruments, especially the ESF, were therefore unconditional, resulting from broader normative underpinnings of the EU, or whether recipients, namely states, regions and individual project holders, were subject to a set of conditions for benefitting from European solidarity. The answer to that question is threefold. First, a historical perspective on the development of the ESF and the related instruments shows that cohesion policy can be regarded as an unconditional commitment from Europeans acting collectively. The desired convergence has only happened slowly and its progress can even be halted – if not reversed – by major economic downturns such as the 2008–10 financial and debt crisis. Despite the relatively weak capacity of the funds to bring about convergence, cohesion policy (and its social string), have remained firmly anchored in the EU toolbox and continue to mobilize a significant share of the EU budget. Financial solidarity has also survived major transformations, especially enlargement, and the political confrontations resulting from drastically increased gaps in levels of prosperity and inequality. After a period of counter-productive austerity and muddling through (Crespy 2020a), the EU is experiencing a new impetus with the adoption of a historically high budget flanked by a recovery package. Financed by common debt, its purpose is to support those countries and regions who suffer most from low economic activity, unemployment and poverty. This, of course, does not mean that the resources are sufficient to tackle the magnitude of the social cohesion problem affecting Europe. But it is fair to say that redistribution is here to stay and, in that sense, can be seen as an unconditional dimension of EU integration. As long as Europeans agree that market integration and competition alone cannot solve Europe's problems, redistribution via the EU funds will remain part of the *raison d'être* of the EU.

Second, from a policy perspective, the ESF has been increasingly assertive in attaching the distribution of funds to the achievement of pre-established objectives. From the outset, the purpose of the ESF was to support requalification and the upgrading of human capital to help regions and workers' adapt to the transformation of production processes and labour markets. Over time, a complex system of multi-level governance and bureaucratic partnership has aimed at ensuring that all actors were geared towards common policy concepts such as activation, inclusion or social investment. Formal conditions have been set out in the funds regulations to ensure compliance with thematic objectives, with EU law or with certain levels of implementation. Increasingly, however, the conditions have no longer been attached to the objectives of cohesion policy as such, namely upward convergence and social cohesion, but to broader economic or even political goals.

Third, this leads us to the perhaps most striking institutional development in the area of redistribution, namely the institutionalization of conditionality as a distinct form of governance. These forms of conditionality tend to use the funds as a stick to punish those states that do not comply with certain policy predicaments. The shift operated in 2013 led to the inclusion of macroeconomic conditionality, that is compliance with rules of the Stability and Growth Pact over deficit and debt levels. The turn to conditionality has been confirmed with the adoption of the 2021–27 budget augmented by NextGenerationEU, with a number of ambiguities. As the rules of the Stability and Growth Pact are suspended, the focus has been placed, yet again, on the alignment of national reforms and investments with the recommendations of the European Semester. If the notion of investment seems now at the core of the EU's agenda, the notion of "structural reforms" has always been very ambiguous and, more often than not, incited cuts in public spending, retrenchment and recommodification, which stand in stark contrast with the very objectives of social cohesion. Finally, both the Commission and the EP have pushed for including a condition related to compliance with the rule of law, on the grounds that EU money could not be well-spent in undemocratic political systems that oppress civil society. This is a significant political step which, as it targets the governments of Poland and Hungary, subjects EU financial redistribution to broader normative considerations across the board. Beyond the fact that this form of conditionality is unlikely to meet its target and lead to enhanced democracy in those two countries, it will surely make for divisive political debates likely to divert Europeans from the pressing issues pertaining to social cohesion.

Further reading

- John Bachtler and Carlos Mendez, "Cohesion and the EU Budget: is conditionality undermining solidarity?" In Ramona Coman, Amandine Crespy and Vivien A. Schmidt (eds), *Governance and Politics in the Post-Crisis European Union* (Cambridge: Cambridge University Press, 2020), 121–39.
- Ramona Coman, "How have EU 'fire-fighters' sought to douse the flames of the eurozone's fast- and slow-burning crises? The 2013 structural funds reform". *British Journal of Politics and International Relations* 20:3 (2018), 540–54.
- Katharina Zimmermann, *Local Policies and the European Social Fund: Employment Policies across Europe* (Bristol: Policy Press, 2019).

Questions to debate

- Does the ESF contribute to the top-down Europeanization of social policy?
- Is conditionality an efficient and legitimate way to enhance the effectiveness of cohesion policy?

IS THE EU FIT FOR THE SOCIAL CHALLENGES OF THE TWENTY-FIRST CENTURY?

Previous chapters have addressed controversies surrounding European social policy by looking at developments in governance, politics and policies following the creation of the EEC in the aftermath of the Second World War, with a particular emphasis on the contemporary period. The purpose of this chapter is to look to the future and assess whether the EU is well-equipped to enable Europeans to manage collectively the social challenges that have been posed most acutely since the turn of the twenty-first century. Since 2008, the EU has experienced a period of turbulence described by political actors (notably Jean-Claude Juncker) and social scientists alike as a "polycrisis". The financial and debt crisis of 2008–10, the sudden influx of migrants in 2015, the protracted Brexit, recurrent conflicts over democracy and the rule of law and the ongoing Covid-19 pandemic have all questioned the capacity of the EU to sustain its multi-level social, economic and political order against the backdrop of ever-more polarized societies. Reacting rather than acting, Brussels technocrats and national leaders have mostly "improvised" new policy instruments and procedures while forging hard-fought compromises in emergency situations (van Middelaar 2019). In many ways, the European social question lies at the heart of those moments of existential crisis. Successive crises have exacerbated social challenges as young people, women, immigrants and the self-employed are hit hardest by the second historic recession faced by Europe in just over a decade.

Can the EU take the lead in the struggle for social cohesion? Is it fit for purpose in a post-Covid-19 world with simultaneous challenges? Or is it doomed to be a powerless spectator of deteriorating national social models? To address these questions, this chapter looks at three particular issues that, while they can at first sight seem peripheral to the social policy agenda, nevertheless contribute to shape it in important ways. First, this chapter will attempt to draw from the lessons of the Brexit referendum by analysing the links between social policy and the UK's decision to leave the EU. Second, the coronavirus pandemic has placed health at the centre of the social policy debate. Although health policy was never an important field of action for the EU, we have seen it conquer new competences and initiate new policies in the midst of the health crisis. How likely is the EU to become a key player in this field? Third, we have witnessed the rise of the Green Deal as the overarching policy initiative structuring the whole European policy agenda. But how does it articulate with social policy? Can the notion of fair transition ensure that the shift towards an environmentally friendly economy will also enhance social cohesion? Considering the three key topics of Brexit, health and the green transition, a cross-cutting argument will be made regarding the EU's political commitment to social cohesion. Beyond rhetorical gestures, resources and instruments at the EU's disposal are being built-up incrementally. Yet, in the face of the sheer scale of the social issues at stake, it would be too optimistic to conclude that the EU is fit for purpose.

Brexit: "taking back control" for greater social cohesion?

The controversies surrounding the relationship between Brexit and social cohesion are perhaps best illustrated by the debates about the so-called Lexit position, namely a Left Brexit. Lexit was endorsed by those believing that the UK would be best able to implement a political agenda conducive to social cohesion outside of the EU.[1] This view rests to a large extent on the belief that the restoration of (full) national sovereignty would go hand in hand with the restoration of Keynesian or socialist economic policy as "the problems of low investment, stagnant wages and ageing infrastructure that blight our towns and cities require a much more fundamental reconsideration of Britain's economic and political model".[2] More specifically, Lexit is underpinned by a threefold argument: (a) the EU has locked in neoliberal policies by constitutionalizing the four freedoms and competition policy in the treaties, which has led to the privatization of public services and the undermining of workers' rights – thus, EU membership is the major obstacle to a far-reaching transformation and definancialization of the British socio-economic model; (b) the EU is impossible to reform; and (c) progressive change will therefore be possible once the British people enjoy full sovereignty to decide in favour of a more just social model. All three claims are highly debatable. Adopting a nuanced approach, this book has provided arguments regarding the direct and indirect constraints exerted by the EU on national social policy. It has also shed light on why the politics and institutions of the EU may favour the status quo, or

---

1. Although a minority in the centre-left, the Lexit position proved influential in Jeremy Corbyn's entourage. A number of observers and academics have also identified as supporting Lexit, for instance by publicizing their analyses on the website www.thefullbrexit.com.
2. The Full Brexit founding statement, www.thefullbrexit.com/about (accessed 6 September 2021).

incremental change, over radical reform. The perspective adopted here also departs from deterministic legal-institutionalist analyses, which leave little room for politics and the struggle of ideas. Picturing the UK as a victim of the EU's neoliberal straitjacket seems ironic given that the country has in fact been fairly successful at "uploading" its own recipes towards Brussels and was long considered the good pupil of European socio-economic coordination. However, the purpose here is not to prove Lexit wrong. This section will seek to enrich the debate from three different perspectives: looking at how the lack of social cohesion has to a large extent led to the Brexit referendum result, focusing on whether social rights will find themselves under threat in a post-Brexit UK, and finally trying to figure out whether or not we should expect intensified social dumping at the EU's doorstep.

The social roots of Brexit

One of the main ideas conveyed by the Leave campaign was that EU membership was associated with two intolerable burdens: financial contributions to the EU budget and migrations flows. Often interpreted as indicators of parochial egoism or even outright xenophobia, the common denominator to both concerns was, however, less often pointed out, namely that the Brexit vote was arguably a reaction to the degradation of social cohesion and social welfare in the UK. The budget and the immigration issues both converge when we consider dislocations in some areas of public services and infrastructure under pressure from highly dynamic demographic changes. The most notable exploitation of this social malaise by the Leave campaign was its claim that the £350 million allegedly sent to the EU every week would instead be invested in the National Health Service (NHS) post-Brexit, a claim famously depicted on the side of a Leave campaign tour bus.

With New Labour in government in the 1990s, the UK adopted an open policy stance to mass migration, spurring the arrival of approximately 3.3 million immigrants between 2001 and 2014 (Coleman 2016: 201). When the eastern enlargement of the EU occurred in 2004, Tony Blair's government decided to not place any restrictions on the free movement of workers coming from the new member states, unlike the French and German governments. Important migratory inflows from central and eastern Europe thus added to pre-existing flows from outside Europe. In fact,

> intra-EU mobility is an essential and functional aspect of the UK's hegemonic role in Europe. The British strategy in Europe consisted of the promotion of EU workers' mobility in order to operate an efficient allocation of skills for the UK (and other "core countries") within the European economy. (Antonucci & Varriale 2020: 47)

By 2013, the immigrant population from eastern Europe living in the UK had increased from 170,000 in 2004 to 1.24 million. This rapid demographic change was, however, not matched by large-scale investments in public services. In several urban areas, hospitals and schools came under pressure while housing prices were driven up, exacerbating Britain's housing issue. Furthermore, this degradation of social welfare was accompanied by a feeling of cultural dislocation and of new perceived threats to British national identity, as increased immigration made British society more multicultural than ever.

Studies of the referendum vote have made clear that British citizens at the bottom of the social ladder and/or living in economically depressed areas had been more inclined to cast a Leave vote. Lower education levels, occupation in the manufacturing sector, low wages or unemployment proved to be key drivers explaining the vote at the individual level. The sociology of Brexit is therefore in tune with the larger body of literature in comparative politics that identifies the "losers" of Europeanization and globalization as the main constituency behind the success of the far right, with cultural and economic threats making a "return to the nation" appealing. This further echoes the research on welfare chauvinism and its sociological drivers (Greve 2019).

Digging deeper into the British social model helps explain the social roots of Brexit. Behind the high employment level lies an activation model underpinning labour market policy that has implied a significant deterioration of working conditions and pay, unwanted part-time contracts and in-work poverty (Clegg 2017). This sense of impoverishment was not only felt by those most in need or at the very bottom of the social ladder but was shared to a large extent by voters in the "squeezed middle", namely workers with intermediate rather than low levels of education, part of a middle class caught in a downward spiral of social decline (Antonucci *et al.* 2017). The liberal, highly commodifying welfare model of the UK suffered further after the 2008 financial crisis as the British government adopted austerity. As a non-member of the eurozone and free of any Troika bailouts, pressure from the EU was low. Yet the UK government opted for strict fiscal discipline and important cuts in social spending. As early as 2009, the British government set the target of saving £9 billion a year for a total of £35 billion by 2014. When it took office in 2010, the coalition government of Conservatives and Liberal Democrats led by David Cameron designed a large-scale austerity plan combining tax increases and cuts in spending amounting to a historic 13 per cent retrenchment in public expenditure (Taylor-Gooby 2012). Austerity was also combined with far-reaching restructuring of welfare services, pushing the marketization of welfare further. This mainly occurred through:

> a root-and-branch reform of non-pension cash benefits, the radical reorganization of the NHS and of higher education, and the substitution

of private for-profit and not-for-profit agencies for state services in social housing, social welfare provision, aspects of health, education and welfare to work, across local government and possibly throughout the public sector. (Taylor-Gooby 2012: 65)

Retrenchment in welfare benefits and public services accelerated the typically neoliberal "great risk shift" from the welfare state to local government and households, which particularly affected the most vulnerable territories and individuals (Kennett *et al.* 2015). The UK government's austeritarian response to the 2008 financial crisis contributed to a considerable deterioration of social cohesion in the country. Although this policy did not plant the seeds of Brexit, which may well have been present already, it certainly made the ground more fertile for them to germinate and take root.

Social welfare in the post-Brexit UK

Whether Brexit will lead to a deterioration of social rights in the UK remains an open question that will only find a definite answer in the years to come. Ever since its accession to the EEC in 1973, the UK had been a strong opponent of the development of social policy, a pattern consistent with a broader reticence vis-à-vis any moves towards political and social integration that might lead the EU towards increased federalization (Hantrais 2019). The UK government consistently opposed policy proposals implying more EU regulation and intervention or increased resources. After Thatcher's cabinet had to concede the extension of qualified majority voting to health and safety issues for the single market to go ahead with the 1986 Single European Act, Major kept the country out of monetary and social integration when the Maastricht Treaty was negotiated in 1992. Although Blair eventually accepted the integration of the social protocol's provisions into the treaty, meaning they would also apply to the UK, the country promoted above all decentralization and soft-law based coordination in the social policy realm. British activism in the contentious negotiations over the revision of the Working Time Directive between 2004 and 2009 is highly illustrative of the country's reticence towards EU social regulation. In that debate, the UK adamantly spearheaded the group of member states objecting to the suppression of the opt-out from the directive's key provision limiting working time to 48 hours per week. Unlike the government, British social scientists, officials and trade unionists have promoted EU social policy in various ways, as Hantrais (2019) stresses.

Overall, the social impact of Brexit will mainly come as a result of "the pledge to 'take back control' of money, borders and laws" (Stewart *et al.* 2020).

The importance of EU law for enhancing social rights in the UK is itself controversial. On one hand, analyses from the House of Commons, the Institute of Employment Rights (Coutouris & Ewing 2019) or Dublin University's Brexit Institute (Velutti 2020) point to how the EU has served to either create rights that did not exist in the country beforehand – such as the right to statutory paid annual leave enshrined in the 2003 Working Time Directive or protections included in the 2008 Temporary Agency Work Directive – or to the extension of existing rights – such as the Pregnant Workers Directive (92/85/EC) increasing the coverage of workers entitled to a 14-week maternity leave (Ferguson 2020). In many instances, however, social standards in UK law have been above minimum EU requirements, an argument that has often been put forward by Conservative decision-makers in Brexit debates. Still, EU legislation often serves to "fill important gaps" in the UK's existing social provisions, such as in the example of the 2019 directive on work–life balance, which will not be applied in the UK (De la Porte *et al.* 2020).[3]

Since all EU social regulations have been retained in the British national legal order, no dramatic change is expected in the immediate aftermath of the country's departure from the EU. The social effects of Brexit may instead unfold as legislation connected to retained EU law is freely changed by the British parliament in the future. This is less likely for those provisions that are also enshrined in the UK's primary law, such as the Equality Act 2010 that includes provisions set in the two EU anti-discrimination directives from 2000.[4] Together with the CJEU's case law, these EU directives have significantly enhanced UK anti-discrimination law (Wintemute 2016). There is an important caveat to be considered in that the European Charter of Fundamental Rights was itself not retained. Admittedly, while the CJEU has not always used the charter to advance workers' rights in a progressive fashion,[5] the neutralization of the charter in the UK may entail "significant gaps in substantive rights that do not have direct equivalents in other UK human rights law" (Shannon & Nayak-Oliver 2021).

The trade and cooperation agreement signed on 24 December 2020 includes some minimal safeguards as to the rights of Europeans in the UK. They relate essentially to the coordination of social security, including the right to transfer

---

3. The net gains implied by the transposition of the EU directive would have concerned especially *paid* parental leave and five (unpaid) carer days per year.
4. Council Directive 2000/43/EC of 29 June 2000 implementing the principle of equal treatment between persons irrespective of racial or ethnic origin, Official Journal L 180 (19 July 2000); and Council Directive 2000/78/EC of 27 November 2000 establishing a general framework for equal treatment in employment and occupation, Official Journal L 303 (2 December 2000).
5. For instance, in the *Alemo Herron* case, which emerged in the UK in 2012–13, the CJEU used Article 16 of the charter – regarding the freedom to conduct business – to undermine the application of collective agreements in the contracting out of public services.

pension benefits to and from the UK. Foreign citizens living in the UK may nevertheless see their rights undermined after Brexit, as both freedom of movement and the provisions linked to EU citizenship are no longer in force. The so-called settled status (residency) accessible to all those working for over five years and residing in the country implies that their full access to social benefits is guaranteed. Entitlements will in contrast be granted on a case-by-case basis for those with the "pre-settled" status (residents for less than five years). In this regard, Brexit will reinforce Europe's unequal migration and citizenship patterns as "core–periphery inequalities intersect with class, gender and racism" (Antonucci & Varriale 2020: 49). A blatant illustration of this can be found in the difficulties faced by female migrants from central and eastern Europe working in the low-wage sector – often part-time – in proving their residence and thus access to social benefits (Shutes & Walker 2018). They are all the more likely to struggle to secure the settled status and are likely to suffer a loss of welfare in post-Brexit Britain.

Turning to "borders", there is an expectation that disruption will occur in the labour market, in particular for the healthcare and social care sectors as migration flows change as a result of Brexit. With significant numbers leaving the UK (and arriving in lower numbers), labour shortages might occur. Asking whether the post-Brexit UK is becoming more "Americanized", Gingrich and King (2019) point to two trends in particular. The first is that the UK has followed a broader trend of the welfare state reform in Europe, which has consisted of linking social benefits to work. The second trend they observe is that the UK has developed an increasingly restrictive approach to welfare rights, increasingly depriving non-citizens of welfare entitlements. Both trends converge to accentuate social segregation between the "deserving" and the "undeserving" of social protection.

Considering "money", the interruption of EU redistributive policies may deprive vulnerable groups or areas from resources. In 2014–20, £14.6 billion were allocated to the UK through all European structural and investment funds (including the Youth Unemployment Initiative), with the main beneficiaries being regions in Wales and northern England. To compensate the anticipated loss, Boris Johnson's government has pledged to create a UK Shared Prosperity Fund matching the former EU funding. While discussions about the design of the fund are ongoing, the Welsh government has already expressed its opposition to the fund being administered from Westminster (Brien 2021). Moreover, it is not clear if the UK Prosperity Fund will provide the same level of resources to its constituent regions that the EU budget under NextGenerationEU would have – including all its new instruments and earmarking for spending the money on social exclusion and promoting the green transition. If it failed to do so, it would undeniably put the UK's less well-off territories and communities in a more unfavourable position than if they had remained in the EU.

Towards social dumping?

At first, there were good grounds to argue that disentangling EU social policy regulations from UK law may prove very tricky (Hantrais 2019). In contrast to Theresa May, who left office in 2019, Boris Johnson took a much more adversarial approach in the negotiations over the UK's withdrawal from the EU and subsequently to the negotiations around the new free trade agreement. Disagreement between the UK and the bloc crystallized on, among other things, the EU's demand to guarantee a "level playing field" in trade relations, as Johnson refused to commit to align UK law with EU law. As a result, the EU–UK Trade and Cooperation Agreement contains sophisticated provisions aimed at safeguarding the level playing field in the future (see Box 9.1). Beyond a principled commitment not to weaken social standards in ways that would affect trade, the novel provisions also outline the procedure for resolving conflicts, leading some to the conclusion that "this is uniquely an agreement to manage divergence and not to promote convergence" (Van den Hende & White 2021). Concerns also rise from the fact that it may be very difficult in disputes to *prove* that changes in regulation impede fair competition, thus potentially making the provisions in the agreement ineffective in preventing the erosion of workers' rights and of environmental protection standards (Morris 2020).

BOX 9.1 THE EU–UK TRADE AND COOPERATION AGREEMENT AND SOCIAL STANDARDS

The LPF [level playing field] provisions are set out under Title XI of Part One and cover six fields: competition, subsidy control (state aid), state-owned enterprises and designated monopolies, taxation, labour and social standards, environment and climate. The initial general provisions recognise the "common understanding" of mutual benefits of the LPF that prevents distortion of "trade or investment", and stress that the objective is not to "harmonise" standards. [...]

The "non-regression" principle applies in the two chapters regarding labour and social standards, and environment and climate. [Article 6.2 of the agreement states that] "a party shall not weaken or reduce, in a manner affecting trade or investment between parties, its labour and social protection below the levels in place at the end of the transition period, including by failing to effectively enforce its laws and standards". [...]

Chapter 9 [...] envisages that should parties be unable to address disagreements through consultation and dialogue, a party may request that a panel of experts be created to examine the case [...] The list of 15 experts is to be composed of two sub-lists of five experts, each designated by one party, plus a sub-list of five non-nationals of the EU or the UK. […]

Article 9.4 makes provision for rebalancing measures in cases where "significant divergences" arise in the areas of labour and social, environmental or climate protection, or with respect to subsidy control, and which result in "material impacts on trade and investment" […] Should no mutually acceptable solution be reached, the concerned party may adopt strictly necessary and proportionate "rebalancing measures" to remedy the "material impact", unless the other party requests the establishment of an arbitration tribunal. If after 30 days the arbitration tribunal has not delivered its final ruling, the party concerned may adopt rebalancing measures, and in that case, the other party may take proportionate counter-measures, until the tribunal delivers its ruling.

Source: Hallak (2021: 14–17).

It is also difficult to imagine how Brexit will not bring about intensified competition between the UK and the EU in the attraction of capital. Finding itself in a more vulnerable position, the UK may want to compensate any losses induced by reduced access to the EU single market by reducing costs for businesses by lowering quality standards as well as social and environmental regulatory requirements. Freed from EU state-aid rules, the UK may also engage in corporate welfare programmes involving direct financial support to companies (Farnsworth 2017). Thus, there are good reasons to expect that the UK will "drift apart" further (Ebbinghaus 2020) from regulated capitalism. This is likely to be visible, for instance, in the area of pensions. Given the paramount importance of the financial sector in the British economy, post-Brexit competition with the continent to attract pension funds will mean an intensified strategy promoting private pensions. In Ebbinghaus's words:

> the City's pro-Brexit financial interests will push further for less regulated financialization of pensions, making a large share of British retirement income subject to more volatility. Departing from a Social Europe that puts more brakes on funded pension capitalism, Brexit has thus made UK pension futures less, not more, secure. (Ebbinghaus 2020: 76)

Although there has been a lot of speculation, the concerns that exist about regulatory competition between the EU and the UK leading to decreasing social standards is not baseless. Just a few weeks after the Trade and Cooperation Agreement was reached in January 2021, Johnson's cabinet admitted that it was conducting a review of employment regulations linked to EU law – such as the

EU Working Time Directive – with a view towards possible suppressions or revisions; potential objections from the EU about breaches of the level playing field provisions would be dealt with through the existing mechanisms for dispute settlements in the agreement (Gallardo 2021).

To conclude, the idea that Brexit will only alter the UK's social system at the margins, affecting migrants in particular, will need to be reassessed as time passes. The social impact of Brexit will depend on parliamentary majorities, prevailing policy ideas and selected strategies for the country to deal with its trade relations with the EU. Five years after the referendum and the Lexit controversy, current events seem to confirm the view that "the damage that Brexit [will] cause to UK labour rights substantially outweighs any (real or imaginary) Brexit dividend" (Coutouris & Ewing 2019: 72). The provisions within the Trade and Cooperation Agreement and current developments also cast doubt on the idea that the EU is well-equipped to face a regulatory competition involving the lowering of social standards.

EU health policy after Covid-19: between interdependency and sovereignty

The area of health policy offers a good illustration of the dynamics underlying the integration of social policy, and why the EU is not fit for purpose to deal with the challenges ahead. A recurrent dynamic is that capacity building at the EU level tends to happen in the wake of "crises"; that is, advances result because of unexpected events, which create policy problems that cannot be resolved within the existing framework. Against a background of often reluctant national elites and sometimes constituencies, the competences, resources and instruments of the EU can be built up in a piecemeal and somewhat erratic fashion, resulting in the layering of new procedures on top of older ones. Summing it up, Brooks and Geyer (2020: 1073) have claimed that "the Commission will seek to repeat its 'traditional' reaction to public health crises: creating and strengthening technocratic agencies, and carefully laying the groundwork for potential expansion of its areas of activity, whilst avoiding formal treaty change".

Capacity building as a result of health crises

As pointed in Chapter 4, most of EU regulation in public health was the result of the contaminated blood crisis in the 1980s and the "mad cow" crisis in the 1990s. This pattern was repeated in 2003 when severe acute respiratory syndrome (SARs) prompted the set-up of the European Centre for Disease

Prevention and Control. In 2013, the swine flu epidemic led to introduction of a joint mechanism for vaccine procurement. Likewise, the Covid-19 pandemic has prompted new initiatives in the field of health; these have been built to a large extent because of the weakness of existing procedures. Policy-wise, innovations cover three areas: the prevention and management of cross-border health threats, securing market supply of medicines and medical products and strengthening healthcare systems. Governance-wise, this new step in the Europeanization of health relies on intensified coordination of national actions, the build-up of European resources and the expansion of EU agencies. The 2013 decision on serious cross-border health threats (1082/2013/EU) has created a loose network of national representatives – the Health Security Committee – which has largely been neglected by the member states. Intergovernmental and voluntary procedures have at their end failed to ensure adequate preparedness and coordination to prevent or tackle epidemics. When Covid-19 broke out in early 2020, the initial responses of governments were largely uncoordinated and unilateral. The ineffectiveness of the European civil protection mechanism was most cruelly illustrated when there was no answer to Italy's desperate calls for help as Lombardy was ravaged by the virus. The fact that France and Germany blocked their exports of medical equipment, while China was rescuing Italy, badly damaged the idea of European solidarity.

Against this background, the European Commission has sought to use the window of opportunity provided by the Covid-19 pandemic to strengthen European capacity in the area of health. The first example of this has been the extension of the scope of RescEU (the European civil protection mechanism) to matters of public health alongside the prevention and management of natural disasters as well as chemical, biological, radiological and nuclear incidents. RescEU now has reserves of medical supplies located in six member states, including masks, protective gear, ventilators and more, which can be distributed swiftly throughout Europe in case of emergencies. However the piecemeal, progressive build-up of EU health policy is most noticeable in EU4Health, a major new programme put forward by the European Commission. Endowed with €5.1 billion, covered primarily by NextGenerationEU, it constitutes the largest ever EU health instrument. Its purpose is to fill gaps in national actions along three lines: (a) to improve preparedness, coordination and crisis management in dealing with epidemics; (b) to support the weaker healthcare systems to especially ensure access and affordability for people and enhance prevention policies; and (c) to guarantee the availability and affordability of medicines. Other objectives of EU4Health include the supervision of development of e-health, ranging from the digitalization of healthcare systems to the development of a vaccination passport. For instance, the Digital Europe and Connecting Europe Facility will serve to develop the infrastructure needed for the development of digital health tools.

In November 2020, the European Commission put forward a package of regulations aimed at strengthening European capacity to act against cross-border heath threats. To do so, it has pursued the typical "agencification" model, which can also be observed in other policy areas (Rittberger & Wonka 2011). Following an EP resolution, as well as a Franco-German call, a regulation proposal to strengthen the mandate of the European Centre for Disease Prevention and Control was put forward in November 2020.[6] Likewise, the mandate of the EMA, initially centred on the regulation of the European medicines market, will be extended to preparedness, risk management and the surveillance of epidemics (see Box 9.2). Finally, the Commission announced it will propose the creation of a new agency, the Health Emergency Response Authority, by the end of 2021, in order to facilitate the fight against cross-border health threats.

BOX 9.2 THE EUROPEAN MEDICINE AGENCY

Council Regulation (EEC) No 2309/93 of 22 July 1993 established a European Agency for the Evaluation of Medicinal Products and laid down community procedures for the authorization and supervision of medicinal products, with the goal of harmonizing the work of existing medicine regulatory bodies in member states. The European Medicine Agency (EMA) facilitates the development and access of medicines, evaluates applications for marketing authorization, monitors the safety of vaccines across their life cycle and provides reliable information on human and veterinary medicines in lay language. Although EMA's evaluations commonly provide the basis for authorization in member states, respective member states' authorities may also do so independently. In fact, most medicinal authorizations in the EU are taken at member-state level. EMA has, however, established itself as the competent authority and enjoys a de facto or quasi-regulatory power.

EMA is at the heart of the European medicines regulatory network, which assembles more than 50 competent national authorities (human and veterinary), the Commission and EMA. The Commission takes binding decisions that are based on EMA's evaluations.

---

6. The new tasks of the agency include "epidemiological surveillance via integrated systems enabling real-time surveillance; preparedness and response planning, reporting and auditing; provision of non-binding recommendations and options for risk management; capacity to mobilize and deploy an EU Health Task Force to assist local response in the member states; building a network of EU reference laboratories and a network for substances of human origin" (European Parliament 2021).

EMA has come under the spotlight for its role in vaccine authorization in the Covid-19 pandemic. The agency has set up a Covid-19 taskforce dealing with commercial and clinical aspects related to vaccines. In November 2020, the Commission put forward a proposal to reinforce the role of EMA, notably in the area of monitoring and mitigating shortages of medicinal products.

Source: www.ema.europa.eu (accessed 15 September 2021).

Besides EU4Health, support for national healthcare systems will also be provided via other EU financial instruments, in particular the ESF+ (which supports vulnerable groups having access to healthcare), the European Regional Development Fund (to improve regional healthcare facilities) and Horizon Europe (for health-related research). The current Commission's health entrepreneurship, geared towards investment, comes after a long era of liberalization and fiscal discipline, where DG ECFIN's concerns about the financial sustainability of healthcare systems and calls for "efficiency gains" were conducive of social retrenchment and the weakening of welfare systems. It will be interesting to see how health will be handled in the framework of fiscal governance in the future.

A final line of action concerns the assertion of the EU in the global governance of health. The EU, having shunned the World Health Organization (WHO) to a certain extent in recent times, preferring to set up its own initiatives and funding structures with more clearly defined goals such as the Global Vaccine Alliance, seemed to reinforce its commitment to WHO, particularly after Donald Trump withdrew the United States from the organization (later re-established under the presidency of Joe Biden) (Van Schaik *et al.* 2020). Although France and Germany have committed to increased funding and made proposals in the ongoing fuzzy debate about reforming the WHO, there is no clear European consensus (Van Schaik *et al.* 2020). Furthermore, Europeans find themselves between a rock and a hard place regarding the distribution of vaccines. European countries plus the European Commission form the second largest group of contributors to COVAX, an initiative of the Global Vaccine Alliance to provide vaccines to poorer countries.[7] Yet, this attempt to promote equitable access to vaccines globally is clearly in contradiction to their activism to secure as many doses as possible for Europe, with governments under pressure. A high-level commitment might not be sufficient to radically change the role of the EU in global health governance, as limited willingness to significantly increase spending and the low interest of partner countries (notably in the framework of neighbourhood policy and development

---

7. GAVI, donors' table, "Commitments to GAVI 2021–2025", www.gavi.org (accessed 15 March 2021).

cooperation) for health concerns continue to be major obstacles to efficiency (Veron & Di Ciommo 2020).

Political resistance to competence creep

Timid calls for treaty change aimed at extending the EU competences in the area of health – for example by ETUC or the European Commission – have largely been ignored and there are no prospects currently for any major changes (Brookes *et al.* 2020: 45). The key legal basis for the EU action in the field of health is Article 168 TFEU. The complicated ambivalent content and structure of the article reflects the same genuine reluctance as can be observed towards social policy integration. The EU's health competences are clearly defined as supporting competences geared towards "complementing national policies" and "encouraging cooperation" among member states who shall "coordinate among themselves". The article also insists on subsidiarity and the primacy of national competences. The regulatory competence (hard law) reluctantly granted to the EU in paragraphs 4 and 5 is narrowly circumscribed to quality standards for human substances, veterinary, phytosanitary and medical products, and to the fight against cross-border health threats. Current ambitions to exploit these competences to their fullest may very well run into serious obstacles and little political will. This possibility was recently illustrated by the manner in which EU4Health was trumped by national leaders. Whereas the European Commission initially put forward a budget of €9.4 billion for the programme, it was slashed down to €1.4 billion in the budget negotiations of the European Council in July 2020, before rising once more to €5.4 billion after negotiations between the Council and the EP in December 2020.

Following De Ruijter (2019), it is nevertheless possible to turn the argument around. The development of EU health policy over time could amount to a "silent revolution", with the EU intervening in numerous matters ranging from medicine authorization to the reimbursement of treatments or the shaping of insurance markets. This is taking place without any comprehensive constitutional recognition of EU competence in the area of health. Such a phenomenon is also referred to as "competence creep", which occurs when the EU manages to impose rules and gain influence without the treaty granting it a specific competence in a particular domain (Garben 2019). From the perspective of the human rights and values involved with health policy adopted by De Ruijter, competence creep in health policy could lead to important legitimacy gaps in the EU's action. This is owed to the fact that EU health policy is detached from the questions of fundamental rights and values and is instead grounded in depoliticized and scientific understanding of health and internal market objectives (Garben 2019: ch. 7).

Combining this angle with the important functional drivers for more integration explained earlier, the absence of treaty change (or of political debates) can only serve to exacerbate the legitimacy gaps of the EU's action.

In any event, this new extension in the EU's scope of action has been continuously disputed by unilateral national actions over the past two years. As EU institutions failed to react quickly enough to coordinate an immediate response to the outbreak of Covid-19, governments engaged in a "rush to defensive rebordering" (Genschel & Jachtenfuchs 2021). In February and March 2020, 10 member states banned exports of medical products (especially protective personal equipment such as face masks), 20 put some entry bans in place and 13 reintroduced border controls in contradiction with Schengen rules. During March 2020, governments also decided on school closures and lockdowns in an erratic manner. In a race to catch up on coordination, the European Commission fought hard in June to take the lead in the negotiations with pharmaceutical companies to purchase vaccines. The Commission was given a mandate to purchase jabs through a single solidarity-based procurement procedure and to distribute them to the member states on a pro-rata population basis. This implied convincing France, Germany, Italy and the Netherlands, who had already started to form a group of wealthy buyers, to join the EU common procedure.

Although the Commission succeeded in this endeavour, it has been constantly blamed for its strategy ever since. The Commission's insistence on low prices and securing the legal responsibility of pharmaceutical companies in case of medical issues with the vaccines has been widely seen as a cause for Europe lagging behind both the United States and the UK in the race to secure doses and advance the vaccination campaign (Deutsch & Wheaton 2021). Likewise, the EMA's authorization procedure for vaccines has been repeatedly criticized for being too slow. With vaccines becoming a geopolitical issue, tensions and disputes were common not only between the EU and Russia, but also within the EU itself. Whereas Ursula von der Leyen questioned publicly the efficiency of the Russian vaccine Sputnik V, Hungary bypassed common procedures to authorize the Russian vaccine, as well as a Chinese and an Indian vaccine not (yet) cleared by the EMA. Croatia and Slovakia have also indicated a desire to do the same. At the time of writing, the EMA is only now beginning its review of Sputnik V. In the same vein, governments imposing travel prohibitions and border closures (especially Belgium, Germany and Denmark) were pressured by the European Commission to implement disproportionate (and ineffective?) measures to curb the spread of the virus.

In a nutshell, the outbreak of Covid-19 has undeniably set an EU health policy in motion in a significant and multidimensional fashion. Yet, it is unlikely to be a game changer as capacity building remains limited and piecemeal, with an underlying resistance to any leap towards the centralization of health policy.

The EU's attempt to provide a unified response to the pandemic has taken the form of a difficult tug of war to assert the moral and practical superiority of multilateralism over "sovereigntist instincts" (Benoît & Hay forthcoming). With a number of new procedures and instruments now in place, the EU is arguably more fit than it ever was to face the health challenges of the twenty-first century, the EU health policy still exhibits major issues with regard to its efficiency and legitimacy.

A socially just ecological transition: limited ambitions in the face of great challenges

The need to engage with a profound change of the contemporary capitalist socio-economic model in the face of climate change undeniably constitutes a great civilizational challenge. After years of too much talk and too little action, EU institutions have put the "European Green Deal" at the top of their political agenda. While relatively recent, debates about the social dimension of this transformation process have flourished over the past few years. They have crystallized on the notion of "just transition" originating in US union circles in the 1990s and promoted by international organizations, especially the ILO. The European social question intersects in various and complex ways with the ecological transition, spurring the emergence of new political conflict lines. As put by Pochet (2019: 309):

> There is a gap between those who think that technology can to a large extent bring solutions and those underlining that the issue is in the first place societal and that only a deep change of our consumption practices can allow a sufficient decrease in CO_2 emissions.

This section looks at the emerging distributional conflicts and provides a critical account of the policy issues and the politics underlying the European Green Deal.

New distributional and political conflicts

There are basically two ways to conceive of how the ecological transition plays out in terms of social cohesion. On the one hand, climate change and social inequality reinforce each other, requiring policy-makers to deal with both simultaneously. A flourishing literature shows how both globally and locally, the poor and the vulnerable are disproportionately impacted by climate change and the destruction of the environment. This is illustrated by unequal access to potable water, quality air, energy or food. The ongoing Covid-19 pandemic, ensuing from human damage to ecosystems and excessive proximity to animals, has disproportionately killed people in the working classes and those living in deprived areas, a trend reinforced by other sources of inequality such as ethnic origin or gender (Stafford & Deeny 2020). On the other hand, the realization that the planet can only provide limited resources in a bounded ecological system (Raworth 2017) can trigger various reactions at the individual and societal level. Although certainly desirable, the shift towards "sustainable consumption", fostering frugal and reflective consumption departing from twentieth-century-style overconsumption, is not likely to happen at a large scale if left to individual incentives and beliefs (Jackson 2005: 437). There is a great danger that European societies may follow a non-egalitarian path where increasingly scarce and/or expensive goods and services will only be available for the wealthy. In that sense, many aspects of the European lifestyle, which have been considered as improvements and are the result of twentieth-century successes, such as healthy nutrition or long-haul flights, may become less accessible.

The crux of the matter lies in the institutional and financial arrangements that underpin the transition and whether they will make it socially just. Two problematic areas have emerged in particular. The first is the issue of the inevitable destruction of employment involved in the decarbonization of the economy. The economic and social significance of coal mines in Germany or Poland, for instance, have come under the spotlight. Yet, beyond fossil fuel sectors, a wide range of activities ranging from road, air and maritime transport to the automotive industry will also be affected. Thus, a just transition does not only imply the need for policies to operate territorial, sectoral and individual reconversions, but also a more comprehensive industrial policy framework generating new green value chains (Denis 2020). Furthermore, as posited by Pochet (2019), the new jobs created in the green economy (as in the energy or recycling sectors) are not guaranteed to have high standards in terms of working conditions and pay.

Another crucial issue concerns the taxation of carbon-laden activities. How ill-conceived measures can degenerate into massive anti-establishment protests was best illustrated by the yellow vests movement (*gilets jaunes*), which practically paralysed France for months on end in 2018–19. The trigger was the government decision in October 2018 to increase the tax on fuel for cars in the framework of a broader law aiming to raise taxes on energy products. The movement developed spontaneously and started with the occupation of roundabouts in rural and suburban areas. Large demonstrations also took place in large cities, including Paris, where violence between demonstrators and the police escalated to levels long-unseen in the country, resulting in 12 deaths and thousands of casualties. Beyond the particular issue of fuel, the grievances of the movement rapidly grew to encompass a broad "reformulation of the social question" around the issue of tax justice (Spire 2019). Particular demands were diverse, ranging from the suppression of certain taxes, increasing the minimum wage to €1,300 per month, effectively tackling homelessness, to the introduction of a popular initiative referendum. More generally, demands were made for increased resources for all public services, especially in rural and suburban areas described as being abandoned by Parisian elites.

This leads to the question of how distributional conflicts will shape the political constituencies likely to support or resist the ecological transition if it fails to be socially just. In this regard, three flashpoints appear. First, as in the case of Brexit, the sociology of the yellow vests movement shows that it mobilized, above all, the "squeezed" middle class, rather than just the most deprived in French society, as it led the revolt against work insecurity combined with unbearable fiscal burdens. This indicates the limitations of various "tax shifts" from capital and progressive taxes to socially undifferentiated sources of fiscal revenue. A just transition must rely on new fiscal strategies in which the EU certainly has an important role to play. Second, the mass youth mobilization of 2018–19, epitomized by Greta Thunberg's revolt against the political establishment, shed light on the generational aspect of the transition. Although it may be unfair to stigmatize baby boomers for consumption practices that had become the norm across the western world, younger generations seem more concerned with the prospect of uncontrolled climate change. A word of caution is nevertheless necessary here since this awareness seems typically higher among educated, urban young people. Third, political scientists have typically seen climate change as a matter of "new politics" anchored into post-materialist values. Thus, it might only reinforce the Green/ alternative/libertarian versus traditional/authoritarian/nationalist cleavage that has powerfully restructured European politics over the past few decades (Hooghe *et al.* 2002). Cutting across the left/right cleavage, this could be a problem for many political parties, especially large government parties who may be divided on how to deal with the green transition and how to address the social justice element.

Social justice: the blind spot of the European Green Deal?

Drawing from older reflections on the green economy, calls for a Green Deal have emanated from various activist circles, intellectual platforms in the UK, the United States and Europe, as well as international organizations in the aftermath of the 2008 financial crisis.[8] After years of inertia, the European Commission

8. These include the Green New Deal Group (notably around Tim Jackson) in the UK, the Center for American Progress, the Green European Foundation (linked to the European Green Party) and the United Nations Environment Programme (see Herman 2015).

made a historic move to spearhead the fight against climate change both internally and globally as it issued its communication for the European Green Deal in December 2019. The Green Deal's purpose is to "design deeply transformative policies" in order to achieve a set of key goals ranging from clean energy to the protection of eco-systems or the acceleration of smart mobility (European Commission 2020). The most striking measure deployed is the so-called European Climate Law passed in June 2021,[9] which makes the commitment to climate neutrality in terms of CO_2 emissions by 2050 a legal obligation for all EU member states. In addition, a range of actions are planned to achieve the goals set in the Green Deal, such as:

- investing in environmentally friendly technologies;
- supporting industry to innovate;
- rolling out cleaner, cheaper and healthier forms of private and public transport;
- decarbonizing the energy sector;
- ensuring buildings are more energy efficient; and
- working with international partners to improve global environmental standards.[10]

At the discursive level, the European Commission has largely embraced the notion of just transition, as its vice president in charge of the Green Deal, Frans Timmermans, repeatedly insisted that the ecological transition should "leave no one behind". The main instrument set up in the framework of the Green Deal is the Just Transition Mechanism (see Box 9.3), which rests on three pillars: the Just Transition Fund, serving to distribute €40 billion to regions with the most carbon-dependent economies; €30 billion from InvestEU to leverage private money; and €10 billion in loans from the European Investment Bank directed to the public sector. Beyond the Green Deal, a further tool that has been developed is the green conditionality for spending the resources under the multi-annual budget and NextGenerationEU in 2021–27 (see Chapter 8). The December 2020 agreement foresees that 40 per cent of all spending should be earmarked as green. Since this involves all structural and investment funds it means that the ESF+, for instance, will be used to re-skill workers in green sectors or to fund initiatives promoting the circular economy. Finally, after a series of consultation with organized civil society, the European Commission

---

9. Regulation (EU) 2021/1119 of the European Parliament and of the Council of 30 June 2021 Establishing the Framework for Achieving Climate Neutrality and Amending Regulations (EC) No. 401/2009 and (EU) 2018/1999 ("European Climate Law").

10. European Commission, "A European Green Deal", https://ec.europa.eu/info/strategy/priorities-2019-2024/european-green-deal_en (accessed 15 September 2021).

BOX 9.3 THE JUST TRANSITION MECHANISM

The idea of a fund aimed at financially supporting regions relying on fossil fuel energy was put forward by the European Commission and the EP in 2017 and 2018 respectively, in the run-up to the talks on the multi-annual financial framework for 2021–27. The European Commission proposed a regulation establishing a Just Transition Fund in January 2020 endowed with €7.5 billion, an amount increased to €40 billion in the framework of NextGenerationEU in May 2020, then cut down to €17.5 billion in the European Council negotiations in July 2020.

The fund is part of the EU's cohesion policy and specifically targets regions extracting coal, petrol, natural gas, shale gas and lignite. In the framework of the European Semester, governments will have to submit territorial just transition plans in tune with their national climate and energy plans. The identification of eligible territories and measures laid down in the plans will occur through a dialogue between national administrations and European Commission services.

Besides the fund itself, the Just Transition Mechanism has two further pillars: (a) a €20 billion investment package under InvestEU (the investment instrument of the EU aiming at leveraging private investment) targeting sustainable transport and energy infrastructures; and (b) a €30 billion loan facility from the European Investment Bank dedicated to the public sector for projects related to infrastructure, urban heating and energy efficiency in buildings.

Source: Spina (2010).

---

issued a communication entitled "A Strong Social Europe for Just Transitions" (COM(2020)14) in January 2020. Here, the emphasis lies on the EPSR and how it should bring about enhanced social cohesion after an action plan is adopted. However, the absence of articulation with the Green Deal is striking.

What emerges from this complex picture is the difficulty in finding a consistent and convincing intellectual frame articulating ecological and social goals. There are four main weaknesses in these new EU policy instruments, which raise doubts regarding the EU's ability to bring about a just transition (Denis & Denuit 2020). First, the overall amount of money dedicated to the "just" dimension of the transition is insufficient. Although 40 per cent of NextGenerationEU will be dedicated to the ecological transition (approximately €100 billion a year), the European Court of Auditors estimated that about €1,115 billion a year is necessary to allow the EU to meet its objectives. Because the devil often lies in the detail, the methodology foreseen to assess whether expenses from the governments will be counted as "green" seems particularly problematic. Based on indicators developed by the OECD, the so-called climate tracking system used by the Commission leads to overestimates of the share of sustainable expenditure (European Court of Auditors 2020). Moreover, EU institutions are ready to take a particularly lax approach to the way in which national governments will use the money, since they will "consider an investment to be a sustainable investment if it does not *significantly harm* any environmental or social objective" of the Green Deal (European Court of Auditors 2020: n.p., emphasis added).

Second, whereas the European Commission had proposed to endow the Just Transition Fund with €40 billion, it was significantly cut down to €17.5 billion by the European Council in the negotiations on the multi-annual financial framework in July 2020. Moreover, the fund will be the main financial instrument backing the European Green Deal, indicating a narrow strategy to compensate the most carbon-dependent sectors and territories in a targeted fashion, as opposed to comprehensive action aimed at fostering wider socio-economic change (Sabato & Fronteddu 2020: 16–17).

Third, the notion of inequality is conspicuously absent from EU policy-making. Neither the unequal distribution of environmental damage nor the costs associated with the transition have a prominent place in the Green Deal. How taxes should be used to make the transition "just" is a particularly dramatic blind spot, as deplored by the European Anti-Poverty Network, one of the largest European platforms of social NGOs (EAPN 2020)

Fourth, green national spending will be operated through the European Semester, which was originally conceived to monitor the excessive deficit and debts and recommend structural reforms (see Chapter 7). In spite of an increased focus on investment and recovery, the European Semester still appears ill-equipped to allow the implementation of a comprehensive strategy for tackling inequality in the ecological transition. Recognizing that "measuring and assessing (social) sustainability are still at their infancy", work on elaborating an analytical toolkit considering social and environmental sustainability together is underway in DG EMPL (Jaksic *et al.* 2019: 65). Yet this has barely percolated through to the political level and the European Green Deal remains typically focused on human capital and employability. In turn, the existing apparatus for assessing environmental and climate issues (e.g. indicators) still needs to be integrated into the European Semester, in synergy with the social scoreboard (Charveriat & Bodin 2020). Finally, as underscored by Sabato and Fronteddu (2020: 21), neither the DG for the Environment (DG ENV) nor the DG for Climate Action (DG CLIMA) have so far been involved in the European Semester, which is steered by DG ECFIN and DG EMPL.

In sum, it seems fair to say that the Green Deal exhibits an expected pro-market bias in its approach to the just transition. Ideologically, it aims primarily at defining a new growth strategy. Intellectually, it still relies on old concepts and indicators (e.g. GDP) and market instruments (e.g. the pricing of carbon, financial compensation of the "losers") (Laurent 2020). EU policy-making therefore seems to concentrate on solutions to perceived *trade-offs* between economic efficiency, social welfare and ecological transition, rather than developing a deeper reflection on how to foster *synergies* between them in a way that puts human and environmental welfare first.

Old politics and temptation of greenwashing

The philosophical and interest-based divergences over the European Green Deal have fed political battles at the European level. However, none of them appear to be very new as the just transition agenda reactivates well-known conflicts among EU institutions, member states, political parties and societal interests. This is also typical of the way in which EU policy-making forges compromises that integrate – more or less successfully – a number of policy ideas and instruments, and neutralizes more radical alternatives.

With the European Green Deal, Ursula von der Leyen has clearly shown entrepreneurship in a move to reassert the purpose and legitimacy of the European Commission. This was done, first, by capitalizing on the political momentum created by the youth mobilization for climate change in 2018–19 and, second, by using the window of opportunity opened by the Covid-19 pandemic to significantly increase the funding available for the green transition and link economic recovery to a forward-looking transformational agenda (Dupont *et al.* 2020). The political responses triggered by the Commission's offensive have reactivated classical patterns of conflict in the EU. The EP has (overall) played a cheerleader role for an ambitious Green Deal. The EP and the Commission have nevertheless had to face the reluctance of heads of state and government who typically tend to water down legal obligations or financial commitments stemming from the EU. This was illustrated during the negotiations on the multi-annual financial framework, as the European Council slashed the budget of the Just Transition Fund by 42 per cent in July 2020. These negotiations were the stage for a confrontation between net contributors – illustrated by the tenacity of the "frugal four" – and net recipients to the EU budget, with a special emphasis on the Just Transition Fund; whereas deliberations on the European Climate Law unveiled the same left–right divide, which appears in the EP on most socio-economic matters. Although far-right Eurosceptics reject the idea of binding commitments at EU level in the name of national sovereignty and economic efficiency, the Conservatives favoured softer regulation, arguing that "if Europe wants to create jobs and remain an industrial continent, it is crucial to maintain realistic CO_2

emission targets".[11] In contrast, the Greens and the far-left have requested an increase in the Climate Law's objectives, aiming for emission reductions of up to 65 per cent by 2050. As for the Social Democrats, they have mainly pursued ambitious regulation, insisting on implementation issues. A lot is at stake with the European Green Deal for a social democracy that is in decline across Europe and in need of recasting some of its ideological fundaments through the prism of the just transition: "the elements of active government, collective goods and social inclusion chime with the social democratic tradition, yet it needs to overcome the contradictory baggage on utopianism, on the one hand, [and] industrialism, on the other" (Bloomfield & Steward 2020: 775).

Fundamentally, party politics have reflected oppositions between various societal interest groups. While admitting that the decarbonization of the industry was a necessary step, industry representatives have asked that EU regulation should be kept to a minimum, avoiding overly ambitious targets (Simon 2020). They insisted that massive (public?) investment and a comprehensive industrial strategy were needed to reach the ambitious objectives set and raised concerns about a loss of competitiveness at the global level. Although trade unions have also called for an ambitious industrial strategy that secures value chains and jobs, social NGOs have criticized the economic bias of the Green Deal and stressed that public goods and the fight against inequalities should be at the top of the EU's agenda (EAPN 2020).

Ultimately, the dilemmas and compromises involved have emerged in a number of policy areas. The EU's Common Agricultural Policy (CAP) is perhaps most illustrative of the resistance to the ecological transition within European economies and societies. Since the 1990s, the successive reforms of CAP have aimed to transform it from a productivist policy, having supported intensive agriculture, to one encouraging a new environmentally friendly agricultural model. However, the necessary compromises among the EU institutions, member states and political parties have amounted more to "greenwashing" than a proper "greening" of CAP (Alons 2017). As a result, CAP has kept its redistributive bias, whereby it benefits wealthier farmers disproportionately and has so far failed to provide a tangible springboard for smaller farmers wanting to develop, among other things, organic agriculture. The ongoing discussions about CAP post-2020 show little change in this regard. Both the Council and the EP have considerably watered down the green ambitions of the European Commission by "diluting 'environmental spending' with interventions which are not proven to positively contribute to the environment; by excluding 40 per cent of agricultural land subject to make space for nature; by excluding or postponing mandatory support for

---

11. "Make stronger CO_2 curbs, but don't kill jobs", EPP group in the EP, 10 September 2020, www.eppgroup.eu (accessed 15 September 2021).

'eco-schemes'" (Metta 2020: n.p.). These developments have raised a great deal of criticism regarding the incompatibility of CAP with the European Green Deal.

Last but not least, the role of finance in the green transition remains controversial. In its 2018 "Action Plan: Financing Sustainable Growth", the European Commission envisaged recasting the role of finance in order to see capital flows redirected towards the green economy. As Asian central banks have been at the forefront in considering climate change as a major risk for financial stability, this has now also become a major concern for the ECB. Since 2018, the president of the ECB, Christine Lagarde, has made various statements indicating her willingness to "go green". In January 2021, she announced the set-up of a climate team to reflect on new possible instruments such as green bonds, with one of the key issues being the central bank's credo of "market neutrality", which denies the distributive consequences of monetary policy (Van't Klooster & Fontan 2020). Central banks' corporate bond purchase schemes have been illustrative of this, as through trying to reproduce seemingly neutral market structures while buying bonds from all companies, central banks have massively supported the fossil fuel industry along with air transport and the arms industry, among others (Van't Klooster & Fontan 2021). Over the past few years, various citizens' groups, NGOs and academics have criticized the negative contribution made by central banks through their financing of multinationals that exploit fossil fuel and, more broadly, activities damaging the environment.[12] In March 2021, the Bank of England announced that it would abandon "market neutrality" to consider the environmental impact of the corporations from whom it is buying bonds. While the ECB is expected to follow suit, it remains to be seen how it can come up with effective new tools to bring the just transition forward.

Conclusion

After years of muddling through and regressive socio-economic policy-making, the EU has arguably been moving faster over the past few years to tackle the great challenges it is facing in the twenty-first century. This chapter has looked at how new policy concepts, resources and regulations have emerged around three issues: the social consequences of Brexit, health policy after Covid-19 and the ecological transition. Ironically, all these issues question "our European way of life" that the European Commission has pledged to defend and promote. The account provided here shows that, despite recent decisions and an increased awareness of rising inequality, the EU is not really fit for purpose in that sense.

---

12. For instance, 350.org hosts a global campaign advocating "a just recovery for all", which targets the role of banks. See https://350.org (accessed 6 September 2021).

Brexit is likely to weaken social regulation through the back door, against a historic pandemic-induced recessionary background. The European Green Deal seems disappointing to those hoping for a decisive shift towards tackling inequality, striving for tax justice and public investment in environmentally friendly collective goods. The risk of capture by the economic and societal forces resistant to change is great, as much of the Green Deal relies on incentivizing economic actors to invest in green growth and compensating the "losers" of decarbonization. If it remains so, it might prove insufficient to tackle climate change and the socially unequal impact of health threats. Ultimately, the danger is that most Europeans are left on their own with everyday choices to make between – as the *gilets jaunes* put it – "the end of the month" and "the end of the world".

Further reading

- Eleanor Brooks and Robert Geyer, "The development of EU health policy and the Covid-19 pandemic: trends and implications". *Journal of European Integration* 42:8 (2020), 1057–76.
- Linda Hantrais, *What Brexit Means for EU and UK Social Policy* (Bristol: Policy Press, 2019).
- Sebastiano Sabato and Boris Fronteddu, "A socially just transition through the European Green Deal?" OSE Working Paper (Brussels: European Trade Union Institute, 2020).

Questions to debate

- Has the EU asserted effective leadership in the management of the Covid-19 pandemic?
- Does the European Green Deal constitute a critical juncture in the EU's approach to the ecological transition?

CONCLUSION: FROM THE SOCIAL QUESTION TO THE DEMOCRATIC QUESTION

As a new political constellation has arisen out of the recovery agenda, we see the EU building its role in socio-economic governance. Brexit, the Covid-19 pandemic and the climate emergency not only make the European social question more acute, they also pose it in new ways that emphasize the interdependency binding European societies together. Over the past few years, EU institutions have operated a non-negligible relaunch of their social agenda, stressing the need for social cohesion; ventured into new social territories such as minimum incomes; strengthened their regulatory and bureaucratic capacities, as in the field of health; and significantly increased the budgetary resources of the EU, looking to introduce new sources of fiscal revenue in the near future. All of this, however, happened without much debate in national arenas. The role of the EU in the social realm remains a political taboo and even more so a formalization of such a role in legal terms. Yet, in order to allow the EU to address the European social question in an effective and legitimate fashion, generating a widely shared understanding of what the EU is *actually doing* and what it *should do* in the future constitutes a key endeavour. To conclude this book, it is therefore argued that the normative basis of EU social policy needs to be strengthened, from a conceptual and democratic point of view.

As a starting point, it is useful to consider the four ideal-typical models distinguished by Claassen *et al.* (2019) to rethink the role of the EU in social policy. First, the EU could be a *passive spectator* if both the formulation of normative ideals and consequential institutional arrangements were to remain exclusively with national governments. Yet, as this book has shown, the state of EU integration has already overtaken this model and a return to full national sovereignty in social policy would require deconstructing all existing EU instruments and resources, as some "defenders of nation states" have claimed (see the Introduction). Against the backdrop of the pandemic, however, Europeans are currently moving in the opposite direction by endowing the EU with more tasks and resources.

Second, in the *patron of nations* model, the key choices for the social models lie entirely with nation states and the EU is only in charge of enabling them by tackling negative externalities, on the one hand, and organizing only (limited) redistribution when necessary, on the other. In line with Crum's proposals, this model sees the main duty of the EU as (a) guaranteeing equal access for citizens and states to the economic opportunities of the single market, (b) supporting national welfare states in fulfilling European social values and goals and (c) preserving one's autonomy to decide on social policy arrangements (Crum 2015). The main political problem arising from this model, however, is that member states are not likely to agree to pooling a significant amount of resources without a certain degree of mutual control over social policy. Although the idea of national *autonomy* is appealing from a democratic point of view, it is debatable whether all national models should be put on an equal footing. For a whole set of historic, cultural, economic and political reasons, some governments are unwilling or unable to effectively address the lack of social cohesion across Europe. Above all, European ambitions and values do not exist as such, but rather float above national welfare states. These are reshaped as national social models change, insofar as national and European social institutions are already more closely embedded with each other than one might think at first sight. Because who is the *European patron* if not the member states themselves? The Council of the EU and the European Council remain not only the collective master of the treaties, but also the prevailing political authority (van Middelaar 2014), unmatched neither by the European Commission nor by the CJEU, let alone the EP.

Third, the EU could be a *guarantor of social rights*, defining rights and minimum standards enjoyed by citizens but leaving member states responsible for implementing the policies to achieve objectives and comply to standards. To a large extent, this is the logic that already underpins social regulation, the European social dialogue and the OMC. Yet, relying on that approach alone does not seem viable from a political point of view. The reason being that, in such a configuration, the EU only imposes *constraints* on national governments, without providing incentives. In other words, it uses the stick, but does not offer any carrot for national governments to comply with European social rights. Then, further dilemmas arise as to whether the stick should continue to operate with a soft touch (soft law) or be potentially coercive (hard law and sanctions for non-compliance). In the former case, as for instance with the calls for governments to engage with social investment in the recommendations of the European Semester, it easily turns to ineffective incantations. In the latter case, the legitimacy of sanctions or court proceedings will be questioned by those states that find themselves in the impossible position of having to meet the standards due to insufficient resources. Thus, if one accepts that social policy is a core state power, it needs to rely on two pillars: one regulatory (settings standards and rules), the other redistributive (providing resources).

This leads us to the fourth model put forward by Claassen *et al.* (2019), which conceives of the EU as a *protector of citizens* performing all the classic functions of social protection. As the authors admit, this model is highly unrealistic. Regardless of the key legitimacy issues at stake, it is hard to see why replacing national welfare states with a supranational one could be feasible or desirable.

Against this conceptual background, it is argued that none of these models *alone* can serve as a reference to address the European social question. Rather, the features of all models (except perhaps for the first) need to be combined in a way that allows the EU to provide added value and play a more effective and positive role in the multi-layered governance of social cohesion. Beyond the notion of "shared competence" that defines social policy in the TFEU, the normative foundations – both from a philosophical and a legal point of view – will need to be consolidated along a *three-dimensional model*. The EU conceives of itself as a union of states and citizens, who are simultaneously national *and* European citizens. The EU's social competence can therefore not be rooted in a monistic vision. It necessarily has to be articulated in a way that not only focus on the recipients of social policy (i.e. states or citizens), but also on the *relationship among actors in a given space*. As argued by Ferrera (2005), territoriality and political boundedness have been key in the institutionalization of social policy. Social cohesion can thus only be assessed in terms of cohesiveness of constitutive parts in given boundaries. Following Sangiovanni (2013), it is therefore useful to conceptualize the role of the EU along the lines of a "tripartite model" aiming at ensuring national, inter-national and transnational social cohesion.

1. *National cohesion concerns the relationship among national citizens within the boundaries of the nation state or national societies*
Here, the EU performs a duty of helping and constraining its member states in achieving a satisfactory level of social cohesion at the national level. To do so, however, it cannot rely on setting standards alone. In contrast with what we have experienced in the aftermath of the 2008 financial crisis, the EU needs to be much more effective in preventing a degradation of national social cohesion as a result of major economic downturns. With NextGenerationEU, the EU is de facto moving beyond the model of a regulatory state and strengthens the redistributive string to its repertoire of action in a significant way. If the EU is to be a "guarantor of social rights" using not only sticks but also carrots grown in the common garden, then the choices pertaining to it should be made democratically. For with redistribution comes accountability. On the one hand, this implies

a democratic debate at European level about the objectives pursued through commonly provided resources (top-down accountability). If one accepts that parliamentarism remains a main source of democratic legitimacy in Europe, those debates should include not only the executives elected at the national level and debating among themselves (in the Council), but also representatives elected in national parliaments as well as the EP. On the other hand, it does not seem illegitimate to envisage mechanisms for (bottom-up) accountability of member states, both through their peers (Council) and elected representatives (EP) over how the common money is spent.

An important degree of diversity in national arrangements is bound to remain and is as such fully legitimate. But only the public explication of national policies and deliberation can serve to preserve and enhance diversity instead of implicit pressure and forked-tongued politics of national administrations. In this regard, the bilateral bureaucratic dialogue between the services of the European Commission and national administrations underpinning, for instance, the European Semester does not do justice to the political and societal importance of the recovery agenda. Nor can the punctual and tense grand bargains occurring in the European Council be considered as an open and democratic deliberation about alternative policy options. Across the board, the EP as well as national parliaments should be more involved in squaring the circle of taxation and representation (Crum 2020). In this area, the EU is therefore the guarantor of national cohesion. But owing to its redistributive nature, the role of the EU is inextricably linked to its role regarding international cohesion.

2. International cohesion concerns the relationship among states (and regions) within the boundaries of the EU
In Article 151 TFEU cited earlier, the EU has set itself the duty to address gaps in social cohesion between national societies. The long-standing EU objective of convergence clearly taps into that dimension by targeting not only nation states but also regions. This dimension clearly relates to the existence of unpalatable interdependencies and potentially asymmetric externalities. The notion that risks and opportunities related to economic integration (the monetary union), geopolitical configurations (migration) or unexpected events (such as a pandemic) are not distributed equally across member states should be democratically acknowledged; and the related debates should serve as a basis to set up redistribution mechanisms between countries. Here, two archetypical counter-models have crystallized fears and objections. On one side of the spectrum, we find the *transfer union* whereby wealthy countries would only sacrifice their own welfare for ineffective policies tapping into moral hazards and resistance

to change among the "laggards". On the other side of the spectrum is the idea that a "one-size-fits-all" policy model (e.g. the export-led state) is dogmatically enforced through more or less coercive means in spite of obvious structural socio-economic diversity. There is thus a tension to be resolved between the balancing of particular strengths and weaknesses across states and regions and coherent action for operating a just socio-ecological transition.

3. Transnational cohesion concerns the relationship among European citizens within the boundaries of the EU

Through this dimension, the EU is creating a direct bond as a "protector of citizens" regardless of where they come from. Mainly through the principle of non-discrimination, the EU has pioneered the creation of a set of transnational rights in terms of free movement and individual social and societal rights. To a limited extent, these rights have fleshed out the idea of European citizenship. The jurisprudence of the CJEU in particular has been a main driver of new pan-European rights. This process has nevertheless produced two fundamental imbalances. The first is a strong dependence on market-making, as rights have mainly been justified by the existence of a common market and the freedom of movement (for the purpose of labour mobility) within it. Insofar as European citizenship can be qualified as a market citizenship (Magnette 1999), it runs the risk of subordination to and dependence on the versatile needs of the market. The second imbalance pertains to the fact that most of the EU's transnational rights in fact rely on the mutual granting of national rights and the opening of welfare states to non-national EU citizens. This is what happens when, for instance, Europeans go to study or seek healthcare in other EU countries than their country of nationality. Therefore, they are an extension of national rights beyond national boundaries rather than genuine new rights or entitlements granted through the EU itself.

This is problematic in several respects. First, this makes rights a matter of reciprocity leaving open the question as to whether all rights should always be granted to all Europeans (De Witte 2012). In this regard, research has provided evidence that the de facto difference in levels of welfare across member states prevents the theoretical opening of national welfare boundaries to materialize as substantive equal rights for all Europeans (Bruzelius & Seeleib-Kaiser 2019). Even these theoretical rights to reciprocity can be called into question. Since the 2014 *Dano* case, the CJEU has clearly reversed its jurisprudence and increasingly granted national governments the possibility to curtail non-national EU citizens' access to social benefits such as unemployment or child benefits. Linking to the first issue identified, namely market dependence, the reasoning holds that if they are not sufficiently economically active, EU citizens can be seen as an excessive burden for national social systems in which case even expulsion from the territory may be justified. This undermines the rights to freely live and work in the EU entailed in the 2004 so-called citizenship directive. To conclude, then, the EU needs to leave the era of market citizenship behind to substantiate EU citizenship with a social string and transnational rights, which cannot be withdrawn or denied by member states' governments. This is not to say that the EU should become a fully fledged supranational welfare state, but that it ought to develop some capacity to develop and sustain pan-European rights *as such*. Arguably, the EU will only be able to address the pressing social issues of the twenty-first century if it asserts its three-pronged role.

Addressing the European social question through democratization

That being said, substantiating the social dimension of European citizenship in the national, international and transnational realms is not likely to result from the current form of EU politics. As argued by scholars of social movements, the intergovernmental turn accentuated by the politics of emergency and grand summits in the face of "crises" accompanied by the marginalization of the EP in socio-economic governance has meant the closing down of channels for mediating grievances from the grassroots towards the EU institutions (Della Porta & Parks 2018). This has fuelled further resentment vis-à-vis establishments at all levels of governance and the expression of movements who have experimented (e.g. by occupying camps) with forms of participation and claimed contempt towards traditional intermediary institutions such as parties or trade unions (Della Porta 2015; Della Porta 2017). In many respects, Peter Mair's prediction that the absence of channels mediating classical opposition to policies at the EU level would turn it into anti-system opposition to the EU polity itself became the reality of today's European politics (Mair 2007). What we have observed overall is the rise of executive politics, in the form of occasional grand summits of the European Council backed by a multi-level bureaucratic machinery associating national administrations and the European Commission in the making of policies, while parliamentarism and popular participation largely side-lined or at best instrumentalized to forge legitimacy. The European Semester, which has become the most central framework with regard to socio-economic governance, is illustrative of this development. Against this background, the strengthening of the EU's prerogatives in the social realm may arguably only deepen its deficit of democratic legitimacy. The technocratic build-up of "Social Europe" may well backlash in different ways, if no democratic procedure ensures the necessary popular support for deciding over matters of justice, solidarity and redistribution. Globalization, European integration and the latest financial crisis together have contributed heavily to de-politicize the social question, not least by using law as "an important instrument for lifting the social questions outside of political contestation" (De Witte 2019: 581).

What is needed then, is a democratization of EU socio-economic governance in order to enable citizens to "reappropriate the social question" (De Witte 2019: n.p.). How this can be done is of course one of the most difficult questions of our time, which not only concerns the EU but also domestic politics. To be sure, the two strategies pursued so far by the EU institutions are arguably democratic dead ends. The first is the strengthening of the European "stakeholders' democracy" (Aldrin & Hubé 2016) in which the European social agenda is co-managed by the EU institutions and interest groups representing diffuse citizens' interests. The main problem here is that this kind of politics is very much confined to the Brussels bubble in a way that is disconnected from grassroots grievances and, as such, it accentuates the elitist bias of EU integration. Moreover, the multiple procedures and fora for dialogue, consultation, etc. have no binding procedures ensuring that organized civil society is not only heard but also listened to. A consequence is that its power is limited to agenda setting and persuasion but is often toothless with regard to decision-making. A second direction has seen the rise of soft coordination – through the OMC and then the European Semester – which has considerably augmented the multi-level executive and administrative network deciding and implementing social policy. From a democratic point of view, this is problematic because it amounts to a confiscation of deliberation by epistemic communities and networks of decision-makers who operate out of sight of the public sphere. Eventually, channels of accountability are blurred, and it is virtually impossible for the citizen to know who is responsible for bad (or good!) policies.

Two different avenues may be more promising with a view of addressing the European social question in a more democratic manner. Historically, parliamentary representation has proved an effective way. While there is a lot to say about the problems involved with representation at all territorial levels of governments, the relevance of parliamentarism as such has been further weakened by EU integration. In the realm of socio-economic governance, perhaps more than in any other policy domain, the EU needs an effective multi-level parliamentary system that has the power to steer and legitimize decisions. Instead of being symbolic (such as the Conference of Parliamentary Committees for Union Affairs [COSAC]) or an EP that is too often restricted to the role of spectator. For a starter, the EP needs to be fully empowered with decision-making powers, including on matters addressed through soft coordination and the European Semester. This also means granting it a genuine right of initiative to propose legislation. Additionally, we now live in an age in which the Covid-19 pandemic has led European leaders – like many others! – to convene regularly via videoconference. Why not build a permanent electronic infra-structure allowing national parliaments to deliberate and vote on matters falling under their scope of competence (e.g. labour market reforms of social rights)? Along with representation, participation can form a second string to bring social policy back into the realm of democratic politics. Because of the bureaucratic constraints and resources needed to participate, the European Citizen Initiative launched with the Lisbon Treaty only constitutes a weak form of democratic par-ticipation involving, again, mainly very organized groups. And again, it has been very disappointing in terms of response from the European Commission. In the same vein, the Conference on the Future of Europe taking place in May and June 2021 is not likely to help alleviate the legitimacy crisis of the EU. Without a tangible objective or mechanism binding decision-makers, it is hard to see how it will amount to anything else than another instrumental staging of citizen deliberation. In contrast, one could think of testing new procedures allowing citizens (selected randomly) to take part in decision-making or using European referenda (as opposed to national referenda) on key redistributive or institu-tional issues.

In any event, it is hard to see at this point how the EU could fully address the social question and assert its three-pronged role without undertaking sub-stantial democratizing steps. Both the lack of political impulse and democratic grounds would undermine its legitimacy. As history shows, the social question and the democratic question are bound to remain closely intertwined.

INDEX OF CJEU JUDGMENTS

REFERENCES

Abdelal, R. 2006. "Writing the rules of global finance: France, Europe, and capital liberalization". *Review of International Political Economy* 13(1): 1–27.

Adranghi, A. *et al.* 2019. "Stuck on the Rubicon? 'Socializing' the European Semester through the European Pillar of Social Rights". Working Paper, Foundation for European Progressive Studies and the Renner Institute, www.feps-europe.eu/attachments/publications/wg%20social%20europe%20-%20paper%20final.pdf.

Agostini, C. *et al.* 2017. "Conclusion". In C. Agostini *et al.*, *Balancing Protection and Investment: Structural Reforms in Five Countries*, 109–11. Brussels: ETUI.

Aldrin, P. & N. Hubé 2016. "The European Union, a stakeholders' democracy: from participationism laboratories to democratic experiments". *Gouvernement et action publique* 2(2): 125–52.

Alons, G. 2017. "Environmental policy integration in the EU's common agricultural policy: greening or greenwashing?" *Journal of European Public Policy* 24(11): 1604–22.

Anderson, K. 2015. *Social Policy in the European Union*. Basingstoke: Palgrave Macmillan.

Andor, L. 2020. "Labour markets and mobility: how to reconcile competitiveness and social justice?" In A. Crespy *et al.* (eds), *Governance and Politics in the Post-Crisis European Union*, 217–37. Cambridge: Cambridge University Press.

Andor, L. *et al.* 2014. "Designing a European unemployment insurance scheme". *Intereconomics* 49(4): 184–203.

André, C. & C. Hermann 2009. "Privatisation and marketisation of health care systems in Europe". In M. Frangakis *et al.* (eds), *Privatisation Against the European Social Model*, 129–44. Basingstoke: Palgrave Macmillan.

Antonucci, L. & F. Corti 2020. "Inequalities in the European Semester". Policy study, Foundation for European Progressive Studies, www.feps-europe.eu/attachments/publications/inequalities_in_the_european_semester%20online.pdf.

Antonucci, L. *et al.* 2017. "The malaise of the squeezed middle: challenging the narrative of the 'left behind' Brexiter". *Competition & Change* 21(3): 211–29.

Antonucci, L. & S. Varriale 2020. "Unequal Europe, unequal Brexit: how intra-European inequalities shape the unfolding and framing of Brexit". *Current Sociology* 68(1): 41–59.

Armstrong, K. 2010. *Governing Social Inclusion Europeanization through Policy Coordination*. Oxford: Oxford University Press.

Arpe, J., S. Milio & A. Stuchlik 2015. "Social policy reforms in the EU: a cross-national comparison". *Social Inclusion Monitor Europe (SIM):Reform Barometer*, www.bertelsmann-stiftung.de/fileadmin/files/user_upload/Study_EZ_SIM_Europe_Reformbarometer_2015.pdf.

Baccaro, L. & C. Howell 2011. "A common neoliberal trajectory: the transformation of industrial relations in advanced capitalism". *Politics & Society* 39(4): 521–63.

Bache, I. *et al.* 2011. *Politics in the European Union*. Oxford: Oxford University Press.

Bachtler, J. *et al.* 2017. "Introduction: reassessing the performance and direction of EU cohesion policy in 2014–2020". In J. Bachtler *et al.* (eds), *EU Cohesion Policy: Reassessing Performance and Direction*, 1–8. Abingdon: Routledge.

Bachtler, J. & C. Mendez 2020. "Cohesion and the EU budget: is conditionality undermining solidarity?" In J. Bachtler *et al.* (eds), *Governance and Politics in the Post-Crisis European Union*, 121–39. Cambridge: Cambridge University Press.

Bailey, D. 2005. "Obfuscation through integration: legitimating 'new' social democracy in the European Union". *Journal of Common Market Studies* 43(1): 13–35.

Bailey, D. 2017. "Obstacles to 'Social Europe' ". In P. Kent & N. Lendvai-Bainton (eds), *Handbook of European Social Policy*, 108–25. Cheltenham: Edward Elgar.

Bailey, D. *et al.* (eds) 2017. *European Social Democracy During the Global Economic Crisis: Renovation or Resignation?* Manchester: Manchester University Press.

Bailleux, A. 2014. "La Cour de justice, la Charte des droits fondamentaux et l'intensité normative des droits sociaux". *Tijdschrift voor sociaal recht (TSR)/Revue de droit social (RDS)* 2014(3): 281–308.

Barbier, J. 2015. *La longue marche vers l'Europe sociale*. Paris: PUF.

Barcevicius, E., T. Weishaupt & J. Zeitlin 2014a. "Institutional design and national influence of EU social policy coordination: advancing a contradictory debate". In E. Barcevicius *et al.* (eds), *Assessing the Open Method of Coordination*, 1–15. Basingstoke: Palgrave Macmillan.

Barcevicius, E., T. Weishaupt & J. Zeitlin 2014b. "Tracing the social OMC from its origins to Europe 2020". In E. Barcevicius *et al.* (eds), *Assessing the Open Method of Coordination*, 16–39. Basingstoke: Palgrave Macmillan.

Bartolini, S. 2005. *Restructuring Europe*. Oxford: Oxford University Press.

Baun, M. & D. Marek 2014. *Cohesion Policy in the European Union*. Basingstoke: Palgrave Macmillan.

Bekker, S. 2018. "Flexicurity in the European Semester: still a relevant policy concept?" *Journal of European Public Policy* 25(2): 175–92.

Bekker, S. 2020. "The European Semester: understanding an innovative governance model". In P. Cardwell & M. Granger (eds), *Research Handbook on the Politics of EU Law*, 67–81. Cheltenham: Edward Elgar.

Bellamy, R. 2013. "'An ever-closer union among the peoples of Europe': republican intergovernmentalism and democratic representation within the EU". *Journal of European Integration* 35(5): 499–516.

Bellamy, R. & J. Lacey 2017. "The nature of European solidarity: how national citizenship is supplemented by and constrains European citizenship". In F. de Quadros & D. Sidjanski (eds), *The Future of Europe: The Reform of the Eurozone and the Deepening of Political Union*, 517–22. Lisbon: Editoria.

Benlolo-Carabot, M. 2012. "Les droits sociaux dans l'ordre juridique de l'Union Européenne". *La Revue des droits de l'homme* 2012(1): 84–102.

Benoît, C. & C. Hay forthcoming. "The Covid-19 crisis and the antinomies of sovereignty in European advanced capitalist economies". *Comparative European Politics*.

Bernaciak, M. 2014. "Social dumping and the EU integration process". ETUI Working Paper, 2014/6, www.etui.org/Publications2/Working-Papers/Social-dumping-political-catchphrase-or-threat-to-labour-standards.

Bieler, A. 2005. "Class struggle over the EU model of capitalism: neo-Gramscian perspectives and the EU model of capitalism". *Critical Review of International Social and Political Philosophy* 8(4): 513–26.

Bieler, A. 2015. "Social Europe and the eurozone crisis: the importance of the balance of class power in society". In A. Crespy, *The Elusive Pursuit of Social Europe in the Eurocrisis*, 22–44. Basingstoke: Palgrave Macmillan.

Bieler, A. *et al.* (eds) 2015. *Labour and Transnational Action in Times of Crisis*. London: Rowman & Littlefield.

Bieler, A., J. Jordan & A. Morton 2019. "EU aggregate demand as a way out of crisis? Engaging the post-Keynesian critique". *Journal of Common Market Studies* 57(4): 805–22.

Blauberger, M. & S. Schmidt 2017. "Free movement, the welfare state, and the European Union's over-constitutionalization: administrating contradictions". *Public Administration* 95(2): 437–49.

Blauberger, M. *et al.* 2018. "ECJ judges read the morning papers: explaining the turnaround of European citizenship jurisprudence". *Journal of European Public Policy* 25(10): 1422–41.

Bloomfield, J. & F. Steward 2020. "The politics of the Green New Deal". *Political Quarterly* 91(4): 770–9.

Blyth, M. 2013. *Austerity: The History of a Dangerous Idea*. Oxford: Oxford University Press.

Borriello, A. 2017. "'There is no alternative': how Italian and Spanish leaders' discourse obscured the political nature of austerity". *Discourse and Society* 28(3): 241–61.

Bouget, D. *et al.* 2015. *Social Investment in Europe: A Study of National Policies*. Brussels: European Social Policy Network.

Brack, N., R. Coman & A. Crespy 2019. "Unpacking old and new conflicts of sovereignty in the European polity". *Journal of European Integration* 41(7): 817–32.

Braun, B. 2018. "Central banking and the infrastructural power of finance: the case of ECB support for repo and securitization markets". *Socio-Economic Review* 18(2): 395–418.

Bribosia, E. *et al.* 2019. *The Charter's Social and Non-Discrimination Provisions in the Employment Field: E-NACT Handbook No. 2*. Florence: EUI Centre for Judicial Cooperation.

Brien, P. 2021. "The UK Shared Prosperity Fund". House of Commons Library, No. 08527, https://commonslibrary.parliament.uk/research-briefings/cbp-8527/.

Brookes, E., A. de Ruijter & S. Greer 2020. "Covid-19 and European Union health policy: from crisis to collective action". In B. Vanhercke, S. Spasova & B. Fronteddu (eds), *Social Policy in the European Union: State of Play 2020*, 33–52. Brussels: ETUI.

Brooks, E. & R. Geyer 2020. "The development of EU health policy and the Covid-19 pandemic: trends and implications". *Journal of European Integration* 42(8): 1057–76.

Browne, M. 2004. "La stratégie européenne pour l'emploi: nouveau modèle ou faux semblant?" In R. Harmattan, *L'Europe sans Bruxelles? Une analyse de la méthode ouverte de coordination*, 57–73. Paris: L'Harmattan.

Bruzelius, C. & M. Seeleib-Kaiser 2019. "European citizenship and social rights". In P. Kennett & N. Lendvai-Bainton (eds), *Handbook of European Social Policy*, 155–66. Cheltenham: Edward Elgar.

Bulmer, S. *et al.* 2007. *Policy Transfer in European Union Governance: Regulating the Utilities*. London: Routledge.

Bussi, M., B. Hvinden & M. Schoyen 2019. "Has the European Social Fund been effective in supporting young people?" In B. Hvinden *et al.* (eds), *Youth Unemployment and Job Insecurity in Europe*, 206–29. Cheltenham: Edward Elgar.

Cantillon, B. 2019. "The European Pillar of Social Rights: ten arguments for prioritising principle 14 on minimum incomes". Herman Delleck Centre for Social Policy Working Paper, University of Antwerp, https://medialibrary.uantwerpen.be/oldcontent/container2453/files/CSB%20WP%202019/CSBWorkingPaper1902.pdf.

Caporaso, J. & S. Tarrow 2009. "Polanyi in Brussels: supranational institutions and the transnational embedding of markets". *International Organization* 63(4): 593–620.

Careja, R., P. Emmeneger & N. Giger (eds) 2020. *The European Social Model Under Pressure*. Wiesbaden: Springer.

Carrieri, M., M. Ambra & A. Ciarini 2018. "The 'resistable' rise of decentralised bargaining: a cross-country and inter-sectoral comparison". In S. Leonardi & R. Pedersini, *Multi-Employer Bargaining Under Pressure: Decentralisation Trends in Five European Countries*, 39–66. Brussels: ETUI.

Carruba, C. & M. Gabel 2014. *International Courts and the Performance of International Agreements: A General Theory with Evidence from the European Union*. Cambridge: Cambridge University Press.

Caune, H. 2014. "Le modèle danois et la flexicurité européenne: une stratégie en deux bandes de persuasion par l'expertise". *Gouvernement et action publique* 3(2): 55–79.

Chalmers, D., M. Jachtenfuchs & C. Joerges (eds) 2016. *The End of the Eurocrats' Dream: Adjusting to European Diversity*. Cambridge: Cambridge University Press.

Charveriat, C. & E. Bodin 2020. *Delivering the Green Deal: The Role of a Reformed Semester within a New Sustainable Growth Strategy for the EU*. Brussels: Institute for European Environmental Policy.

Cheneval, F. & K. Nicolaïdis 2017. "The social construction of *demoi*cracy in the European Union". *European Journal of Political Theory* 16(2): 235–60.

Cheneval, F. & F. Schimmelfennig 2013. "The case for *demoi*cracy in the European Union". *Journal of Common Market Studies* 51(2): 334–50.

CIRIEC 2004. "Contribution of services of general interest to economic and social cohesion". *Report for the European Commission DG Regio*, www.psiru.org/reports/Ciriec-DGRegio-SGEI.doc.

Claassen, R. *et al.* 2019. "Four models of protecting citizenship and social rights in Europe: conclusions to the special issue 'Rethinking the European Social Market Economy'". *Journal of Common Market Studies* 57(1): 159–74.

Clegg, D. 2017. "Brexit, the UK labour market and the lessons for Social Europe". In B. Vanhercke, S. Sabato & D. Bouget (eds), *Social Policy in the European Union: State of Play 2017*, 33–49. Brussels: ETUI.

Cocks, P. 1980. "Towards a Marxist theory of European integration". *International Organization* 34(1): 1–40.

Cohen, A. & A. Vauchez 2011. "The social construction of law: the European Court of Justice and its legal revolution revisited". *Annual Review of Law and Social Science* 7(1): 417–31.

Coleman, D. 2016. "A demographic rationale for Brexit". *Population and Development Review* 42(4): 681–92.

Coman, R. 2017. "Intergovernmental method, community method and open method of coordination: the resilience, efficiency and legitimacy of the EU's modes of governance". In A. Grimmel (ed.), *The Crisis of the European Union: Challenges, Analyses, Solutions*, 173–95. Abingdon: Routledge.

Coman, R., L. Fromont & A. Weyembergh (eds) 2019. *Les solidarités européennes. Entre enjeux, tensions et reconfigurations*. Brussels: Bruylant.

Coman, R. & F. Ponjaert 2016. "From one Semester to the next: towards the hybridization of new modes of governance in EU policy". Cahiers du CEVIPOL/Brussels Working Papers, 5/2016, http://cevipol.ulb.ac.be/sites/default/files/bxl_working_paper_5_2016_issue_on_eu_economic_governance.pdf.

Coman, R. & F. Sbaraglia 2018. "Gouverner par la conditionnalité ou la flexibilité? La réforme de la politique de cohésion de l'Union européenne (2014–2020)". *Gouvernement et action publique* 2018(3): 35–55.

Conter, B. 2007. "Plein emploi ou chômage nécessaire: la stratégie européenne pour l'emploi, entre utopie et pragmatisme". *Politique européenne* 1(21): 21–40.

Copeland, P. 2014. *EU Enlargement, the Clash of Capitalisms and the European Social Dimension*. Manchester: Manchester University Press.

Copeland, P. 2020. *Governance and the European Social Dimension*. Abingdon: Routledge.

Copeland, P. & M. Daly 2014. "Poverty and social policy in Europe 2020: ungovernable and ungoverned". *Policy & Politics* 42(3): 341–65.

Copeland, P. & M. Daly 2015. "Social Europe: from 'add-on' to 'dependence-upon' economic integration". In A. Crespy & G. Menz (eds), *Social Policy and the Eurocrisis: Quo Vadis Social Europe*, 140–60. Basingstoke: Palgrave Macmillan.

Copeland, P. & M. Daly 2018. "The European Semester and EU social policy". *Journal of Common Market Studies* 56(5): 1001–18.

Copeland, P. & B. Ter Haar 2013. "A toothless bite? The effectiveness of the European employment strategy". *Journal of European Social Policy* 23(1): 21–36.

Corti, F., S. Sabato & B. Vanhercke 2019. "The European (Social) Union is in need of a 'social imbalances procedure'". EuVisions, www.euvisions.eu/european-social-union-social-imbalances-procedure-corti-vanhercke-sabato/.

Coutouris, N. & K. Ewing 2019. "Brexit and workers' rights". Institute of Employment Rights, www.ier.org.uk/product/brexit-and-workers-rights.

Cram, L. 1993. "Calling the tune without paying the piper? Social policy regulation: the role of the Commission in European Community social policy". *Policy & Politics* 21(2): 135–46.

Cremers, J. 2020. "The European Labour Authority and rights-based labour mobility". *ERA Forum* 21: 21–34.

Crespy, A. 2010. "When Bolkestein is trapped by the French anti-liberal discourse: a discursive-institutionalist account of preference formation in the realm of EU multi-level politics". *Journal of European Public Policy* 17(8): 1253–70.

Crespy, A. 2012. *Qui a peur de Bolkestein? Conflit, résistances et démocratie dans l'Union européenne.* Paris: Economica.

Crespy, A. 2016. *Welfare Markets in Europe: The Democratic Challenge of European Integration.* Basingstoke: Palgrave Macmillan.

Crespy, A. 2020a. "The EU's socioeconomic governance 10 years after the crisis: muddling through and the revolt against austerity". *Journal of Common Market Studies* 58: 133–46.

Crespy, A. 2020b. "Salaires minimaux: l'Union européenne opte (encore) pour la gouvernance par les données". *The Conversation*, 30 November, https://theconversation.com/salaires-minimaux-lunion-europeenne-opte-encore-pour-la-gouvernance-par-les-donnees-150219.

Crespy, A. & K. Gajewska 2010. "New parliament, new cleavages after the eastern enlargement? The conflict over the Services Directive as an opposition between the liberals and the regulators". *Journal of Common Market Studies* 48(5): 1185–208.

Crespy, A. & G. Menz 2015a. "Commission entrepreneurship and the debasing of Social Europe before and after the Eurocrisis". *Journal of Common Market Studies* 53(4): 753–68.

Crespy, A. & G. Menz 2015b. "Social Europe is dead: what's next?" In A. Crespy & G. Menz (eds), *Social Policy and the Euro Crisis: Quo Vadis Social Europe?* 182–210. Basingstoke: Palgrave Macmillan.

Crespy, A. & G. Menz (eds) 2015c. *Social Policy and the Euro Crisis: Quo Vadis Social Europe?* Basingstoke: Palgrave Macmillan.

Crespy, A. & L. Parks 2017. "The connection between parliamentary and extraparliamentary opposition in the EU: from ACTA to the financial crisis". *Journal of European Integration* 39(4): 453–67.

Crespy, A. & V. Schmidt 2017. "The EU's economic governance in 2016: beyond austerity?" In B. Vanhercke, S. Sabato & D. Bouget (eds), *Social Policy in the European Union: State of Play 2017*, 99–114. Brussels: ETUI.

Crespy, A. & P. Vanheuverzwijn 2017. "What 'Brussels' means by structural reforms: empty signifier or constructive ambiguity?" *Comparative European Politics* 17(2): 92–111.

Crouch, C. 2020. "Social Europe: a manifesto". *Social Europe*, www.socialeurope.eu/book/social-europe-a-manifesto.

Crum, B. 2015. "A multi-layered Social Europe? Three emerging transnational social duties in the EU". In A. Crespy & G. Menz (eds), *Social Policy and the Eurocrisis: Quo Vadis Social Europe*, 161–81. Basingstoke: Palgrave Macmillan.

Crum, B. 2020. *How to Provide Political Guidance to the Recovery and Resilience Facility?* Brussels: Economic Government Support Unit.

Daly, M. 2006. "EU social policy after Lisbon". *Journal of Common Market Studies* 44(3): 461–81.

Daly, M. 2017. "The dynamics of European Union social policy". In P. Kent & N. Lendvai-Bainton (eds), *Handbook of European Social Policy*, 93–107. Cheltenham: Edward Elgar.

Dawson, M. 2018. "New governance and the displacement of Social Europe: the case of the European Semester". *European Constitutional Law Review* 14(1): 191–209.

De la Porte, C. 2011. "Principal–agent theory and the open method of co-ordination: the case of the European Employment Strategy". *Journal of European Public Policy* 18(4): 485–503.

De la Porte, C. 2019a. "The European Pillar of Social Rights meets the Nordic model". European Policy Analysis, Swedish Institute for European Policy Studies, January, www.sipotra.it/old/wp-content/uploads/2019/01/The-European-Pillar-of-Social-Rights-meets-the-Nordic-model.pdf.

De la Porte, C. 2019b. "The European Social Union: addressing challenges on the labour market". EUVisions, www.euvisions.eu/esu-debate-addressing-challenges-labour-market-de-la-porte/.

De la Porte, C. & E. Heins (eds) 2016. *The Sovereign Debt Crisis, the EU and Welfare State Reform*. Basingstoke: Palgrave Macmillan.

De la Porte, C., T. Larsen & D. Szelewa 2020. "The EU's work–life balance directive: a lost opportunity for the UK in gender equality?" In M. Donoghue & M. Kuisma (eds), *Whither Social Rights in (Post-)Brexit Europe?* 94–9. Munich: Social Europe.

De la Porte, C. & P. Nanz 2011. "The OMC – a deliberative-democratic mode of governance? The cases of employment and pensions". *Journal of European Public Policy* 11(2): 267–88.

De la Porte, C. & B. Palier forthcoming. "The politics of European Union social investment initiatives". In J. Garritzmann, S. Häusermann & B. Palier (eds), *The World Politics of Social Investment*. Oxford: Oxford University Press.

De la Porte, C. & P. Pochet 2002. *Building Social Europe Through the Open Method of Coordination*. Brussels: Peter Lang.

De Ruijter, A. 2019. *EU Health Law and Policy: The Expansion of EU Power in Public Health and Health Care*. Oxford: Oxford University Press.

De Schutter, O. 2006. "L'équilibre entre l'économique et le social dans les traités européens". *Revue française des affaires sociales* 2006(1): 131–57.

De Spiegelaere, S. & J. Waddington 2017. "Has the recast made a difference? An examination of the content of European Works Council agreements". *European Journal of Industrial Relations* 23(3): 293–308.

De Witte, F. 2012. "Transnational solidarity and the mediation of conflicts of justice in Europe". *European Law Journal* 18(5): 694–710.

De Witte, F. 2015. *Justice in the EU: The Emergence of Transnational Solidarity*. Oxford: Oxford University Press.

De Witte, F. 2019. "EU law, politics, and the social question". *German Law Journal* 14(5): 581–611.

Degryse, C. 2006. "Historical and institutional background to the cross-industry social dialogue". In A. Dufresne *et al.* (eds), *The European Sectoral Social Dialogue: Actors, Developments and Challenges*, 31–47. Brussels: Peter Lang.

Degryse, C. 2017. "The relaunch of European social dialogue: what has been achieved up to now?" In B. Vanhercke, S. Sabato & D. Bouget (eds), *Social Policy in the European Union: State of Play 2017*, 115–32. Brussels: ETUI.

Degryse, C. & P. Pochet 2011. "Has European sectoral social dialogue improved since the establishment of SSDCs in 1998?" *Transfer* 17(2): 145–58.

Della Porta, D. 2015. *Social Movements in Times of Austerity*. Cambridge: Polity.

Della Porta, D. 2017. "Late neoliberalism and its discontents in the economic crisis: an introduction". In D. Della Porta *et al.* (eds), *Late Neoliberalism and Its Discontents in the Economic Crisis*, 1–39. Basingstoke: Palgrave Macmillan.

Della Porta, D. & L. Parks 2018. "Social movements, the European crisis, and EU political opportunities". *Comparative European Politics* 16(1): 85–102.

Delwit, P. 1995. *Les partis socialistes et l'intégration européenne: France, Grande-Bretagne, Belgique*. Brussels: Editions de l'Université libre de Bruxelles.

Denis, B. 2020. "La 'neutralité climatique' européenne est-elle socialement juste?" *La Revue politique* 114: 11479–85.

Denis, G. & F. Denuit 2020. "L'Europe face au défi climatique". *La Revue politique* 114: 11470–72.

Denord, F. & A. Schwartz 2009. *L'Europe sociale n'aura pas lieu*. Paris: Raison d'agir.

Denuit, F. 2020. "Le revenu universel européen: une nouvelle voie pour l'Europe sociale". In R. Coman *et al.* (eds), *Les solidarités européennes: Entre enjeux, tensions et reconfigurations*, 227–55. Brussels: Bruylant.

De Schutter, O. 2021. "Statement by Olivier De Schutter", United Nations special rapporteur on extreme poverty and human rights, on his visit to the European Union (25 November 2020 to 29 January 2021), www.ohchr.org/EN/NewsEvents/Pages/DisplayNews.aspx?NewsID=26693&LangID=E.

Deutsch, J. & S. Wheaton 2021. "How Europe fell behind on vaccines". *Politico.* 27 January.

Dietsch, P., F. Claveau & C. Fontan 2018. *Do Central Banks Serve the People?* Cambridge: Polity.

Dubel, P. 2019. "Analysis of the impact of the European Social Fund on the SME sector in Poland". *Problemy Zarzadzania* 17(6): 120–32.

Dufresne, A. 2006. "The evolution of sectoral industrial relations structures in Europe". In A. Dufresne, C. Degryse & P. Pochet (eds), *The European Sectoral Social Dialogue*, 49–82. Brussels: Peter Lang.

Dufresne, A. 2015. "Euro-unionism and wage policy: the German paradox – a driving force, but also a brake?" In A. Crespy & G. Menz (eds), *Social Policy and the Eurocrisis: Quo Vadis Social Europe*, 83–113. Basingstoke: Palgrave Macmillan.

Dufresne, A. & C. Gobin 2016. "Le dialogue social européen ou la déconstruction du droit social et la transformation des relations professionnelles". In P. Lapointe (ed.), *L'avantage du dialogue social?* 23–63. Québec: Presses de l'Université Laval.

Dufresne, A. & J. Pernot 2013. "Les syndicats européens à l'épreuve de la nouvelle gouvernance économique". *Chronique internationale de l'IRES*, November, www.ires.fr/publications/chronique-internationale-de-l-ires/item/3577-europe-les-syndicats-europeens-a-l-epreuve-de-la-nouvelle-gouvernance-economique.

Dunlop, C. & C. Radaelli 2016. "Policy learning in the Eurozone crisis: modes, power and functionality". *Policy Sciences* 49(2): 107–24.

Dupont, C., S. Oberthür & I. von Homeyer 2020. "The Covid-19 crisis: a critical juncture for EU climate policy development?" *Journal of European Integration* 42(8): 1095–110.

Ebbinghaus, B. 1999. "Does a European social model exist and can it survive?" In G. Huemer, F. Traxler & M. Mesch (eds), *The Role of Employer Associations and Labour Unions in the EMU: Institutional Requirements for European Economic Policies*, 1–26. Aldershot: Ashgate.

Ebbinghaus, B. 2020. "Uncertain futures of post-Brexit pensions: three paradoxical implications". In M. Donoghue & M. Kuisma (eds), *Whither Social Rights in (Post-)Brexit Europe?* 70–6. Munich: Social Europe.

Erne, R. 2008. *European Unions: Labors' Quest for a Transnational Democracy.* Ithaca, NY: Cornell University Press.

Esping-Andersen, G. 1990. *The Three Worlds of Welfare Capitalism.* Princeton, NJ: Princeton University Press.

European Anti-Poverty Network (EAPN) 2020. "Key messages on the European Green Deal and the 'Just Transition'", EAPN Reflection Paper, www.eapn.eu/wp-content/uploads/2020/08/EAPN-2020_EAPN-Green-Deal-Key-Messages-Reflection-Paper-4601.pdf.

European Commission 1993. "Growth, competitiveness, employment: the challenges and ways forward into the 21st century". White Paper, 5 December, https://op.europa.eu/en/publication-detail/-/publication/0d563bc1-f17e-48ab-bb2a-9dd9a31d5004.

European Commission 2004. "Facing the challenge: the Lisbon Strategy for growth and employment". Report from the High-Level Group chaired by Wim Kok, 12 November. KA-62-04-260-EN-C, https://op.europa.eu/en/publication-detail/-/publication/88b6bc81-e3ad-4156-960f-f549369aa9d4.

European Commission 2013. "Towards social investment for growth and cohesion – including implementing the European Social Fund 2014–2020", 22 February, https://ec.europa.eu/eip/ageing/library/towards-social-investment-growth-and-cohesion-including-implementing-european-social-fund_en.html.

European Commission 2020. "The European Green Deal". COM(2019) 640 final, 11 December, https://eur-lex.europa.eu/legal-content/EN/TXT/?uri=CELEX:52019DC0640.

European Commission 2021. "The European Pillar of Social Rights Action Plan", 4 March, https://ec.europa.eu/info/strategy/priorities-2019-2024/economy-works-people/jobs-growth-and-investment/european-pillar-social-rights/european-pillar-social-rights-action-plan_en.

European Council 2000. "Conclusions of the presidency: Lisbon meeting of 23–4 March 2000", www.europarl.europa.eu/summits/lis1_en.htm.

European Court of Auditors 2020. "Tracking climate spending in the EU budget", www.eca.europa.eu/en/Pages/DocItem.aspx?did=54194.

European Parliament 2021. "Extension of the mandate of the European Centre for Disease Prevention and Control", legislative train schedule, December 2020, www.europarl.europa.eu/legislative-train/theme-promoting-our-european-way-of-life/file-ecdc-mandate-extension.

European Trade Union Institute (ETUI) 2020. "Benchmarking Working Europe 2020", www.etui.org/publications/benchmarking-working-europe-2020.

European Union 2021. "Regulation (EU) 2021/241 of the European Parliament and of the Council establishing the Recovery and Resilience Facility". 12 February, http://data.europa.eu/eli/reg/2021/241/oj.

Everson, M. & C. Joerges 2012. "Reconfiguring the politics–law relationship in the integration project through conflicts–law constitutionalism". *European Law Journal* 18(5): 644–66.

Ewing, K. 2015. "The death of Social Europe". *King's Law Journal* 26(1): 76–98.

Fabbrini, S. 2016. "From consensus to domination: the intergovernmental union in a crisis situation". *Journal of European Integration* 38(5): 587–99.

Faist, T. 2001. "Social citizenship in the European Union: nested membership". *Journal of Common Market Studies* 39(1): 37–58.

Falkner, G. 1998. *EU Social Policy in the 1990s: Towards a Corporatist Policy Community*. London: Routledge.

Falkner, G. 2000. "The Treaty on European Union and its revision: sea change or empty shell for European social policies?" In S. Kuhnle (ed.), *Survival of the European Welfare State*, 185–201. London: Routledge.

Falkner, G. 2010. "European Union". In F. Castles *et al.* (eds), *The Oxford Handbook of the Welfare State*, 292–305. Oxford: Oxford University Press.

Falkner, G., M. Hartlapp & O. Treib 2007. "Worlds of compliance: why leading approaches to European Union implementation are only 'sometimes-true theories'". *European Journal of Political Research* 46(3): 395–416.

Farnsworth, K. 2017. "Taking back control or empowering big business? New risks to the welfare state in the post-Brexit competition for investment". *Journal of Social Policy* 46(4): 699–718.

Fasone, C. 2014. "European economic governance and parliamentary representation: what place for the European Parliament?" *European Law Journal* 20(2): 164–85.

Ferguson, D. 2020. "End of Brexit transition: workers' rights". Briefing Paper, House of Commons Library, https://commonslibrary.parliament.uk/research-briefings/cbp-9099/.

Ferrera, M. 1996. "The 'southern model' of welfare in Social Europe". *Journal of European Social Policy* 9(1): 17–37.

Ferrera, M. 2003. "European integration and national social citizenship: changing boundaries, new structuring?" *Comparative Political Studies* 36(6): 611–52.

Ferrera, M. 2005. *The Boundaries of Welfare: European Integration and the New Spatial Politics of Social Protection*. Oxford: Oxford University Press.

Ferrera, M. 2017. "The European Social Union: a missing but necessary 'political good'". In F. Vandenbroucke, C. Barnard & G. De Basere (eds), *A European Social Union After the Crisis*, 47–67. Cambridge: Cambridge University Press.

Ferrera, M. 2018. "Crafting the ESU": towards a roadmap for delivery". EUVisions, www.euvisions.eu/crafting-the-european-social-union-ferrera/.

Fertikh, K. 2016. "La construction d'un 'droit social européen': socio-histoire d'une catégorie transnationale (années 1950–années 1970)". *Politix* 115(3): 201–24.

Fertikh, K. 2017. "L'Europe sociale au ras du sol: sociologie des pratiques ordinaires d'interprétation du traité de Rome". *Raisons politiques* 67(3): 141–63.

Flecker, J. & C. Hermann (eds) 2012. *Privatization of Public Services: Impacts for Employment, Working Conditions, and Service Quality in Europe*. Abingdon: Routledge.

Flora, P. (ed.) 1999. *State Formation, Nation-Building and Mass Politics in Europe: The Theory of Stein Rokkan*. Oxford: Oxford University Press.

Fontan, C. 2013. "Frankentstein en Europe. L'impact de la Banque centrale européenne sur la gestion de la crise de la zone euro". *Politique européenne* 2013(4): 22–45.

Fontan, C. 2014. "L'art du grand écart. La Banque centrale européenne face aux dilemmes provoqués par la crise de la zone euro". *Gouvernement et action publique* 2014(2): 103–23.

Frangakis, M. *et al.* (eds) 2008. *Privatisation Against the European Social Model: A Critique of European Policies and Proposals for Alternatives*. Basingstoke: Palgrave Macmillan.

Gajewska, K. 2008. "The emergence of a European labour protest movement?" *European Journal of Industrial Relations* 14(1): 104–21.

Gajewska, K. 2009. *Transnational Labour Solidarity: Mechanisms of Commitment to Cooperation within the European Trade Union Movement*. Abingdon: Routledge.

Gallardo, C. 2021. "UK confirms post-Brexit review of employment laws". *Politico.* 19 January, www.politico.eu/article/uk-government-confirms-post-brexit-review-of-eu-derived-employment-laws/.

Garben, S. 2018. "The European Pillar of Social Rights: effectively addressing displacement?" *European Constitutional Law Review* 14(1): 210–30.

Garben, S. 2019. "Competence creep revisited". *Journal of Common Market Studies* 57(2): 205–22.

Genschel, P. & M. Jachtenfuchs 2021. "Postfunctionalism reversed: solidarity and rebordering during the corona-crisis". *Journal of European Public Policy* 28(3): 350–69.

Geyer, R. 2000. *Exploring European Social Policy*. Cambridge: Polity.

Gingrich, J. 2011. *Making Markets in the Welfare State: The Politics of Varying Market Reforms*. Cambridge: Cambridge University Press.

Gingrich, J. 2021. "Changing states, changing citizens, changing Politics?" In C. Ledoux, K. Shire & F. van Hooren (eds), *The Dynamics of Welfare Markets*, 49–75. London: Palgrave Macmillan.

Gingrich, J. & D. King 2019. "Americanising Brexit Britain's welfare state?" *Political Quarterly* 90(1): 89–98.

Gobin, C. 1997. *L'Europe syndicale entre désir et réalité. Essai sur le syndicalisme et la construction européenne à l'aube du XXIème siècle*. Brussels: Labor.

Goetschy, J. 1999. "The European Employment Strategy: genesis and development". *European Journal of Industrial Relations* 5(2): 117–37.

Goetschy, J. 2004. "L'apport de la méthode ouverte de coordination à l'intégration européenne: des fondements au bilan". In P. Magnette (ed.), *La grande Europe*, 213–55. Brussels: Editions de l'Université de Bruxelles.

Goetschy, J. 2005. "The open method of coordination and the Lisbon Strategy: the difficult road from potential to results". *Transfer* 11(1): 64–80.

Golden, D. 2019. "A fairer Europe for workers … or else? Some observations from the ETUC Congress 2019, Vienna, 21–24 May 2019". *Transfer* 25(4): 489–93.

González-Alegre, J. 2018. "Active labour market policies and the efficiency of the European Social Fund in Spanish regions". *Regional Studies* 52(3): 430–43.

Graziano, P. 2007. "Adapting to the European Employment Strategy? Continuity and change in recent Italian employment policy". *International Journal of Comparative Labour Law and Industrial Relations* 23(4): 543–65.

Graziano, P. & M. Hartlapp 2019. "The end of Social Europe? Understanding EU social policy change". *Journal of European Public Policy* 26(10): 1484–501.

Graziano, P., S. Jacquot & B. Palier (eds) 2011. *The EU and the Domestic Politics of Welfare State Reforms: Europa, Europae*. Basingstoke: Palgrave Macmillan.

Greenwood, J. & J. Dreger 2013. "The transparency register: a European vanguard of strong lobby regulation?". *Interest Groups & Advocacy* 2(2): 139–62.

Greve, B. 2019. *Welfare, Populism and Welfare Chauvinism*. Bristol: Policy Press.

Guillen, A. & B. Palier 2004. "Introduction: does Europe matter? Accession to EU and social policy developments in recent and new member states". *Journal of European Social Policy* 14(3): 203–9.

Gumbrell-McCormick, R. & R. Hyman 2015. "International trade union solidarity and the impact of the crisis". Swedish Institute for European Policy Analysis, www.sieps.se/en/publications/2015/international-trade-union-solidarity-and-the-impact-of-the-crisis-20151epa/.

Haas, P. 1992. "Epistemic communities and international policy coordination". *International Organization* 46(1): 1–35.

Habermas, J. 1998. *Die postnationale Konstellation: Politische Essays*. Frankfurt am Main: Suhrkamp.

Habermas, J. 2013a. *The Crisis of the European Union: A Response*. Cambridge: Polity.

Habermas, J. 2013b. "Democracy, solidarity and the European crisis". *Roadmap to a Social Europe: Social Europe Report*, www.ictu.ie/download/pdf/roadmap_to_social_europe_sej_oct_2013.pdf#page=9.

Hallak, I. 2021. "EU–UK Trade and Cooperation Agreement". February, European Parliament Research Service, PE 679.071, www.europarl.europa.eu/RegData/etudes/IDAN/2021/679071/EPRS_IDA(2021)679071_EN.pdf.

Hantrais, L. 1995. *Social Policy in the European Union*. Basingstoke: Palgrave Macmillan.

Hantrais, L. 2019. *What Brexit Means for EU and UK Social Policy*. Bristol: Policy Press.

Hartlapp, M. 2019. "European Union social policy". In S. Blum, J. Kuhlmann & K. Schubert (eds), *Routledge Handbook of European Welfare Systems*, 545–59. London: Routledge.

Hartlapp, M., J. Metz & C. Rauh 2014. *Which Policy for Europe? Power and Conflict Inside the European Commission*. Oxford: Oxford University Press.

Hatzopoulos, D. 2012. *Regulating Services in the European Union*. Oxford: Oxford University Press.

Hatzopoulos, V. 2007. "Why the open method of coordination is bad for you: a letter to the EU". *European Law Journal* 13(3): 309–42.

Hay, C. & B. Rosamond 2002. "Globalisation, European integration and the discursive construction of economic imperatives". *Journal of European Public Policy* 9(2): 147–67.

Heidenreich, M. & J. Zeitlin (eds) 2009. *Changing European Employment and Welfare Regimes: The Influence of the Open Method of Coordination on National Reforms*. Abingdon: Routledge.

Hemerijck, A. 2016. "New EMU governance: not (yet) ready for social investment?" Institute for European Integration Research, Working Paper 01/2016, https://eif.univie.ac.at/downloads/workingpapers/wp2016-01.pdf.

Hennette, S. *et al.* 2017. "Treaty on the democratization of the economic and social government of the European Union ('T-Dem')", http://tdem.eu/en/treaty/.

Hennette, S. *et al.* (eds) 2019. *How to Democratize Europe*. Cambridge, MA: Harvard University Press.

Hermann, C. 2015. "Green new deal and the question of environmental justice". ILO Working Paper No. 31, February, https://global-labour-university.org/fileadmin/GLU_Working_Papers/GLU_WP_No.31.pdf.

Hilal, N. 2007. *L'eurosyndicalisme par l'action. Cheminots et routiers en Europe*. Paris: L'Harmattan.

Hodson, D. & I. Mahler 2001. "The open method of co-ordination as a new mode of governance: the case of soft economic policy co-ordination". *Journal of Common Market Studies* 39(4): 719–46.

Holman, O., H. Overbeek & M. Ryner 2004. "Neoliberal hegemony and the political economy of European restructuring". *International Journal of Political Economy* 28(1/2).

Hooghe, L., G. Marks & C. Wilson 2002. "Does left/right structure party positions on European integration?" *Comparative Political Studies* 35(8): 965–89.

Höpner, M. 2018. "Social Europe is a myth". *Social Europe*, 5 November, https://socialeurope.eu/social-europe-is-a-myth.

Höpner, M. & A. Schäfer 2010. "Polanyi in Brussels? Embeddedness and the three dimensions of European economic integration". MPIfG Discussion Paper No. 10/8, www.mpifg.de/pu/mpifg_dp/dp10-8.pdf.

Horn, L. 2009. "Organic intellectuals at work: The high-level group of company law experts in European corporate governance regulation". In B. van Apeldoorn & J. Drahokoupil (eds), *Contradictions and Limits of Neoliberal European Governance: From Lisbon to Lisbon*, 125–41. Basingstoke: Palgrave Macmillan.

Horn, L. & A. Wigger 2016. "Business as usual: the EU is (still) driven by corporate interests". In H. Zimmermann & A. Dür (eds), *Key Controversies in European Integration*, 116–20. Basingstoke: Palgrave Macmillan.

Hugrée, C., E. Pénissat & A. Spire 2020. *Social Class in Europe*. London: Verso.

Hyman, R. 2015. "Austeritarianism in Europe: what options for resistance?" In D. Natali & B. Vanhercke (eds), *Social Policy in the European Union: State of Play 2015*, 97–126. Brussels: ETUI/OSE.

Jackson, T. 2005. "Live better by consuming less? Is there a 'double dividend' in sustainable consumption?" *Journal of Industrial Ecology* 9(1–2): 19–36.

Jacquot, S. 2013. "Les effets de l'européanisation dans le domaine social. Entre influence européenne et usages nationaux". *Politique européenne* 40: 409–21.

Jacquot, S. 2014. "L'Europe sociale". In R. Dehousse (ed.), *L'Union européenne*, 201–14. Paris: La Documentation française.

Jacquot, S. 2015. *Transformations in EU Gender Equality: From Emergence to Dismantling*. Basingstoke: Palgrave Macmillan.

Jacquot, S. & C. Woll (eds) 2004. *Les usages de l'Europe*. Paris: L'Harmattan.

Jacquot, S. & C. Woll 2010. "Using Europe: strategic action in multi-level politics". *Comparative European Politics* 8: 110–26.

Jaksic, K., J. Peschner & A. Pisiotis 2019. "Sustainable growth and development in the EU: concepts and challenges". In European Commission, *2021 Report on Sustainable Development in the European Union*, 62–89, https://ec.europa.eu/social/BlobServlet?docId=21414&langId=en.

Joerges, C. 2017. "Social justice in an ever more diverse union". In F. Vandenbroucke, C. Barnard & G. De Basere (eds), *A European Social Union after the Crisis*, 68–91. Cambridge: Cambridge University Press.

Joerges, C. & F. Rödl 2009. "Informal politics, formalised law and the 'social deficit' of European integration: reflections after the judgments of the ECJ in *Viking* and *Laval*". *European Law Journal* 15(1): 1–19.

Jordan, J., V. Maccarone & R. Erne 2020. "Towards a socialization of the EU's new economic governance regime? EU labour policy interventions in Germany, Ireland, Italy and Romania (2009–2019)". *British Journal of Industrial Relations* 59(1): 191–213.

Kenner, J. 2003. "Economic and social rights in the EU legal order: the mirage of indivisibility". In T. Harvey & J. Kenner (eds), *Economic and Social Rights under the EU Charter of Fundamental Rights: A Legal Perspective*, 1–26. Oxford: Hart.

Kennett, P. *et al.* 2015. "Recession, austerity and the 'Great Risk Shift': local government and household impacts and responses in Bristol and Liverpool". *Local Government Studies* 41(4): 622–44.

Keune, M., J. Leschke & A. Watt (eds) 2008. *Privatisation and Liberalisation of Public Services in Europe: An Analysis of Economic and Labour Impact*. Brussels: ETUI-REHS.

Kleinman, M. 2002. *A European Welfare State? European Union Social Policy in Context*. Basingstoke: Palgrave Macmillan.

Kohler-Koch, B. 2012. "Post-Maastricht civil society and participatory democracy". *Journal of European Integration* 34(7): 809–24.

Kröger, S. 2007. "The end of democracy as we know it? The legitimacy deficits of bureaucratic social policy governance". *Journal of European Integration* 29(5): 565–82.

Kuitto, K. 2016. *Post-Communist Welfare States in European Context*. Cheltenham: Edward Elgar.

Larsson, B. *et al.* 2020. "What's the point of European sectoral social dialogue? Effectiveness and polycontexturality in the hospital and metal sectors". *Industrial Relations Journal* 51(5): 410–26.

Laurent, E. 2020. "The European Green Deal: from growth strategy to social-ecological transition?" In B. Vanhercke, S. Spasova & B. Fronteddu (eds), *Social Policy in the European Union: State of Play 2020*, 97–111. Brussels: ETUI.

Leboutte, R. 2008. *Histoire économique et sociale de la construction européenne*. Brussels: Peter Lang.

Lechevalier, A. & J. Wielgohs (eds) 2015. *Social Europe – a Dead End: What the Eurozone Crisis is Doing to Europe's Social Dimension*. Copenhagen: Djof Publishing.

Ledoux, C., K. Shire & F. van Hooren 2020. "Introduction: from the emergence to the dynamics of welfare markets". In C. Ledoux, K. Shire & F. van Hooren (eds), *The Dynamics of Welfare Markets*, 3–48. Basingstoke: Palgrave Macmillan.

Leiber, S. 2007. "Transposition of EU social policy in Poland: are there different 'worlds of compliance' in east and west?" *Journal of European Social Policy* 37(4): 349–60.

Leibfried, S. 2005. "Social policy: left to the judges and the markets?" In H. Wallace, W. Wallace & M. Pollack (eds), *Policy Making in the European Union* (5th ed.), 243–77. Oxford: Oxford University Press.

Leibfried, S. & P. Pierson (eds) 1995. *European Social Policy: Between Fragmentation and Integration*. Washington, DC: Brookings Institution.

Leibried, S. & P. Pierson 2000. "Social policy: left to courts and markets?" In H. Wallace & W. Wallace (eds), *Policy-Making in the European Union* (4th ed.), 267–92. Oxford: Oxford University Press.

Leino-Sandberg, P. & F. Losada Fraga 2020. "How to make the European Semester more effective and more legitimate?" PE 651.365, www.europarl.europa.eu/RegData/etudes/IDAN/2020/651365/IPOL_IDA(2020)651365_EN.pdf.

Lenaerts, K. & P. Foubert 2001. "Social rights in the case law of the European Court of Justice". *Legal Issues of Economic Integration* 28(3): 267–96.

Leonardi, S. & R. Pedersini (eds) 2018. *Multi-Employer Bargaining Under Pressure: Decentralisation Trends in Five European Countries*. Brussels: ETUI.

Loefler, E., D. Sobszak & F. Hine-Hugh 2012. *Liberalisation and Privatisation in the EU: Services of General Interest and the Roles of the Public Sector*. Brentwood: Multi-Science Publishing.

Lubow, A. & S. Schmidt 2019. "A hidden champion? The European Court of Justice as an agenda-setter in the case of posted workers". *Public Administration* 99(2): 321–34.

Magnette, P. 1999. *La citoyenneté européenne*. Brussels: Editions de l'Université de Bruxelles.

Mair, P. 2007. "Political opposition and the European Union". *Government and Opposition* 1: 1–17.

Makszin, K., G. Medve-Bálint & D. Bohle 2020. "North and south, east and west: is it possible to bridge the gap?" In R. Coman, A. Crespy & V. Schmidt (eds), *Governance and Politics in the Post-Crisis European Union*, 335–57. Cambridge: Cambridge University Press.

Martin, A. & G. Ross. 1999. *The Brave New World of European Labor: European Trade Unions at the Millennium*. New York: Berghahn Books.

Martinsen, D. 2015. *An Ever More Powerful Court? The Political Constraints on Legal Integration in the European Union*. Oxford: Oxford University Press.

Martinsen, D. & A. Wessel 2014. "On the path to differentiation: upward transfer, logic of variation and sub-optimality in EU social policy". *Journal of European Public Policy* 21(9): 1255–72.

McNamara?, K. 1998. *The Currency of Ideas*. Ithaca, NY: Cornell University Press.

McNamara, K. 2006. "Economic governance, ideas and EMU: what currency does policy consensus have today?" *Journal of Common Market Studies* 44(4): 803–21.

Menz, G. 2015. "Whatever happened to Social Europe? The three-pronged attack on European social policy". In A. Crespy & G. Menz (eds), *Social Policy and the Eurocrisis: Quo Vadis Social Europe*, 45–62. Basingstoke: Palgrave Macmillan.

Metta, M. 2020. "The EU's Common Agricultural Policy after 2020: high ambition, low reform!" *Heinrich Böll Stiftung CAP Strategic Plans*, 3 November, https://eu.boell.org/en/2020/11/03/cap-post-2020-high-ambition-low-reform.

Mias, A. 2004. "Du dialogue social européen au travail législatif communautaire: Maastricht, ou le syndical saisi par le politique". *Droit et société* 58: 657–79.

Moreira Ramalho, T. 2020. "The Troika in its own words: responding to the politicisation of the southern European crises". *Journal of European Integration* 42(5): 677–93.

Morin, M. 2014. "Le compromis a minima de la directive de 2009 sur les comités d'entreprise européens: asymétries informationnelles et freins au dialogue social". *La Revue des Sciences de Gestion* 2014(5): 21–33.

Morris, M. 2020. "The agreement on the future relationship: a first analysis". Institute for Public Policy Research, briefing, December, www.ippr.org/files/2020-12/agreement-on-future-relationship-ippr-assessment-1-.pdf.

Moury, C. *et al.* 2021. *Capitalising on Constraint: The Politics of Conditionality in Bailed-Out Countries During and After the Eurozone Crisis.* Manchester: Manchester University Press.

Natali, D. 2004. "Europeanization, policy arenas, and creative opportunism: the politics of welfare state reforms in Italy". *Journal of European Public Policy* 11(4): 1077–95.

Nicolaïdis, K. 2007. "Trusting the Poles? Constructing Europe through mutual recognition". *Journal of European Public Policy* 14(5): 682–98.

Nicolaïdis, K. 2013. "European democracy and its crisis". *Journal of Common Market Studies* 51(2): 351–69.

Nolke, A. & A. Vliegenhart 2009. "Enlarging the varieties of capitalism: the emergence of dependent market economies in east central Europe". *World Politics* 61(4): 670–702.

Organization for Economic Cooperation and Development (OECD) 2017. *Understanding the Socio-Economic Divide in Europe: Background Report*, www.oecd.org/els/soc/cope-divide-europe-2017-background-report.pdf.

Offe, C. 2000. "The democratic welfare state: a European regime under the strain of European integration". Working paper, HIS Political Science Series 2000, No. 68, http://nbn-resolving.de/urn:nbn:de:0168-ssoar-246586.

Offe, C. 2003. "The European model of 'social' capitalism: can it survive European integration?" *Journal of Political Philosophy* 11(4): 437–69.

Palier, B. 2000. "Does Europe matter? Européanisation et réforme des politiques sociales des pays de l'Union européenne". *Politique européenne* 2: 27–8.

Palier, B. 2010. "The long conservative corporatist road to welfare reforms". In B. Palier (ed.), *A Long Goodbye to Bismarck? The Politics of Welfare Reform in Continental Europe*, 333–87. Amsterdam: Amsterdam University Press.

Papadopoulos, Y. & S. Piattoni. 2019. "The European Semester: democratic weaknesses as limits to learning". *European Policy Analysis* 5(1): 58–79.

Parks, L. 2015. *Social Movement Campaigns on EU Policy: In the Corridors and in the Streets.* Basingstoke: Palgrave Macmillan.

Pelucha, M., V. Kveton & O. Potlukac 2019. "Using mixed method approach in measuring effects of training in firms: case study of the European Social Fund support". *Evaluation and Program Planning* 73(1): 146–55.

Perin, E. & E. Léonard 2016. "Soft procedures for hard impacts: the European sectoral social dialogue's potential for regulation". *Transfer* 22(4): 475–90.

Pianta, M. & P. Gerbaudo 2016. "In search of European alternatives: anti-austerity protests in Europe". In M. Kaldor & S. Selchow (eds), *Subterranean Politics in Europe*, 31–59. Basingstoke: Palgrave.

Pierson, P. 1996. "The path to European integration: a historical institutionalist analysis". *Comparative Political Studies* 29(2): 123–63.

Pochet, P. 2019. *A la recherche de l'Europe sociale*. Paris: Presses universitaires de France.

Pochet, P. & C. Degryse 2016. "Dialogue social européen: une relance 'de la dernière chance?'". *OSE Paper Series* 17, www.ose.be/files/publication/OSEPaperSeries/Pochet_Degryse_2016_OpinionPaper17.pdf.

Pochet, P. & C. Degryse 2017. "La dynamique sociale européenne au prisme d'une approche quantitative". *Politique européenne* 58(4): 72–108.

Prosser, T. 2005. "Competition and public services: from single market to citizenship?" *European Public Law* 11(4): 543–63.

Prosser, T. 2016. "Economic union without social union: the strange case of the European social dialogue". *Journal of European Social Policy* 26(5): 460–72.

Prosser, T. 2017. "Insiders and outsiders on a European scale". *European Journal of Industrial Relations* 23(2): 135–50.

Puetter, U. 2014. *The European Council and the Council*. Oxford: Oxford University Press.

Radaelli, C. & S. Borras 2010. *Recalibrating the Open Method of Coordination: Towards Diverse and More Effective Usages*. Stockholm: Swedish Institute for European Policy Studies.

Ramírez Pérez, S. 2020. "Esperando a Godot? Los ciclos de la Europa social en la historiografía de la integración europea". *Lavoro e diritto* 2020(3): 369–91.

Rawls, J. 1971. *A Theory of Justice*. Cambridge, MA: Harvard University Press.

Rawls, J. & P. van Parijs 2003. "Three letters on the law of peoples and the European Union". *Revue de philosophie économique* 7: 7–20.

Raworth, K. 2017. *Doughnut Economics: Seven Ways to Think Like a 21st-Century Economist*. London: Random House.

Rittberger, B. & A. Wonka 2011. "Introduction: agency governance in the European Union". *Journal of European Public Policy* 18(6): 780–9.

Rodrigues, M. (ed.) 2002. *The New Knowledge Economy in Europe: A Strategy for International Competitiveness and Social Cohesion*. Cheltenham: Edward Elgar.

Rorive, I. & E. Bribosia 2015. "Droit de l'égalité et de la non-discrimination". *Journal européen des droits de l'homme/European Journal of Human Rights* 2016(2): 254–68.

Rorive, I. & E. Bribosia 2017. "Droit de l'égalité et de la non-discrimination". *Journal européen des droits de l'homme/European Journal of Human Rights* 2017(2): 191–213.

Rosamond, B. 2002. "Imagining the European economy: 'competitiveness' and the social construction of 'Europe' as an economic space". *New Political Economy* 7(2): 157–77.

Ryner, M., H. Overbeek & O. Holman 1998. "Guest editors' introduction". *International Journal of Political Economy* 28(1): 3–11.

Sabato, S. & F. Corti 2018. "'The times they are a-changin'?' The European pillar of social rights from debates to reality check". In B. Vanhercke, D. Ghailani & S. Sabato (eds), *Social Policy in the European Union: State of Play 2018*, 51–70. Brussels: ETUI.

Sabato, S. & B. Fronteddu 2020. "A socially just transition through the European Green Deal?" OSE Working Paper, www.etui.org/publications/socially-just-transition-through-european-green-deal.

Sabato, S. & B. Vanhercke 2017. "Towards a European Pillar of Social Rights: from a preliminary outline to a commission recommendation". In B. Vanhercke, S. Sabato & D. Bouget, *Social Policy in the European Union: State of Play 2017*, 73–96. Brussels: ETUI/OSE.

Sabato, S., B. Vanhercke & S. Spasova 2017. "Social partners' involvement in the European Semester". *European Social Observatory Research Paper* 35, www.ose.be/files/publication/OSEPaperSeries/Sabato_Vanhercke_Spasova_2017_OseResearchPaper35.pdf.

Sabel, C. & J. Zeitlin (eds) 2008. *Experimentalist Governance in the European Union*. Oxford: Oxford University Press.

Salais, R. 2013. *Le viol d'Europe*. Paris: Presses Universitaires de France.

Sanchez Salgado, R. 2014. "Rebalancing EU interest representation? Associative democracy and EU funding of civil society organizations". *Journal of Common Market Studies* 52(2): 337–53.

Sangiovanni, A. 2013. "Solidarity in the European Union". *Oxford Journal of Legal Studies* 33(2): 213–41.

Sapir, A. (ed.) 2004. *An Agenda for a Growing Europe: The Sapir Report*. Cambridge: Cambridge University Press.

Saurugger, S. 2008. "Interest groups and democracy in the EU". *West European Politics* 36(1): 1272–89.

Saurugger, S. & F. Terpan 2017. *The Court of Justice of the European Union and the Politics of Law*. Basingstoke: Palgrave Macmillan.

Savevska, M. 2014. "Polanyian reading of the socio-economic transformations of the European Union". *Journal of Contemporary European Studies* 22(4): 395–410.

Sbaraglia, F. 2016. "Who makes European cohesion policy: a practitioners' learning perspective". *Regional Studies, Regional Science* 3(1): 420–7.

Sbaraglia, F. 2018. *"C'est arrivé près de chez vous": une analyse de l'émergence du modèle d'investissement social européen en Région wallonne saisie par les instruments*. Brussels: Université libre de Bruxelles.

Scharpf, F. 1988. "The joint-decision trap: lessons from German federalism and European integration". *Public Administration* 66: 239–78.

Scharpf, F. 1999. *Governing in Europe: Effective and democratic?* Oxford: Oxford University Press.

Scharpf, F. 2010. "The asymmetry of European integration, or why the EU cannot be a 'social market economy'". *Socio-Economic Review* 8(2): 211–50.

Scharpf, F. 2015. "After the crash: a perspective on multi-level European democracy". *European Law Journal* 21(3): 384–405.

Scharpf, F. 2016. "Forced structural convergence in the eurozone: or a differentiated European monetary community". MPIfG Discussion Paper No. 16/15, www.econstor.eu/handle/10419/150047.

Schmidt, S., M. Blauberger & D. Martinsen 2018. "Free movement and equal treatment in an unequal union". *Journal of European Public Policy* 25(10): 1391–402.

Schmidt, V. 2018. "Rethinking EU governance: from 'old' to 'new' approaches to who steers integration". *Journal of Common Market Studies* 56(7): 1544–61.

Schmidt, V. 2020. *Europe's Crisis of Legitimacy: Governing by Rules and Ruling by Numbers in the Eurozone*. Oxford: Oxford University Press.

Seeliger, M. & J. Kiess. 2019. *Trade Unions and European Integration*. Abingdon: Routledge.

Seikel, D. 2015. "Class struggle in the shadow of Luxembourg: the domestic impact of the European Court of Justice's case law on the regulation of working conditions". *Journal of European Public Policy* 22(8): 1166–85.

Shannon, L. & M. Nayak-Oliver 2021. "Our economic and social rights after Brexit". Just Fair blog, http://justfair.org.uk/our-rights-after-brexit/.

Shutes, I. & S. Walker 2018. "Gender and free movement: EU migrant women's access to residence and social rights in the UK". *Journal of Ethnic and Migration Studies* 44(1): 137–53.

Simon, F. 2020. "Electricity boss: 'EU climate law should be kept short and simple'". *Euractiv*, 3 March, www.euractiv.com/section/energy-environment/interview/electricity-boss-eu-climate-law-should-be-kept-short-and-simple/.

Smismans, S. 2008. "The European social dialogue in the shadow of hierarchy". *Journal of Public Policy* 28(1): 161–80.

Smith, R. *et al.* 2012. "Medical tourism the European way". In J. Hodges, L. Turner & A. Kimball (eds), *Risks and Challenges in Medical Tourism: Understanding the Global Market for Health Services*, 37–55. Santa Barbara: CA: ABC Clio.

Spina, A. 2010. "The institutional growth of the European Medicines Agency". *European Journal of Risk Regulation* 1(1): 81–2.

Spire, A. 2019. "Reformuler la question sociale". In J. Confavreux (ed.), *Le fond de l'air est jaune: Comprendre une révolte inédite*, 91–8. Paris: Seuil.

Stafford, M. & S. Deeny 2020. "Inequalities and deaths involving Covid-19". Health Foundation blog, 21 May, www.health.org.uk/news-and-comment/blogs/inequalities-and-deaths-involving-covid-19.

Stewart, K., K. Cooper & I. Shutes 2020. "What will 'taking back control' mean for social policy in the UK? Brexit, public services and social rights". *Journal of European Social Policy* 30(4): 509–17.

Strath, B. & L. Magnusson 2004. *A European Social Citizenship? Preconditions for Future Policies from a Historical Perspective*. Brussels: Peter Lang.

Streeck, W. 1994. "European social policy after Maastricht: the 'social dialogue' and 'subsidiarity'". *Economic and Industrial Democracy* 15(2): 151–77.

Streeck, W. 2014. "Small-state nostalgia? The currency union, Germany, and Europe: a reply to Jurgen Habermas". *Constellations* 21(2): 213–21.

Streeck, W. 2019. "Progressive regression: metamorphoses of European social policy". *New Left Review* 118: 117–39.

Supiot, A. 2015. *La gouvernance par les nombres. Cours au Collège de France (2012–2014)*. Paris: Fayard.

Szyszczak, E. & J. van de Gronden (eds) 2013. *Financing Services of General Interest*. The Hague: Asser Press.

Taylor-Gooby, P. 2012. "Root and branch restructuring to achieve major cuts: the social policy programme of the 2010 UK Coalition Government". *Social Policy & Administration* 46(1): 61–82.

Terpan, F. & S. Saurugger 2021. "Soft and hard law in times of crisis: budget monitoring, migration and cybersecurity". *West European Politics* 44(1): 21–48.

Theodoropoulou, S. 2018. "Drifting into market insecurity? Labour market reforms in Europe after 2010". ETUI Working Paper 2018.03, https://papers.ssrn.com/sol3/papers.cfm?abstract_id=3168383.

Tosun, J. *et al.* 2017. "The absorption of structural and investment funds and youth unemployment: an empirical test". In J. Bachtler *et al.* (eds), *EU Cohesion Policy: Reassessing Performance and Direction*, 151–68. Abingdon: Routledge.

Tricard, J. 2020. "Once upon a time there was the European social dialogue". In B. Vanhercke *et al.* (eds), *Social Policy in the European Union 1999–2019: The Long and Winding Road*, 71–98. Brussels: ETUI.

Van Apeldoorn, B. 2003. *Transnational Capitalism and the Struggle Over European Integration*. London: Routledge.

Van Apeldoorn, B., J. Drahokoupil & L. Horn (eds) 2009. *Contradictions and Limits of Neoliberal European Governance*. Basingstoke: Palgrave Macmillan.

Van de Gronden, J. 2013. "Conclusion". In E. Szyzczak & J. van de Gronden (eds), *Financing Services of General Economic Interest: Reform and Modernization*, 273–84. The Hague: Asser Press.

Vandenbroucke, F. 2017. "The idea of a European Social Union: a normative introduction". In F. Vandenbroucke, C. Barnard & G. De Basere (eds), *A European Social Union After the Crisis*, 3–46. Cambridge: Cambridge University Press.

Vandenbroucke, F., C. Barnard & G. De Baere (eds) 2016. *A European Social Union After the Crisis*. Cambridge: Cambridge University Press.

Vandenbroucke, F., A. Hemerijck & B. Palier 2011. "The EU needs a social investment pact". OSE Opinion Paper, OSE European Social Observatory, https://hal.archives-ouvertes.fr/hal-02190281.

Van den Hende, L. & E. White 2021. "The view from Brussels: EU–UK Trade and Cooperation Agreement level playing field provisions and their enforcement". Herbet Smith Freehills blog, https://hsfnotes.com/brexit/2021/01/04/the-view-from-brussels-eu-uk-trade-and-cooperation-agreement-level-playing-field-provisions-and-their-enforcement/.

Van Gerven, M., B. Vanhercke & S. Gürocak. 2014. "Policy learning, aid conditionality or domestic politics? The Europeanization of Dutch and Spanish activation policies through the European Social Fund". *Journal of European Public Policy* 21(4): 509–27.

Van Gyes, G. 2009. "Liberalising services of general economic interest: the citizen-user perspective in six EU countries". *Policy Paper PIQUE* 5, http://pique.at.

Vanhercke, B. 2009. "Against the odds: the open method of coordination as a selective amplifier for reforming Belgian pensions policies". *European Integration Online Papers* 13/16, www.ose.be/files/publication/bvanhercke/Vanhercke_2009_EiOP%20article_AgainstTheOdds.pdf.

Vanhercke, B. 2020. "From the Lisbon Strategy to the European Pillar of Social Rights: the many lives of the social open method of coordination". In B. Vanhercke *et al.* (eds), *Social Policy in the European Union 1999–2019: The Long and Winding Road*, 99–123. Brussels: ETUI.

Vanheuverzwijn, P. & A. Crespy 2018. "Macro-economic coordination and elusive ownership in the European Union". *Public Administration* 96(3): 578–93.

van Middelaar, L. 2014. *The Passage to Europe: How a Continent Became a Union.* London: Yale University Press.

van Middelaar, L. 2019. *Alarums and Excursions: Improvising Politics on the European Stage.* Newcastle upon Tyne: Agenda Publishing.

Van Parijs, P. & Y. Vanderborght 2017. *Basic Income: A Radical Proposal for a Free Society and a Sane Economy.* Cambridge, MA: Harvard University Press.

Van Schaik, L., K. Jørgensen & R. van de Pas 2020. "Loyal at once? The EU's global health awakening in the Covid-19 pandemic". *Journal of European Integration* 42(8): 1145–60.

Van't Klooster, J. & C. Fontan 2020. "The myth of market neutrality: a comparative study of the European Central Bank's and the Swiss National Bank's corporate security purchases". *New Political Economy* 25(6): 865–79.

Van't Klooster, J. & C. Fontan 2021. "Central bankers remain stuck in the myth of 'market neutrality'". *Social Europe*, 30 March, www.socialeurope.eu/central-bankers-remain-stuck-in-the-myth-of-market-neutrality.

Vauchez, A. 2010. "The transnational politics of judicialization: Van Gend en Loos and the making of EU polity". *European Law Journal* 16(1): 1–28.

Vauchez, A. 2012. "Keeping the dream alive: the European Court of Justice and the transnational fabric of integrationist jurisprudence". *European Political Science Review* 4(1): 51–71.

Velutti, S. 2020. "The potential impact(s) of Brexit on employment rights during the global pandemic". Brexit Institute News, Sussex Law School, http://dcubrexitinstitute.eu/2020/04/the-potential-impacts-of-brexit-on-employment-rights-during-the-global-pandemic/.

Verdun, A. & J. Zeitlin 2017. "Introduction: the European Semester as a new architecture of EU socioeconomic governance in theory and practice". *Journal of European Public Policy* 25(2): 137–48.

Veron, P. & M. Di Ciommo 2020. "Fit for purpose: the EU's role in global health in the era of covid-19". ECDPM Discussion Paper No. 282, https://ecdpm.org/publications/fit-purpose-eu-role-global-health-era-covid-19/.

Verschueren, N. 2013. *Fermer les mines en construisant l'Europe. Une histoire sociale de l'intégration européenne.* Brussels: Peter Lang.

Vesan, P. & F. Corti 2017. *Promoting the Social Dimension of Europe in Adverse Conditions: The European Pillar of Social Rights and the Role of the European Parliament.* Lisbon: ESPANET.

Vesan, P. & F. Corti 2019. "New tensions over Social Europe? The European Pillar of Social Rights and the debate within the European Parliament". *Journal of Common Market Studies* 57(5): 977–94.

Vesan, P., F. Corti & S. Sabato 2021. "The European Commission's entrepreneurship and the social dimension of the European Semester: from the European Pillar of Social Rights to the Covid-19 pandemic". *Comparative European Politics* 3: 277–95.

Vica, V. 2018. "Conditionalities in cohesion policy: research for REGI Committee". PE 617.498, www.europarl.europa.eu/RegData/etudes/STUD/2018/617498/IPOL_STU(2018)617498_EN.pdf.

Vogel, L. 2018. "The fight to protect hairdressers' health: the inside story". *Hesamag: ETUI Health and Safety Magazine*, www.etui.org/sites/default/files/ez_import/Hesamag_17_EN_12-15.pdf.

Vollaard, H. 2017. "Patient mobility, changing territoriality and scale in the EU's internal market". *Comparative European Politics* 15(1): 435–58.

Wagner, A. 2013. "The personnel of the European Trade Union Confederation: specifically European types of capital?" In D. Georgakakis & J. Rowell (eds), *The Field of Eurocracy: Mapping EU Actors and Professionals*, 188–201. Basingstoke: Palgrave Macmillan.

Wall Street Journal 2012. "Interview with Mario Draghi, president of the ECB", 24 February, www.ecb.europa.eu/press/inter/date/2012/html/sp120224.en.html.

Weiss, M. 2011. "The European social dialogue". *European Labour Law Journal* 2: 155–65.

Wendon, B. 1998. "The Commission as image-venue entrepreneur in EU social policy". *Journal of European Public Policy* 5(2): 339–53.

Whyman, P., M. Baimbridge & A. Mullen 2012. *The Political Economy of the European Social Model*. London: Routledge.

Wintemute, R. 2016. "Goodbye EU anti-discrimination law? Hello repeal of the Equality Act 2010?" *King's Law Journal* 27(3): 387–97.

Zeitlin, J. 2005a. "The open method of co-ordination in action: theoretical promise, empirical realities, reform strategy". In J. Zeitlin *et al.* (eds), *The Open Method of Coordination in Action: The European Employment and Social Inclusion Strategies*, 447–503. Brussels: Peter Lang.

Zeitlin, J. 2005b. "Social Europe and experimentalist governance: towards a new constitutional compromise?" In G. de Búrca (ed.), *EU Law and the Welfare State: In Search of Solidarity*, 213–43. Oxford: Oxford University Press.

Zeitlin, J. 2009. "The open method of coordination and national social and employment policy reforms: influences, mechanisms, effects". In M. Heidenreich & J. Zeitlin (eds), *Changing European Employment and Welfare Regimes: The Influence of the Open Method of Coordination on National Reforms*, 214–45. London: Routledge.

Zeitlin, J. & P. Pochet (eds) 2005. *The Open Method of Coordination in Action: The European Employment Strategy and Social Inclusion Strategy*. Brussels: Peter Lang.

Zeitlin, J. & B. Vanhercke 2014. "Socializing the European Semester? Economic governance and social policy coordination in Europe 2020". *Sieps Reports*, Swedish Institute for European Policy Studies, 2014/7, https://papers.ssrn.com/sol3/papers.cfm?abstract_id=2511031.

Zeitlin, J. & B. Vanhercke 2017. "Socializing the European Semester: EU social and economic policy co-ordination in crisis and beyond". *Journal of European Public Policy* 25(2): 149–74.

Zimmermann, K. 2016. "Local responses to the European social fund: a cross-city comparison of usage and change". *Journal of Common Market Studies* 54(6): 1465–84.

INDEX